# After Hope and Change

# Previously Published

*Epic Journey: The 2008 Elections and American Politics*, by James W. Ceaser, Andrew E. Busch, and John J. Pitney Jr.

*Red Over Blue: The 2004 Elections and American Politics*, by James W. Ceaser and Andrew E. Busch

*The Perfect Tie: The True Story of the 2000 Presidential Election*, by James W. Ceaser and Andrew E. Busch

*Losing to Win: The 1996 Elections and American Politics*, by James W. Ceaser and Andrew E. Busch

*Upside Down and Inside Out: The 1992 Elections and American Politics*, by James W. Ceaser and Andrew E. Busch

# After Hope and Change

## *The 2012 Elections and American Politics*

James W. Ceaser, Andrew E. Busch, and
John J. Pitney Jr.

ROWMAN & LITTLEFIELD PUBLISHERS, INC.
Lanham • Boulder • New York • Toronto • Plymouth, UK

Published by Rowman & Littlefield Publishers, Inc.
A wholly owned subsidiary of The Rowman & Littlefield Publishing Group, Inc.
4501 Forbes Boulevard, Suite 200, Lanham, Maryland 20706
www.rowman.com

10 Thornbury Road, Plymouth PL6 7PP, United Kingdom



British Library Cataloguing in Publication Information Available

**Library of Congress Cataloging-in-Publication Data**

Ceaser, James W.
After hope and change : the 2012 elections and American politics / James W. Ceaser, Andrew E. Busch, and John J. Pitney Jr.
pages ; cm
Includes index.
ISBN 978-1-4422-1723-2 (cloth : alk. paper)—ISBN 978-1-4422-1724-9 (pbk. : alk. paper)—ISBN 978-1-4422-1725-6 (electronic)
1. Presidents—United States—Election—2012. 2. Political planning—United States. 3. United States—Politics and government. I. Title.
JK5262012.C43 2013
324.973'0932—dc23
2013005418

∞™ The paper used in this publication meets the minimum requirements of American National Standard for Information Sciences Permanence of Paper for Printed Library Materials, ANSI/NISO Z39.48-1992.

Printed in the United States of America

# Contents

# Acknowledgments

The authors would like to thank Verlan Lewis and John York for their assistance in research and in the preparation of the tables, and Blaire French—yet again—for her careful editing and proofreading of the original manuscript. We are also grateful to Rowman & Littlefield Publishers for its continued support of this election series, which dates back to 1992. Jon Sisk, senior executive editor for political science, has been the guiding force in this venture from the outset, and he was ably assisted in the production of this volume by the editorial staff, in particular by Benjamin Verdi, Julia Loy, and Deborah Hudson, each of whom we gratefully acknowledge.

# ONE

# A Tale of Two Campaigns

It is hard to imagine two electoral campaigns more different than Barack Obama's victories of 2008 and 2012.

The 2008 campaign, featuring "Hope and Change" and "postpartisanship" as its main themes, was built on uplift and inspiration. Millions experienced Obama's epic journey as an event that transcended ordinary politics, opening into higher realms of the cultural or even the "spiritual." The campaign was filled with lofty speeches that galvanized audiences, not only in America but also across large parts of the world. Americans looked forward to the selection of the first African American president and spoke hopefully of the beginning of a post-racial political order. Peoples in other lands saw in Obama a leader who might usher in an era of peace and renewal. Barack Obama the candidate became iconic, a "charismatic" figure who dominated the airwaves and blogosphere throughout the summer and fall of 2008.

Fast forward to 2012. Obama's campaign this time was transparently "political," hard-edged, and brass-knuckled. Operatives who ran the organization made little effort to conceal their tough approach, as they churned out attack ad after attack ad depicting their Republican opponent, Mitt Romney, as a callous oligarch representing a detached slice of the wealthy and powerful. There were no majestic orations this time, and the campaign's slogan, "Forward," was forgotten on November 7, if not before. In the aftermath, friendly analysts were more likely to hail the president's mastery of the electoral "demographics," including the voting blocs of Hispanics and African Americans, than to celebrate post-racialism. Obama also used class and gender divisions to his advantage. Inveighing against the top 1 percent was a perfect thematic fit for an election featuring the wealthiest major party nominee in history, while a righteous defense against an alleged "war on women" kept important social issues alive. Obama still had his supporters in many parts of the world—in France nearly 80 percent backed the President—but there was little of the enthusiasm of 2008 and Obama T-shirts were conspicuously absent. Still, the 2012 Obama campaign got done what needed to be done. It reelected the president. It was an exercise, as athletes sometimes like to say, of "taking care of business."

To describe these two campaigns is not to pronounce a simple value judgment. There is no doubt which campaign Obama found more to his liking—the photos on the cover tell the story. What presidential candidate, after all, would not prefer the grandiose setting of a stage with Greek columns and the adulation of the masses to the sight of arenas with empty seats and audiences cheering on command? Yet it is not clear that the 2012 campaign was worse, either for Barack Obama or for America. The 2008 campaign often imposed on Obama the burden of being measured against impossible standards. Politics has its rare uplifting moments, but for the most part, even when the stakes are high, it is a practical kind of business pursued in a practical way. Loading too much transpolitical baggage onto political life can often end in disappointment or recrimination. The 2012 campaign, a rough-and-tumble affair, was anything but elevating. It will not be remembered or celebrated.[1] Yet by its very normalcy, it returns politics to a more sober and "natural" level.

People will judge these two campaigns in different ways. But one thing is certain. For his second term, Barack Obama will be seen through a new prism. Once the icon, Barack Obama is now the politician. For better or worse, the second term of his presidency will unfold in an era *After Hope and Change*.

## THE MEANING OF THE 2012 ELECTION

The 2012 election looked on the surface to be the perfect status quo event. Americans went through a long and expensive election campaign throughout the summer and fall and in the end chose the same government they had before the election. They reelected the same president and kept the same majority party in the House of Representatives (the Republicans) and in the Senate (the Democrats). The three main powerbrokers in Washington remained at the helm: President Barack Obama, House Speaker John Boehner, and Senate majority leader Harry Reid. Even the minority leaders were the same, Nancy Pelosi in the House and Mitch McConnell in the Senate. An observer from afar might be excused for concluding that nothing had changed.

Yet beneath the surface, it was clear to everyone that the country had become a very different place. By maintaining the political status quo, Americans left intact the great transformations in public policy made during the first two years of the Obama administration. An historic decision was made, even if some might say that it had been reached by default. Given the course of events over the preceding four years, the 2012 election was set up to be a turning point.

In 2008, Americans selected Barack Obama as president together with Democratic majorities in both the House and the Senate. The president and his party, acting almost in parliamentary fashion, went on in 2009 and 2010 to enact legislation that produced a dramatically higher level of federal government involvement in society and that launched a form of nationalized health care. In the midterm elections of 2010, Republicans posed a clear challenge, calling for a repeal of the Affordable Care Act (Obamacare) and a reduction of the role of the federal government to pre-2008 levels. The election results spoke largely in the Republicans' favor. Republicans captured control of the House of Representatives, gaining sixty-three seats (the largest switch since 1948), and picked up six members in the Senate, leaving them just four seats shy of taking over that body. No less important, Republicans made enormous gains in the states, winning many governorships and state legislatures. The momentum, many Republicans felt, had shifted and was now pointing in their direction. Yet with President Obama still in office, and with a Democratic Senate, a reversal of the Democratic program was never in question.

In the aftermath of the midterm election, each party appealed to its respective mandate and continued to press its case. For the next two years the parties went through the motions and engaged in tactical skirmishes. Both sides were marking time, waiting for another election to decide which view should prevail. Under the circumstances, the choice in 2012 was structured so that for Republicans to achieve their objectives, they would have had to win the presidency while calling, as Mitt Romney did, for the rejection of Obama's program. They would probably also have to make further gains in the US Senate, perhaps winning a majority there. Democrats needed merely to hang on. It would not matter whether a majority of voters explicitly intended to endorse the Democratic transformations or not. All President Obama needed to save his change was to keep the keys of the office. And this he did. Republicans lost—they lost much more than an election—by not winning. President Obama won—he won much more than an election—by not losing. The outcome consolidated what Barack Obama had already set in motion and safeguarded the measures that were passed during his first term. House Speaker John Boehner, the most powerful Republican in Washington, acknowledged as much right after the election, stating, "Obamacare is the law of the land."

The greater part of the meaning of the 2012 election related back to the past and to what it already held in store for the future. The election establishes a new baseline of government activity. Barring some huge turnaround, the 2012 result confirms a new stage in American politics, a change not dissimilar to what took place after the New Deal and the Great Society. Politics in America will now revolve around the consequences of this new order, not necessarily to the benefit of Democrats, but that order itself will not easily if ever be undone.

The shape of American politics now resembles more the model found in "blue" states like California, Illinois, and New York, than in the "red" states like Indiana, Wisconsin, and Kansas. Over the years these blue states have embraced the huge new demands built into a larger government and have been seeking new revenues in an effort to meet the added expenses. The red states, which have kept or lowered tax rates, have held the line or scaled back on what government is asked to do. The main examples of the blue model—the United States of America now included—all have executives elected by roughly the same coalition, have promised or locked in benefits that exceed the current capacity of government to fund them, and have created new understandings of what citizens regard as government entitlements. In a political version of creating facts on the ground, every new benefit bestowed tends to build a constituency of supporters who are likely to be resistant to any cutbacks.

Of course the analogy between politics in the United States and politics in the blue states only goes so far. For one thing, because one government is sovereign and the others are not, the common problem of revenue shortfalls is approached in different ways. States have no choice but to keep spending and revenues in some balance, at least as far as current obligations are concerned. The United States government for now operates under no such immediate discipline, as it has been able to finance its debt by continual borrowing and printing money. Numerous analysts have insisted that this way of proceeding is unsustainable, but no one has yet been able to say exactly when the unsustainable becomes unsustainable—or what the unsustainable looks like. For another thing, the political support of the blue model differs between the two levels of government. The major blue state governments today are, politically speaking, blue down to their veins, with strong Democratic majorities in both the executive and legislature. Not so the United States. Democrats have a clear but not overwhelming edge at the national level ("horizontally"), with control of the presidency and the Senate, but Republicans in 2012 won a majority in the House of Representatives while running squarely against the blue model. The national government is thus part red, part blue. America as whole, moreover, is governed under a federal structure. Republicans are strong "vertically" at the state level, with thirty of the fifty governors and full control (both houses of the legislature and the governorship) in twenty-three states compared to thirteen for the Democrats. Politically speaking, the United States remains nearly evenly divided.

The 2012 election result also meant everything to Barack Obama personally. No doubt the sting of defeat is great for any incumbent seeking reelection—it certainly was not easy for either Jimmy Carter or George H. W. Bush. But the stakes in Obama's case were much higher. Even if

Obama accomplishes little in the next four years, his reelection assures him of a place in the Progressive pantheon of major leaders. Like Franklin Roosevelt and Lyndon Johnson, Obama will be remembered as a president who expanded the size and scope of the American welfare state. And he will be celebrated for having done so, in the case of his health care bill, by taking a huge political risk and acting contrary to majority opinion at the time. This outcome for Barack Obama sure beats the prospect of being tucked away in some sinecure, perhaps a college presidency, while watching Mitt Romney and the Republicans dismantle much of what he had enacted.

So much for what the election meant looking back to 2008. What added value, if any, did this election provide to the president and the Democrats going forward? The victor will often speak of a mandate (even if the word is not used) in an effort to use an election result to supply added leverage for enacting parts of his program. The force or weight of such claims will depend on many factors, the two most important being what the president actually emphasized during his campaign and the magnitude of the victory. In a campaign that focused on criticizing his opponent, President Obama offered little by way of setting out a future agenda. But one policy area where he was clear and emphatic was on the need to raise tax rates on the wealthiest. Following his election, he immediately insisted on following through, noting that the election had "sent a very clear message" on this question.[2] His views largely prevailed, as the Republican Party split on the tax issue, allowing a bipartisan majority to enact a tax increase.

Beyond this issue, however, it is unclear what the 2012 election result brings the president and the Democrats by way of a mandate. Here, the important fact going forward, in contrast to looking backward, is the status quo electoral outcome. In contrast to 2008, when his upbeat campaign brought him a reservoir of support and when his party had control of both chambers of Congress, President Obama this time may enjoy less good will and will have to contend with a House of Representatives controlled by the opposition party. The configuration of power, though not the circumstances, is akin to what was in place after the midterm elections of 2010. In addition, the size of Obama's victory hardly speaks the language of a powerful mandate.

## THE SIZE OF OBAMA'S VICTORY

The magnitude of a presidential victory when discussed in the political arena is always subject to interpretation, some of it very creative, with each side presenting the victory as larger or smaller as it suits its political position. Here we undertake an effort at objective electoral analysis by looking at the numbers and by comparing this election to elections in the past. Every election is of course unique, with its own context and its own cast of characters. There are limits to what comparisons to the past can yield, especially since presidential elections today differ so greatly from what they were in other eras. Barack Obama was nominated and elected in 2012 in a way that would have seemed quite unfamiliar to George Washington in 1792 or Ulysses S. Grant in 1872. But certain facts from the past, if handled with care, can contribute to a more balanced understanding of elections and allow for the current election to be seen with the critical distance that comes with an historical perspective.

An initial point that deserves mention, and that demonstrates an important element of strength in Barack Obama's victory, is that he won this election by receiving a majority of the popular vote. It is surprising to recall that in the past six elections three of the winners—Bill Clinton in 1992 and 1996, and Bush in 2000—fell short of winning 50 percent of the vote. Only George W. Bush in 2004 managed to achieve what Barack Obama has now accomplished twice. Obama is by far the biggest vote-getter in the past two decades.

For the best overall measure of the comparative strength of an electoral victory, we turn to the winner's margin over his major opponent. Elections over the past half century range from the great landslides of Lyndon Johnson over Barry Goldwater in 1964 and Richard Nixon over George McGovern in 1972, to the near dead heats of Nixon's squeaker over John Kennedy in 1960 and George Bush's "negative" victory over Al Gore in 2000. Obama's 2012 victory obviously falls into neither of these categories. Situating it within the whole era of "modern" elections, which analysts usually set at 1896, his margin in 2012 (3.85 percent) ranks far down on this list at twenty-fourth out of thirty elections, making it a fairly narrow victory.

To Americans who just lived through the 2012 campaign, Obama's victory probably felt much larger than it was. One reason was that Obama outperformed the polls at the end. The average of the final major polls indicated an election that was headed toward a dead heat in the popular vote.[3] Some of the headlines in the last few day tell the story: "Obama and Romney Deadlocked, Polls Show" (*The Wall Street Journal*), "Polls Show Election Eve Tie" (CNN), and "Obama and Romney Are in a Dead Tie" (*Business Insider*).[4] Obama beat the expectations by about three points. Just as important was the absence of drama on election eve. No one had to master the intricacies of the butterfly ballot or the hanging chad in Florida, as they did in 2000, or worry over broken voting machines and disputed outcomes in obscure counties in Ohio, as they did in 2004. The election was called early, before midnight East Coast time. NBC jumped first at 11:12 p.m., followed by CBS (11:16), CNN and Fox News (11:18), and ABC (11:23). Those who felt no need either to celebrate or to drown their sorrows could enjoy the luxury of a full night's sleep. Probably the biggest surprise, and the one that contributed most to the per-

**Table 1.1. Presidential Victory Margins Since 1896**

| *Rank* | *Year* | *Winner* | *Margin of Victory* |
|---|---|---|---|
| **Landslide** | | | |
| 1 | 1920 | Harding | 26.17 |
| 2 | 1924 | Coolidge | 25.22 |
| 3 | 1936 | FDR | 24.26 |
| 4 | 1972 | Nixon | 23.15 |
| 5 | 1964 | LBJ | 22.58 |
| 6 | 1904 | T.R. | 18.83 |
| 7 | 1984 | Reagan | 18.21 |
| 8 | 1932 | FDR | 17.76 |
| 9 | 1928 | Hoover | 17.41 |
| 10 | 1956 | Eisenhower | 15.4 |
| 11 | 1912 | Wilson | 14.44 |
| **Comfortable Win** | | | |
| 12 | 1952 | Eisenhower | 10.85 |
| 13 | 1940 | FDR | 9.96 |
| 14 | 1980 | Reagan | 9.74 |
| 15 | 1908 | Taft | 8.53 |
| 16 | 1996 | Clinton | 8.51 |
| 17 | 1988 | GHWB | 7.72 |
| 18 | 1944 | FDR | 7.5 |
| 19 | 2008 | Obama | 7.27 |
| 20 | 1900 | McKinley | 6.12 |
| 21 | 1992 | Clinton | 5.56 |
| **Competitive Win** | | | |
| 22 | 1948 | Truman | 4.48 |
| 23 | 1896 | McKinley | 4.31 |
| **24** | ***2012*** | ***Obama*** | ***3.85*** |
| 25 | 1916 | Wilson | 3.12 |
| 26 | 2004 | Bush | 2.46 |
| 27 | 1976 | Carter | 2.06 |
| **Dead Heat** | | | |
| 28 | 1968 | Nixon | 0.7 |
| 29 | 1960 | Kennedy | 0.17 |
| 30 | 2000 | Bush | -0.51 |
| | | *Mean* | 10.86 |
| | | *Median* | 8.52 |

*Note*: In 1912, although Taft was the incumbent, Theodore Roosevelt actually came in second to Woodrow Wilson. Wilson's margin of victory is thus calculated for the difference between him and Roosevelt.

ception of a larger Obama victory, came from the results in the battleground states, those which were contested by the candidates and considered to be potentially in play by the community of electoral analysts. All of these states—Florida, Ohio, Colorado, Virginia, New Hampshire, Nevada, Iowa, Pennsylvania, Wisconsin, Michigan, and Minnesota—went to Obama. Watching them fall one by one was like witnessing a juggernaut. Impressive as this last result was, it does not alter the limited scope of the victory.

Another and perhaps more relevant measure of the magnitude of the 2012 election victory seeks to compare it to "like" cases. Presidential elections fall into two basic types: those in which an incumbent is running and those in which one is not. The presidency is a highly personal office, and elections involving an incumbent invariably focus on the question of whether or not, in Alexander Hamilton's words, "to continue him in his station."[5] Of the fifty-seven presidential elections in American history, slightly more than half (thirty-two) have featured an incumbent—though in five cases the incumbent was a vice president who had ascended to the presidency and in two (FDR in 1940 and 1944) the incumbent was running for a third and fourth term. The comparable incumbent with Obama is the usual case of an elected incumbent president running for a second consecutive term. Table 1.2 lists the presidents in this category since the advent of mass popular voting (1836) according to the popular vote share gained or lost between the first election and the second election bid.

President Obama made history in 2012 by getting reelected while losing vote share. Previous victorious incumbents increased their electoral strength from their first election to their second, while those who lost vote share ended up being defeated. In other words, until 2012 voters had rewarded the winners with more votes, and punished those whom they had approved of less with a loss of the presidency. Obama broke this pattern, and found himself, from an electoral standpoint, in a weaker position in 2012 than in 2008.

This historical fact about the 2012 election helps to highlight some of the features of the campaign. At the beginning of 2012, Obama's election team realized that, barring strong signs of an economic recovery, his reelection bid was going to take place in less than glittering circumstances, with a record of a slow economic recovery, though not a recession, hanging over the campaign. This situation all but eliminated the possibility of framing the election in a triumphalist tone. Republicans would call attention to the deficiencies of the economy, while the president would remind voters of the origin of the economic problems in the policies of his predecessor, speak of the signs of recovery, and ask for patience. In the place of the theme of "Hope and Change," this time the president made sure to point out, "America, I never said this journey would be easy, and I won't promise that now."[6] For the most part, however, the campaign tried to avoid speaking of the performance of the

**Table 1.2. Reelection Contests Since 1836 by Change in Vote Share**

| *Election Year* | *President* | *Change in Vote* | *First Election Vote Share* | *Second Election Vote Share* |
|---|---|---|---|---|
| ***1972*** | ***Nixon*** | ***17.25%*** | ***43.42%*** | ***60.67%*** |
| ***1864*** | ***Lincoln*** | ***15.38%*** | ***39.65%*** | ***55.03%*** |
| ***1984*** | ***Reagan*** | ***8.02%*** | ***50.75%*** | ***58.77%*** |
| ***1916*** | ***Wilson*** | ***7.40%*** | ***41.84%*** | ***49.24%*** |
| ***1996*** | ***Clinton*** | ***6.22%*** | ***43.01%*** | ***49.23%*** |
| ***1936*** | ***FDR*** | ***3.39%*** | ***57.41%*** | ***60.80%*** |
| ***1872*** | ***Grant*** | ***2.92%*** | ***52.66%*** | ***55.58%*** |
| ***2004*** | ***Bush 43*** | ***2.86%*** | ***47.87%*** | ***50.73%*** |
| ***1956*** | ***Eisenhower*** | ***2.19%*** | ***55.18%*** | ***57.37%*** |
| ***1900*** | ***McKinley*** | ***0.62%*** | ***51.02%*** | ***51.64%*** |
| 1888 | Cleveland | -0.22% | 48.85% | 48.63% |
| ***2012*** | ***Obama*** | ***-1.81%*** | ***52.87%*** | ***51.06%*** |
| 1840 | Van Buren | -4.00% | 50.80% | 46.80% |
| 1892 | Harrison | -4.79% | 47.80% | 43.01% |
| 1980 | Carter | -9.07% | 50.08% | 41.01% |
| 1992 | Bush 41 | -15.92% | 53.37% | 37.45% |
| 1932 | Hoover | -18.56% | 58.21% | 39.65% |
| 1912 | Taft | -28.40% | 51.57% | 23.17% |

*Note*: Victorious incumbents are in bold and italics

economy. It focused attention instead on the deficiencies and liabilities of his opponent, on the specific protections or benefits that his opponent's policies threatened, and on the need for the wealthiest to pay their share.

The Obama campaign followed the classic military strategy of yielding ground but tightening defense to save the city. Given his victory margin in 2008, Obama had the luxury of being able to give away votes and yet still win the election. This is exactly what happened. Geographically, Obama lost vote share in nearly every state, but he ended by surrendering only the two most exposed outposts that he had captured in 2008: Indiana and North Carolina.[7] Demographically, Obama gave up vote share among almost every group, Hispanics being a notable exception, but these "losses" were manageable, and he continued to win strong majorities from the main elements of his coalition. In some cases these elements also increased their relative size as a proportion of the total electorate, more than compensating for any fall-off in vote share. Thus, nonmarried women, who gave Barack Obama 67 percent of their vote this time, down from 70 percent in 2008, grew from 20 percent of the electorate in 2008 to 23 percent.[8] All in all, Obama executed the most successful strategic retreat—indeed, the only successful strategic retreat in American electoral history.

A final important measure of the strength of a presidential victory centers on the question of how the president's party fares in holding control of Congress. Table 1.3 lists the eleven presidents reelected to a second term since 1836. Nine of them, Obama included, were initially chosen with their party in control of both houses of Congress (Nixon and Reagan, who were selected in the era of Democratic congressional dominance, entered office under divided government). The record of these nine presidents in keeping unified government is not that stellar: five of them succeeded (Lincoln, Grant, McKinley, FDR, and George W. Bush) and four did not. Eisenhower and Clinton lost control of both chambers, while Wilson and Obama lost just the House.[9]

Obama trails only Woodrow Wilson in the number of House seats he yielded between his two elections. Democrats can celebrate the fact that they picked up strength from the midterm elections in 2010—eight seats in the House and, in a welcome surprise, two seats in the Senate. But the larger fact is that the Democratic Party lost considerable ground between Obama's two victories.[10]

All the measures examined describe an election victory in 2012 that cannot be classified as anything more than modest. Still, a win is a win. Returning to the athletes' jargon mentioned before, it is not hard to imagine the president and his advisors, clinking glasses at 11:30 p.m. on November 6 and telling each other, "We'll take it."

## WAS THE OUTCOME INEVITABLE?

The 2012 election ended in a result that was fairly close. In fact, the poll measurements throughout the campaign indicate it was fairly close all along. Mitt Romney trailed most of the time, and in late September it looked like the race had begun to slip away. But the gap closed following the first presidential debate, which Romney was judged to have won decisively, and in some polls Romney edged ahead. Many analysts saw a possible path to his victory.

The conclusion to which we come is that this election was one that Mitt Romney *could* have won—*could* here being understood in a commonsense way as occurring through less than extraordinary events and actions. Roughly speaking, there are elections in which the preexisting conditions favor one side over another to such a degree that it would take almost a miracle to reverse the anticipated outcome. These are not "could-win" elections, and it is a testimony to either the patriotism or

**Table 1.3. Reelected Presidents Since 1836 with Party's Change in Congress**

| *Reelection Year* | *President* | *Change in Unified or Divided Government* | *Number of Congressional Houses Gained or Lost* | *Change in Senate from First Election* | *Change from First* |
|---|---|---|---|---|---|
| 1864 | Lincoln | U | 0 | 6 | 31 |
| 1872 | Grant | U | 0 | -15 | 37 |
| 1900 | McKinley | U | 0 | 9 | -13 |
| 1916 | Wilson | U→D | -1 | 3 | -64 |
| 1936 | FDR | U | 0 | 17 | 22 |
| 1956 | Eisenhower | U→D | -2 | -2 | -20 |
| 1972 | Nixon | D | 0 | -1 | 0 |
| 1984 | Reagan | D | 0 | 0 | -10 |
| 1996 | Clinton | U→D | -2 | -12 | -51 |
| 2004 | Bush 43 | U | 0 | 5 | 11 |
| 2012 | Obama | U→D | -1 | -4 | -57 |

folly of the losing candidates that they even bother to go through the agony of the campaign. The 2012 election is obviously not in this category. Like the elections of 2000 and 2004, either candidate could have won.

But if either candidate could have won, is it possible to say that one of them *should* have won—*should* here meaning that the advantage lay on his side? This claim might be made on behalf of either man, but since Obama did win, attention after the election focused more on Governor Romney. According to the political columnist David Frum: "When economic conditions are as bad as they were in 2012 and the incumbent wins anyway . . . that's the challenger party throwing away a sure thing."[11] The thesis in a nutshell is that Mitt Romney had an easy path to victory, had he not run so poor a campaign. An adequate examination of this argument must await an account of the campaign itself, which comes in a later chapter. Of interest here, however, is the larger question of the grounds on which it is reasonable to make claims about who "should" have won. Part of the answer, we believe, comes from the use of the method of historical analysis. What is missing from the chorus of claims that Mitt Romney should have won is a consideration of the difficulty of unseating an incumbent president, especially in the modern era.

For the whole of American history two-thirds of all incumbents who ran for a second term—this includes vice presidents who ascended to the presidency—won their second-term bids. The strength of the incumbency advantage, however, has ebbed and flowed across time. It was strong in the early period, from 1789 to 1832, when all seven incumbents ran for a second term, and when all those without the name of Adams were reelected. Included, of course, were the great figures of the Revolution and founding: Washington, Jefferson, and Madison. Beginning in the 1830s, with the development of mass parties having strong nominating institutions (the party conventions) and with the rise of two-party competition, the incumbency advantage vanished. For the fifteen elections from 1836 through 1892, eight incumbents either chose not to run or their party denied them the chance to run for a second term. Just five incumbents were renominated, and only two won reelection: Lincoln and Grant.

Since 1896, with the rise of the modern personal president who stands above his party, the incumbency advantage has reasserted itself. All incumbent presidents—including successor vice presidents—have been renominated for another term. Fifteen won their election, while only five lost: Taft (1912), Hoover (1932), Ford (1976), Carter (1980), and Bush Sr. (1992). To say that Mitt Romney should have won means, of course, that Barack Obama should have joined this small group of exceptional cases. Does his case "fit" with the others?

There are three factors associated with the losses. First, in all of the cases except Hoover, whose 1932 defeat during the Depression explains itself, there were important intra-party primary challenges. Taft faced Teddy Roosevelt in 1912, Ford faced Ronald Reagan in 1976, Carter faced

Ted Kennedy in 1980, and Bush Sr. faced Patrick Buchanan in 1988. These challenges no doubt reflected a certain weakness in these incumbents, but they also added to the incumbents' problems. These challenges exacerbated fault lines within the party, which contributed to defections in the general election, and legitimated lines of attack from the opposite party, which weakened the incumbents' appeal to swing voters.

Second, in two of these cases there was an important third-party candidate who drew support more heavily from the incumbent than the challenger and who was critical in turning the outcome of the election. In 1912, after Teddy Roosevelt failed in his Republican primary challenge to Taft, he bolted to lead the Progressive Party in a campaign that captured massive numbers of Republicans. Taft, in fact, finished third, behind Roosevelt. In 1992 the businessman Ross Perot ran a so-called independent candidacy that siphoned off large portions of the voters from Bush's coalition. T.R. and Perot garnered the greatest vote shares for all third-party challenges since the Civil War. President Carter also faced an independent candidate in 1980, John Anderson, who won a not insignificant 7 percent of the vote. It is less clear how important this candidacy was to Carter's defeat, but Carter himself has had no hesitation in pronouncing it to be decisive.[12]

Finally, all of these incumbents except Carter were seeking another term at the end of long periods of White House control by their party, when general sentiment for change most likely had increased. Taft was going for a fifth consecutive Republican presidential term, Hoover and Bush Sr. for a fourth, and Ford for a third.

Obama enjoyed the incumbency advantage in 2012 without confronting any of these three weakening factors. There was no primary challenge to Obama, who remained extremely popular inside his own party. There was no major third party that operated in 2012, and the small Libertarian Party of Gary Johnson drained votes from Mitt Romney, not Barack Obama. Finally, the Democrats in 2008 had only been in office for one term. There was no sense of fatigue with the Democratic Party. In fact, the public memory of the president before Obama was not of a Democrat, but of the Republican George W. Bush. Democrats sought to keep this memory alive and to cast much of the blame for events on him, just as Democrats had done in the case of Hoover after 1932 and Republicans in the case of Carter after 1980.

These general factors derived from history bring to mind some of the structural advantages that worked for the incumbent in 2012. While Republicans engaged in a tough series of competitive primaries, in which the eventual nominee, Mitt Romney, was subject to some of the same attacks from his competitors as Obama would make later, Obama had the chance to strengthen his organization for the general election campaign and to raise money that could be spent immediately against Romney in the summer months. The incumbent should in any case have the advantage of building an organization for the fall campaign throughout his time in office, while the challenger will have to wait and to rely on what the national party has put into place.

There is, of course, a fourth factor to consider in trying to answer who should have won: the performance of the economy. A poor economy is a frequently cited reason for why party control of the White House switches hands, and it was the main cause of Hoover's loss and important in Carter's defeat. Governor Romney's campaign strategy was to make the 2012 election into a referendum on President Obama's handling of the economy, and poll evidence shows that the economic issue worked to Romney's benefit, though obviously not enough. Many items figure into people's assessment of the economy, including perceptions of how bad the economy is, who bears the fault for poor performance, in what direction things appear to be heading, and which candidate offers greater immediate security to those feeling vulnerable. President Obama had arguments that worked in his favor for each of these questions. The economy was not in recession, nor did it appear to be falling into recession; the origin of the economic collapse lay with his predecessor; the economic situation had clearly improved from the depths of 2009 and showed slight improvement during the final months of the campaign; and Democrats supported benefits, from extended unemployment insurance to food stamps, that Republicans might threaten. Obama never received the kind of good economic news in 2012 that would have put his reelection beyond the reach of a challenger, but Romney never received the bad economic news that could have ensured him victory. The condition of the economy was not decisive.

If an election falls squarely into the "could-win" category, like the election of 2012, it is difficult to say with any great confidence which candidate should have won. This assessment was confirmed by the leading predictive models of political scientists and economists released during the summer of 2012. These models, which try to forecast the results on the basis of different sets of past economic and political patterns, were practically split down the middle in saying which candidate would win.[13] All that can be said is that it is not surprising that an incumbent president strong enough to avoid a primary challenge was also strong enough to defeat his challenger in the general campaign. It is not surprising that even in an economy experiencing a weak recovery, a president who could claim improvement from a crisis that began under his predecessor was reelected. It is also not surprising that in an era of strong party polarization, a very partisan president was able to keep in tow almost all of his adherents. Perhaps in close cases, "the tie goes to the incumbent."

Republicans can certainly lament their failure to take advantage of an opportunity that could have brought victory. But they are being too hard on themselves if they conclude that they threw away an election that they should have won.

## WHAT THE 2012 ELECTION CAN AND CANNOT TELL US ABOUT 2016

No sooner is an election over than analysts begin scouring the exit polls in an effort to forecast which party's candidate will likely be moving into the White House in the next election. The record of such prognostications, however, has not been very impressive. Imagine what such analysts must have said after Herbert Hoover (a Republican) won the 1928 presidential race in a landslide: certainly not that a Democrat would triumph in 1932, and by an even larger landslide. And did those who studied Lyndon Johnson's massive victory in 1964 foresee that a Republican would win in 1968?

There is reason why analysis of the current presidential election proves to be of such limited help in predicting the future. It can say nothing about the most important factors that will influence the upcoming election outcome. No one knows who the candidates will be, and, more importantly, no one knows how well or poorly the just-elected president will perform over the next four years. These things are what most affect the future fate of the party. Gains in strength for the party in presidential elections are connected with the perceived success in the incumbent's performance. Losses have been directly attributable to an incumbent's perceived failures, as in 1932 (the rejection of Hoover), 1968 (disenchantment with Lyndon Johnson), or 1980 (an adverse judgment on Jimmy Carter). New majorities in American presidential politics result not so much from the opposition party candidate winning over the voters as from the incumbent party losing their confidence.

If election results could tell us anything about how well the winner will subsequently do in office, they would have enormous value in predicting the next election. Unfortunately, they cannot. A book on the 2012 presidential election therefore appears at the worst possible moment for offering speculations about 2016. Still, few will fault anyone for trying. Important information is available, if not yet on which party will win, then on some themes—we will mention three of them—that affect the context in the next race.

The first general point to observe is the growing congruence between geography and party support. The 2012 presidential election was a fairly close race nationwide, but it had surprisingly few close races in the states. In an election decided by only 3.85 percent, just four states had victory margins of less than 4 percent and just twelve under 8 percent. Most states recorded huge victories for one candidate or the other. President Obama won Vermont by 36 percent, New York by 28, Maryland by 26, and Massachusetts and California by 23. Governor Romney won Wyoming by 41 percent, Oklahoma by 34, West Virginia by 27, and Nebraska by 22.

A spread along these lines continues a trend that has been in place for a couple of decades. Table 1.4 offers evidence of the change by showing the margins of victories within the states in four presidential elections over the past half century: 1960, 1976, 1988, and 2012.[14] These elections were chosen because they resembled 2012 in their margin of victory, but close elections that were once the exception in the mid-twentieth century (like 1960 and 1976) are now the norm. In the sixty-four years from 1920 to 1984, there were only five elections with single-digit margins of victory (FDR 1944, Truman in 1948, JFK in 1960, Nixon in 1968, and Carter in 1976). Conversely, in the twenty-four years since 1988, all seven elections have been won by less than ten points. Ironically, at the same time that national margins of victory have become smaller, more and more state elections are decided in landslides.

In addition to increasing state margins of victory, swings between the parties by states have also diminished. A geographic sorting has hardened into place, as states now show greater fidelity to one party or another. A half century ago, almost every state could swing between the parties from one election to the next. This was true in the North, East, South, and West. A few examples will illustrate. Today, Louisiana is no longer considered a swing state, but from 1952 to 1980 Louisiana was the ultimate swing state: it never stayed with the same party two elections in a row. Vermont, also no longer a swing state, once swung wildly between the two parties with large margins of victory for whichever party it happened to favor that year: Republican Eisenhower won the state by forty-four points in 1956, Democrat Johnson by thirty-three points in 1964, and Republican Nixon by twenty-six points in 1972. Swaying back and forth with each year's particular winner, California went for Eisenhower in 1952 by a fifteen-point margin, Johnson in 1964 by eighteen points, Reagan in 1984 by seventeen points, and finally settled down with the Democrats and Clinton in 1992 by thirteen points. By contrast, states today tend to stay home. Obama largely won the same states in 2012 that he won in 2008, that Kerry won in 2004, that Gore won in 2000, and that Clinton won in 1996. Similarly, Romney largely won the same states that McCain

**Table 1.4. Presidential Elections by State Margins of Victory**

| *Election* | *Total Margin of Victory* | *Number of States with Margin Under 4%* | *Number of States with Margin 4–8%* | *Number of States with Margin More Than 8%* | *Average State Swing from Previous Election* |
|---|---|---|---|---|---|
| 2012 | 3.85 | 4 | 8 | 39 | 4.84 |
| 1988 | 7.73 | 8 | 11 | 32 | 11.89 |
| 1976 | 2.06 | 18 | 13 | 20 | 26.92 |
| 1960 | 0.16 | 19 | 13 | 18 | 15.11 |

won in 2008, that Bush won in 2004 and 2000, and that Dole won in 1996. Just two states changed between 2008 and 2012, the lowest percent since George Washington won his back-to-back unanimous elections in 1789 and 1792.

Because the electoral college system is based on winning states, "geography" remains the key to capturing the presidency. Republicans, who will be struggling to come back in 2016, will find that the geographical sorting that has taken place in recent decades offers grounds for both hope and despair. The core of the GOP geographical base looks to be relatively safe. Every state Mitt Romney won, except North Carolina, was by a margin of 7.5 percent or more. The problem for Republicans is that Democrats have a similar geographic base that looks equally secure. Barring a huge event that shakes up everything, there is little reason to think that the basic contours of the next election will look that much different from this one. The election will be a battle for the battleground states, with Republicans having a lot of territory to make up.

A second point to emerge from analysis of the 2012 election results relates to underlying changes in demography. After the election Democrats exuded more confidence about the future than the limited magnitude of their victory seemed to warrant, and many Republicans registered more despair. The reason for these reactions related to the previously noted shifts in the relative size of different voting groups. The categories that grew between 2008 and 2012 were on the Democratic side, including the ethnic groups of Hispanics and Asians and the "situational" groups of the unmarried (men and women) and of the nonreligious or secular. The categories that declined were mostly on the Republican side. As Democratic political analyst James Carville has put it, in the most blunt terms, white voters, and white male voters in particular (categories in which Republicans do well), are shrinking: "White voters were 74% of voters in 2008; they were 72% this year. White men comprised just 34% of the electorate."[15] Carville and other Democrats foresee an overall continuation of these trends, leading to the view that there is a demographic wind blowing at the Democrats' back, accentuated by the continuing allegiance of the young to the Democratic Party.

There may be less significance in these forecasts, however, than many now think. Demographic shifts occur at the margin, and the additional help to Democrats in 2016 may not equal that of 2012. Furthermore, the changes in the relative size in these categories in 2012 were not all the result of simple demography, but sometimes of decisions about whether to vote at all. Turnout in some of the favorable categories for Republicans was lower than many analysts expected. According to Sean Trende: "The increased share of the minority vote as a percent of the total vote is not the result of a large increase in minorities in the numerator, it is a function of many fewer whites in the denominator."[16] Preliminary accounts suggest that this decline was among the poorer and underemployed, who could not identify with Romney's candidacy. In any case, surges or declines in turnout in 2016 could easily offset the effects of strictly demographic changes. Finally, demography is not exactly destiny. Ethnic groups can alter their voting tendencies over time as their economic situation or degree of cultural integration changes. For the short term, Mitt Romney's especially poor showing among Hispanics may be attributable in part to his position on self-deportation of immigrants that he embraced during the primary contest. Future Republican candidates, with a different record and background, might be poised to do much better, while it is hard to imagine other Democrats who would have the same appeal among minorities as Barack Obama.

The final point relates to an asymmetry in the electoral support that is generated by the two parties' core positions on an expanding government and welfare state. The Democratic Party's conception of the common good emphasizes social justice, redistributionist policies, and the adoption of more federal government programs. This position helps to create—it may even be designed to foster—faithful electoral constituencies from among those receiving specific benefits and from those who owe their employment to government spending. The favorable political effect for Democrats operates not only in good economic times, but in bad times as well, when the benefits serve as a cushion against difficult conditions: whatever might be the possible beneficial consequences of a different approach, the immediate risks to oneself and one's family ensures support for the pro-government part. The increase in these electoral constituencies, some now believe, has brought the United States closer to a tipping point where so many people benefit from specific programs that arguments about a rollback will fall on deaf ears.

The Republican Party's conception of the public good emphasizes individual liberty in the economic arena, lower taxes, and a smaller federal government. The tangible economic benefits of this position, according to this Republican view, will be general and diffuse: higher levels of overall growth, less unemployment, and ultimately greater prosperity. This approach does less well than the Democratic position in creating specific clientele groups. Where Republicans have enjoyed some success, especially at the state level, has been in linking their position to an overall concern for taxes. Larger government and more programs must lead to higher taxes. But this position was less effective at the national level in 2012, where many Americans now pay no income taxes. In addition, the practice of financing additional programs by borrowing rather than taxing, which both parties over the years have legitimized, allowed putting off any immediate recourse to larger taxes, except now for the wealthy.

The difference in the electoral impact of the core positions of the two parties on welfare state politics now risks placing the Republican Party at a disadvantage. Republicans can hope to counter this disadvantage by convincing voters that a Republican can manage the economy better than

Democrats, which is an argument likely to make a dent only if the economic performance under President Obama should continue to disappoint and if the prospect of higher taxes, not just on the wealthy, becomes more real. Short of such an immediate and tangible reckoning that would convince people by their concrete experience, Republicans have the more difficult option of trying to demonstrate by argument the dangers of a future crisis that will follow from the current policies of incurring massive debt. Not all arguments about the welfare state and economic policy, moreover, turn on strictly economic benefits. Republicans may find grounds for appeal on questions of morality, touching on how much one generation may force the next one to shoulder its debt, and on questions of individual freedom, dealing with how much Americans wish to put up with government policies that direct their lives, even in the name of greater equality and economic security.

These three themes that relate to the next election were derived from looking back to the election of 2012. Important as these issues may be, they are secondary to the more basic determinant in 2016 of the judgment of the incumbent's record of performance. A party in power is running not just against the other party, but against the conditions for which it is held responsible. These conditions in 2016 may well involve questions that go beyond the realm of economic performance that dominated the 2012 election and focus on issues of national debt, foreign policy, or social or cultural matters. The past is prelude to the future so long as one does not look at the past with tunnel vision. The 2012 election was held in neither the best of times nor the worst of times, which helps account for its relatively close result. What sort of times Americans will experience in 2016 no one today can say, but the reality voters face will go a long way to determining the politics of the day.

## NOTES

1. "Overall, 41% of those surveyed—including both voters and nonvoters—said they were happy that Obama was reelected president; 37% were unhappy and 22% neither. A majority of nonvoters (55%) said they were neither happy nor unhappy with the election outcome, while 29% said they were happy and 16% said they were unhappy." ("No Consensus View on Election Outcome," Pew Research online, Nov. 7, 2012, www.people-press.org.)

2. Barack H. Obama, "Transcript of President Obama's News Conference," *New York Times*, Nov. 14, 2012.

3. The final average of the major polls, provided by Real Clear Politics, had Obama up by just 0.7 percent, with a couple of the polls putting Romney ahead.

4. "Polls Show Election Eve Tie," CNN, aired Nov. 5, 2012, 11:00 ET, http://edition.cnn.com; "Obama and Romney Deadlocked, Polls Show," *Wall Street Journal* online, Nov. 6, 2012, http://online.wsj.com; Grace Wyler, "Romney and Obama Are in a Dead Tie," *Business Insider* online, Nov. 6, 2012, www.businessinsider.com.

5. Alexander Hamilton, *Federalist 72*, 1788.

6. Barack H. Obama: "Address Accepting the Presidential Nomination at the Democratic National Convention in Charlotte, NC," Sept. 6, 2012.

7. The two states in which he gained share were New Jersey and Maryland.

8. Final exit poll results from interviews of randomly selected voters as they exited voting places across the country on Tuesday, Nov. 6. Florida, North Carolina, Ohio, and Wisconsin polls included telephone interviews with early voters. The poll was conducted by Edison Media Research for the National Election Pool, the *Washington Post* and other media organizations (www.washingtonpost.com).

9. Wilson lost the House in his 1916 reelection campaign, while all the others lost chambers in the prior midterm election.

10. Republicans during his term also made huge gains at the state level, both in the number of gubernatorial seats that they control and the number of state legislatures under Republican control.

11. David Frum, "How the GOP Got Stuck in the Past," *The Daily Beast*, Nov. 11, 2012, www.thedailybeast.com.

12. James Carter, interview with Chris Matthews, *Hardball*, MSNBC, New York, Oct. 25, 2010.

13. Thirteen political science models can be seen in *PS* 45, no. 4 (October 2012): 591–674. They are summarized in Larry J. Sabato, "Forecasting the Presidential Election: Other Crystal Balls," Center for Politics, Sept. 13, 2012, www.centerforpolitics.org. Economist Ray Fair added his forecast in Marek Ramilo, "Fair Predicts Close Race," *Yale Daily News*, Sept. 25, 2012, accessed Jan. 3, 2013, http://yaledailynews.com.

14. These years were chosen because they had roughly similar margins of victory overall and no significant third-party activity.

15. James Carville and Rebecca Buckwalter-Poza, "Carville: GOP Routed by Reality," CNN online, Nov. 12, 2012, www.cnn.com.

16. Sean Trende, "The Case of the Missing White Voters," Real Clear Politics, Nov. 8, 2012, http://dyn.realclearpolitics.com.

# TWO

# Hanging On

As President Barack Obama prepared for his reelection campaign, he found himself in an uncomfortable gray zone. Although at varying points pundits had declared him either doomed to defeat or preordained to victory, he was neither. Instead, if one looked carefully at the important indicators, it was increasingly clear that Obama would be either the strongest incumbent in the last seventy years to lose a quest for reelection, or the weakest to win.

On balance, the president enjoyed (or suffered from) mediocre approval ratings; a stumbling but slowly growing economy; a political environment characterized by severe polarization that gave him both a solid floor and a hard ceiling of support, with not much room in between; and several big early legislative accomplishments that brought him more public acrimony than acclaim.

First, the economy. Obama was elected in the midst of the financial crisis of late 2008 and took office when the economy seemed to be in a free-fall. A total of 8.8 million jobs were lost from 2007 to the end of 2009, as the unemployment rate shot up.[1] In the first few months of 2009, the Dow Jones Industrial Average continued losing ground, until reaching a twelve-year low point of 6,547.05 on March 9, 2009. Trillions of dollars of wealth disappeared in declining stocks, faltering pension plans, and falling home values. Federal policy had already responded, first in an ad hoc way in early 2008 and then with passage of the $700 billion Troubled Assets Relief Program (TARP), alternately referred to as the "bank rescue" or the "bank bailout," depending on the speaker's point of view. TARP had broad support, and was endorsed by President George W. Bush, Barack Obama, and John McCain. As president, Obama had to administer TARP and decided to go well beyond it to address the crisis.

The crisis itself was not amenable to easy fixing, and soon became known as "The Great Recession" due to its duration and depth. Even after several years, there was no uniform agreement among economists as to the cause of the crisis, though it was clearly connected to the housing bubble of the early 2000s. The list of plausible villains was a long one indeed. Democrats blamed Bush, who presided over the disaster and was said to have encouraged it with lax regulation. This explanation had the benefit of simplicity, and the added benefit (for Democrats) of providing a scapegoat. Some Republicans and conservatives blamed Bill Clinton and other Democrats such as Congressman Barney Frank and Senator Chris Dodd for supporting policies that loosened restrictions on borrowing in a bid to extend home ownership to lower classes. Fannie Mae and Freddie Mac, the two giant federally backed mortgage guarantors, engaged in increasingly risky conduct, and members of Congress from both parties (including then-senator Barack Obama) blocked Bush administration proposals to rein them in. In response to the economic fall after 9/11, the Federal Reserve Board established and long maintained very low interest rates, which some economists contended contributed to an overheated housing market. Many lenders played a part by peddling products such as interest-only loans and so-called subprime mortgages requiring no or very little money down and inadequate income verification; other financial institutions traded in mortgage-backed securities that were so complicated that even financial experts were not entirely certain how they worked. At bottom, millions of Americans willingly took out risky loans to purchase houses they could not afford—though neither Democrats nor Republicans were eager to provoke the anger of the hurting electorate by pointing this out.

From its trough in 2009, the economy stabilized and began to grow slowly. Real GDP shrank by 3.1 percent in 2009, then grew by 2.4 percent in 2010 and 1.8 percent in 2011. The great labor market contraction continued for some time. The seasonally adjusted unemployment rate grew to a high of 10.0 percent in October 2009 and the official rate partially obscured more troubling data. Long-term unemployment, underemployment (people who have to settle for part-time jobs though they would prefer full-time jobs), and minority unemployment soared, and millions became discouraged and stopped looking for work, dropping out of the labor force altogether. Because the ordinarily reported unemployment rate, which the Bureau of Labor Statistics terms the U-1 rate, is based on the percentage of those working or actively seeking work as the denominator, these discouraged workers are not accounted for. For this reason many believed the U-6 unemployment figure, which takes into account discouraged workers and individuals working part-time who would prefer to work full-time, provided a more useful gauge of economic vitality. In the spring of 2010, the U-6 or "real" unemployment rate was closer to 17 percent. Altogether, the number of working Americans fell from

138,028,000 at the beginning of 2008 to a low of 129,244,000 in February of 2010.

Job creation, which most analysts agreed was the key to a lasting recovery, proceeded in fits and starts throughout Obama's presidency. In 2010, 2011, and 2012, there was a brief burst of new jobs created in the early months of the year, leading to hopes that the economy had finally turned the corner; however, in each case, the job numbers quickly fell back again. The slow, unsteady, but, nevertheless, upward trajectory of the employment rate gave both sides ammunition going into the November contest. Because jobs were being created, Obama supporters could point to progress and could compare the present with the depths of 2008/2009. But because they were being created so slowly, his opponents argued that Obama's policies had actually suppressed the naturally resilient American economy, making the latest recession one of the longest and the recovery one of the weakest. To help make this point, Republicans often drew a stark comparison between job creation at the beginning of Ronald Reagan's recovery with that in 2009–2012. In the twenty-seven months following the employment trough under each president, Reagan's economy created 7.7 million net private-sector jobs to 4.4 million under Obama. Measured from the beginning of the official recovery, Reagan's recovery produced 9.1 million additional private-sector jobs to Obama's 3.4 million.[2] The US economic position in the world also slipped. According to the World Economic Forum, the US global competitiveness ranking declined every year from 2009 through 2012.[3]

Associated with the slow economy, both as an effect and (at least for Republicans) as a cause, was the burgeoning federal deficit and debt. The financial crisis and the federal government's response had ballooned the federal deficit from $163 billion in fiscal year 2007 to $438 billion in fiscal year 2008; from 2009 to 2012, Obama era annual deficits never fell below $1 trillion—averaging $1.33 trillion—a figure that would have been unthinkable even a few years before. Overall federal spending grew from 19.7 percent of GDP in 2007 to an estimated 24.3 percent of GDP in 2012. In consequence, the national debt grew from $10.6 trillion on Bush's last day in office to $16 trillion as Democrats held their nominating convention in 2012. Keynesian economists lauded the deficits—some even considered them "too small"—but many others worried about the long-term effects, and even the short-term drag imposed by such an intrusion of the government into the national economy.

Political polarization was apparent from the beginning of the Obama administration. From an early point in his presidency, the gap in Obama's approval rating between self-identified Democrats and self-identified Republicans was the largest ever recorded. The president had taken office on the crest of a campaign in which he portrayed himself as a healer, a "postpartisan" figure, someone who could bring together "red America" and "blue America"; Obama's presidency would not be nearly as transcendent as his candidacy. The goodwill and historic approval ratings that Obama's campaign garnered would quickly dissipate as he began to implement his agenda. By the time he was facing reelection, two passionate and opposing political movements had arisen in response to him and the times: the Tea Party movement, mobilized to stop his health care reform, fight the debt, and (as its adherents saw it) restore limited constitutional government, and the Occupy movement, which protested against Wall Street and the "1 percent" at the top of the income scale. The right claimed that polarization was the result of Obama's unbending resolve to "transform America," the left claimed it was Republicans' obstinacy and jaded gamesmanship that had divided the nation, and still others argued partisan division was simply a reflection of Washington politics since the 1980s. While there was no consensus about the cause—and, in a polarized polity, who would expect that?—few would deny that Obama's postpartisan vision was not realized. As a result, many of Obama's signature domestic achievements were accomplished with limited or no bipartisan support.

While Obama's foreign policy agenda did not divide the country (at least along partisan lines) to the degree that his domestic agenda did, his record was ambiguous. The war in Iraq was ended, though arguably it ended successfully because of late-term strategic decisions (the "surge") made by George W. Bush, which Obama opposed as a senator. Some critics also feared that the terms of US withdrawal gave the United States little capacity to promote stability in post-war Iraq and hence risked the hard-won gains of the war. As he promised, Obama also shifted resources to Afghanistan, but provided fewer troops than the generals thought necessary and imposed a timetable for withdrawal, calling into question the strength of his commitment to victory, a word that rarely passed his lips. When a reporter asked him to define *victory*, he acknowledged that he was avoiding the term, preferring to speak of "success" in a "narrowly drawn" mission.[4]

Obama worked hard, though with little success, to "reset" adversarial relations with Russia and the Muslim world. But in doing so, he was accused of apologizing for America and giving short shrift to close American allies such as Great Britain, Israel, and Poland, which suffered the indignity of the White House announcing cancellation of a proposed joint missile defense system on the seventieth anniversary of the Soviet invasion of Poland in 1939. Obama was, however, able to carry into 2012 anti-terrorism credentials that outweighed, at least in political benefit, all of the rest of his tangled foreign policy. Under his watch, Osama bin Laden was located and killed in a daring commando raid, while dozens of other al-Qaeda operatives were killed in a seemingly endless series of drone strikes in Afghanistan, Pakistan, Yemen, and elsewhere. Obama was also lucky: attempted terrorist attacks, including the Detroit plot to blow up an airliner on Christmas day 2009 and an attempted bombing of

Times Square, failed. Though foreign policy was sure to be secondary to economic concerns in 2012, at least Obama would not have to defend that front—as long as no new crises erupted.

On balance, though, the American people were clearly not impressed with Obama's first term on whatever criteria they deemed most important. Like all presidents, Obama enjoyed a "honeymoon" period with high job approval ratings after taking office. By late November 2009, however, the Real Clear Politics average of his approval ratings had fallen below 50 percent. From late November 2009 up to summer of 2012, Obama's average approval ratings were above 50 percent for exactly four days in January 2011 and for one month after the killing of Osama bin Laden in early May 2011. For the rest of his presidency leading up to the general election, Obama was below 50 percent—that is, for 919 of the 953 days from November 20, 2009, to July 1, 2012. For large swaths of the time, including the last half of 2010, about eight months of 2011, January 2012, and intermittently through the summer of 2012, Obama was not only below 50 percent but also underwater—his negative assessments exceeding his positive assessments. Moreover, when one factored in intensity of feeling—did respondents "strongly" approve or disapprove of Obama's job performance, or only "somewhat" approve or disapprove?—the strong disapprovers outnumbered the strong approvers from July of 2009 without fail, usually by double digits (sometimes as high as a twenty-four percentage-point gap).

Associated with the president's lackluster approval ratings, most Americans believed the country was headed in the wrong direction for the greater part of Obama's term. For obvious reasons, the average so-called right track–wrong track numbers were heavily weighted toward the "wrong track" answer in January 2009. By July, there was an even split, but the trend did not persist very long. Soon, the "wrong track" answer regained the upper hand and did not relinquish its lead. On July 1, 2012, the RCP average showed a polling result of 61.7 percent of respondents saying the country was on the wrong track, compared with only 29.7 percent who thought it was on the right track—numbers not far from the typical responses for the previous three years.

Although the president faced long-term problems with public skepticism, he also enjoyed a floor in difficult times that many presidents would envy. For most of his first term, his average approval ranged between 45 and 49 percent—a danger sign for any incumbent, to be sure, but also far from the lows suffered by presidents including Truman, Nixon, Carter, and George W. Bush, all of whom found themselves in the thirties and even the twenties for extended periods of time. For this floor, Obama could thank several factors. Not least, objective conditions were bad but not terrible, and were improving (if slowly) rather than deteriorating. In addition, despite their lack of appreciation of the president's job performance, most Americans said they liked the president personally. Although they may have found conditions unsatisfactory, many were willing to forgive Obama given the difficult circumstances he inherited. Unlike some presidents in hard economic times, Obama also did not face a torrent of critical news stories about homelessness, black youth unemployment, or other social conditions. And the president benefitted from the loyalty of significant portions of his coalition. Among African Americans, approval of the president ran about 40 percent above the national average.[5]

This combination of circumstances led to a situation in which Obama was in a stronger position than most recent presidents who had lost reelection, but a weaker position than those who had won. This point was made in economical fashion by the American Presidency Project. Its website featured four charts: the approval rating of Obama versus reelected presidents, the approval rating of Obama versus defeated presidents, GDP growth under Obama versus reelected presidents, and GDP growth under Obama versus defeated presidents. In regard to both job approval ratings and economic growth, Obama's trendlines were generally higher than those of the presidents who were defeated in their bids for reelection—and lower than those of the incumbents who won reelection.[6] He was in No Man's Land.

Altogether, "Hope and Change," the Obama formula of 2008, was exhausted before the first year of his presidency was complete. When he entered office, some likened him to Franklin Delano Roosevelt. He had to run for reelection, however, as Harry S. Truman, an embattled incumbent whose chances depended on a combination of sound strategy, ruthless execution, incompetent opposition, and luck. Indeed, by late 2011, the campaign's strategists were openly touting the parallels between Truman in 1948 and Obama.[7] The president, like the haberdasher from Independence, had a strong enough base to win, if it was successfully mobilized through hard-hitting appeals to class, race, age, and gender divisions. Thus policy would be an instrument of campaigning, designed to appeal to the key portions of the Obama coalition—youth, single women, minorities—just as Truman had used policy to build enthusiasm among organized labor, blacks, Jews, and farmers. And, just as Truman waged a relentless negative campaign against Thomas Dewey and the Republican Congress, Obama would, in the parlance of political consultants, "define the opposition," turning a referendum on his presidency—for which he was not well-positioned—into a choice between Obama and something worse.

Along the road from FDR to Truman, from "Hope and Change" to "Just Win, Baby" (the famed motto of Oakland Raiders owner Al Davis), were a number of key inflection points.

## HONEYMOON

Barack Obama entered office enjoying a reservoir of popular goodwill. The nation's first African American president, he was also the first Democratic presidential candidate since Jimmy Carter in 1976 to win more than 50 percent of the nationally aggregated popular vote. Although his congressional coattails were modest by historical standards, they were the longest since Ronald Reagan's in 1980. Aided by Obama's stirring 2008 campaign, Democrats padded their congressional majorities by twenty-eight seats in the House and, after the victorious conclusion of a long and bitter recount in Minnesota, eight seats in the Senate. The recipient of support from a number of high-profile Republicans during the campaign, including former secretary of state Colin Powell and Christopher Buckley, son of *National Review* founder William F. Buckley, Obama also seemed poised to seize the middle and pursue the promise of a "postpartisan" future. In late January 2009, Obama's approval rating stood at 67 percent according to Gallup, and *Time* touted him as the new FDR, heralding the next partisan realignment.[8]

As most analysts perceived, Republicans were in a bind. They could either oppose a popular, history-making president in a time of national crisis, or they could allow themselves to be coopted and swallowed up in a new Obama consensus. Republican congressional leaders promised cooperation when possible; on the other hand, Rush Limbaugh, giving voice to the spirit of resistance that would later animate the Tea Party, frankly admitted that he hoped Obama would fail (in his plans to transform the country). Obama, however, had his own challenges. He would have to deliver. And he, too, had a choice to make. Would he bridge the gap between red and blue America, or would his talk of postpartisanship prove to be merely an attempt to tamp down opposition to a divisive agenda? He could walk through one of three doors: Would he be the conciliator, the hard Chicago pol, or the left-wing academic? His base clearly preferred some combination of the latter two, but there remained a significant part of the country, including the voters who made the difference between John Kerry's 48 percent and Obama's 53 percent, who had found Obama appealing precisely because they thought he would choose Door Number One.

Obama's first task was to propose a large economic stimulus program. With George W. Bush's support, the 110th Congress had already approved a $160 billion stimulus package as the economy slowed in early 2008. Now Obama proposed an $831 billion package divided between tax rebates, transportation projects, aid to state and local governments (to forestall public employee layoffs), supplemental funds for food stamps and other welfare spending, and a variety of "green energy" subsidies. As Obama's chief of staff Rahm Emanuel said, "You never want a serious crisis to go to waste."[9] At least part of the Obama stimulus plan was geared toward using the economic crisis as a lever to implement a number of policies liberals had long called for. After the fact, a variety of voices suggested that Obama had not exerted enough direct control over the construction of the stimulus plan. For example, Michael Gerson argued that "President Obama staked the initial reputation of his administration on the wisdom, restraint, and economic innovation of House Speaker Nancy Pelosi and the rest of the Democratic congressional leadership. It was a mistake."[10] Others, such as congressional scholar Thomas E. Mann, asserted that "Obama's hands were all over this bill from start to finish" and that the final legislative product was "remarkably close to what Obama sought."[11] In any event, there was never any indication that he disapproved of any significant portion of the congressional Democrats' program.

Whatever the direct role of the White House in planning the American Recovery and Reinvestment Act, Obama and his team made two critical miscalculations. One, which would haunt Obama through Election Day 2012, was that they oversold the effectiveness of the program. Among other things, Obama promised a bevy of "shovel-ready projects," as if infrastructure construction could spring forth spontaneously upon passage of the bill. As he would later ruefully acknowledge, "There's no such thing as shovel-ready [projects]."[12] When predicting the economic consequences of the stimulus, the nominee to head Obama's Council of Economic Advisers issued a chart purporting to show the probable unemployment rate with and without the stimulus. When the actual unemployment rate after the stimulus passed exceeded the predicted rate *without* the stimulus—as it did up to and beyond November 6, 2012—critics were handed invaluable political ammunition. Obama's supporters tried to rescue their position by arguing that conditions had been worse than they originally thought, and that the stimulus had "saved" a number of jobs that would have been lost. Nevertheless, the opinion that the stimulus had not met its promises took hold fairly quickly. According to a *Washington Post*/ABC poll in late September and early October, only 29 percent thought that the stimulus money had been mostly well spent, while 68 percent thought that it had mostly been wasted.[13]

Three schools of thought developed around the question of why the stimulus failed to deliver what it promised. On one side were hardline Keynesians, such as Paul Krugman, who argued that the stimulus would have succeeded if it had only been larger. Others suggested that the mix of elements had not been optimal; less should have been spent to satisfy Democratic constituencies, more spent on projects with proven economic value. A third school questioned the entire strategy, likening it to dropping cash from a helicopter in hopes it would somehow produce economic growth. Large stimulus programs in the United States in the 1930s and Japan in the 1990s had failed; why, these critics asked, did we think it would work better this time?

In addition to its dubious economic value, the bill had an extraordinary political cost. House Republicans had no influence in drafting the program and ended up contributing no votes to its passage; Senate Republicans were courted only to the extent that a handful of GOP votes were needed to clear the sixty-vote hurdle. In the end, the overall size of the stimulus was reduced to $787 billion to lure three liberal Republicans—Arlen Specter of Pennsylvania and Susan Collins and Olympia Snowe of Maine. Within a couple of months, Specter would switch parties. Confronted by House Republicans upset at their exclusion from the process and concerned by the heavy spending, Obama responded by telling House Republican Whip Eric Cantor: "Elections have consequences . . . and Eric, I won."[14] This may have been the seminal moment of his first term. On the first major initiative of his presidency, Obama opted not to walk through Door Number One. It would not be the last time.

Given the large Democratic majorities in Congress, Obama's strategic decision had little significance for the outcome of the vote, but it had a large impact on the contours of the vote and on establishing essentially undivided responsibility for the fate of the stimulus. More importantly, it set a tone that put the nation on the course for what one might call the post-postpartisanship of the Obama era.

## THE HEALTH CARE MORASS

While the stimulus debate may have poisoned Obama's relations with congressional Republicans, it was health care that ended the honeymoon. Government-guaranteed universal health care had long been an article of faith on the left. In 1944, Franklin Roosevelt numbered the "right to health care" among the positive guarantees that should constitute an "Economic Bill of Rights" with a status equal to that of the political Bill of Rights in the US Constitution. Harry S. Truman put forward a national health insurance plan that failed in Congress; Lyndon Johnson proceeded incrementally toward the goal with the creation of Medicare and Medicaid; Bill Clinton put forward a comprehensive health reform proposal in 1993–1994, only to see it shelved amid crumbling support. Obama intended to succeed where others had failed, and made health care his top priority after passage of the stimulus.

The development of the health care bill—ultimately called the Patient Protection and Affordable Care Act—followed a course roughly similar to that of the stimulus. The president pushed the issue to the top of the agenda and established general parameters: near-universal coverage, protection for those with preexisting conditions, but no government-run single-payer Canadian-style system. Obama had, as recently as 2008, expressed admiration for the single-payer plan, which has long been the preferred model of the American left, but viewed it as too extreme to command sufficient political support for the time being.[15] Within these parameters, Obama left Democrats in Congress the task of working out the details, while he drummed up public support and made the back-room deals necessary to keep the process moving.

Obama's efforts were largely successful. He was eventually able to secure the support of major interest groups critical to the passage and implementation of a health care overhaul: the insurance industry, represented by America's Health Insurance Plans (AHIP), doctors in the American Medical Association, and the pharmaceutical industry (PhRMA). The AMA was brought along by promises of higher Medicare reimbursement rates, PhRMA by the lure of more customers, and AHIP by a tradeoff that paid for more expensive federal demands regarding who and what would be covered by insurance policies by requiring all Americans to buy health insurance (the "individual insurance mandate"). The large and powerful AARP, representing the retired and near-retired, also signed on early.[16]

With large majorities in Congress, including a suddenly filibuster-proof Senate after the seating of Al Franken from Minnesota, and with the key interest groups trumpeting their approval, Obama seemed set for an easy victory on health care. Despite the aura of inevitability, which had contributed to the interest-group stampede, things began to unravel in July. That month, the Congressional Budget Office estimated that the program would cost $1 trillion, an alarming figure on top of the nearly $1 trillion just allocated to the stimulus. As other details regarding the two-thousand-page bill emerged, the growing backlash intensified. Among the least popular aspects of the bill were the large Medicare cuts proposed to finance the program and the emergence of the Independent Payments Advisory Board (IPAB), which struck some as having powers to impose rationing and limits on treatments. Referring to IPAB, 2008 Republican vice presidential candidate Sarah Palin condemned "death panels" that could deny patients needed treatments if they were too expensive. Over time, the AMA splintered, with seventeen state medical associations rejecting the national organization's endorsement of "Obamacare," and AARP would lose perhaps as many as nine hundred thousand members in protest.[17]

Powerful business groups like the Chamber of Commerce and the National Federation of Independent Business began to push back, voicing discontent over other key elements of Obamacare. They were strongly opposed to the taxes and employer mandates in the legislation. They argued it would impose unbearable costs to employers that would, ultimately, force them to let go of valued employees they could not afford to insure. More importantly, the Tea Party movement came into its own in the debate over health care, rallying and organizing opponents.[18]

The Tea Party movement could be traced to a much-publicized "rant" by CNBC financial analyst Rick Santelli on February 19, 2009, when he expressed frustration over Obama's plan to bail out delinquent homeowners. When Santelli called for modern tea parties to protest big-government policies, the political world was surprised when thousands of citizens around the country showed up for hastily organized rallies. The movement quickly grew to be a significant national phenomenon, a decentralized combination of half a dozen national organizations and some 2,800 local groups taking as its unofficial symbol the Revolutionary War's Gadsden Flag, a yellow banner emblazoned with the motto "Don't Tread on Me."[19] Aside from its clear opposition to Obama's policies, many were unsure of what the Tea Party hoped to accomplish.

Matt Kibbe and Dick Armey, the founders of FreedomWorks, a nonprofit that provides financial support for many Tea Party events and candidates, claimed, "We just want to be free. Free to lead our lives as we please, so long as we do not infringe on the same freedom as others."[20] Kibbe, Armey, and many other Tea Party activists coalesced around three principal platform planks: constitutionally limited government, fiscal responsibility, and free-market economic policies. To many pundits and academics, it was unclear what these broad statements of purpose meant practically. What aspects of the Constitution did they want to return to? What aspects of the current government did they find unconstitutional? Adding to the commentariat's consternation was the fact that the Tea Party, a fairly diffuse mass movement, did not speak with one voice. Despite Nancy Pelosi's insistence that the movement was manufactured "astro-turf" rather than truly grassroots, the Tea Party prided itself on a lack of hierarchical structure or doctrine imposed from on high. While the movement's lack of formal structure may have evinced a certain authenticity, it also complicated efforts to distill the contours of the Tea Party's agenda or theoretical underpinnings. The thread that seemed to tie the movement together was a belief that America's political system had moved away from the Founders' vision. The economic crisis and mounting debt were a result of this trend.

To them, Obama's agenda represented an assault on the idea of limited government. Though many Tea Partiers were upset by TARP (which started under George W. Bush), Wall Street reform, the auto bailout, and mortgage relief, Obamacare drew their especial ire. They saw health care reform as a multidimensional threat to its vision of a good society—Obamacare would add yet another unaffordable entitlement to the nation's fiscal woes, expand the power and reach of the centralized state, and administer the coup de grace to the last vestiges of the constitutional principle of limited government. It would, in short, go far to remaking America along the lines of European social democracies.

As members of Congress returned home for their August recess, they were met with town hall after town hall of citizens irate about health care reform, some spontaneous and some organized by Tea Party groups. Some Democratic members simply stopped holding town hall meetings altogether. Nationally, polls showed that a plurality was now opposed to Obamacare, a fact that would remain true for the next three years. Along with the concerns about government cost and power emphasized by the Tea Party, critics also feared the effects of the reform on insurance prices, choice of insurance, and availability and quality of care, and objected that federal health care dollars might go to pay for abortions or to care for illegal immigrants.

In an attempt to recapture momentum, Obama spoke on health care to a joint session of Congress on September 9, 2009. Up to this point, he had remained largely quiet about what details he preferred. The speech was yet another opportunity to mediate between the entrenched Republicans and ardent Democrats, leveraging his still-formidable popularity and institutional power to broker a bipartisan deal. Instead, he again bypassed Door Number One, simply repeating his arguments, commending congressional Democrats for their progress, and calling on Americans for support. Americans were underwhelmed and after a short-lived boost, support was back where it was before, well below levels of opposition. A few days after Obama's speech to Congress, Tea Party activists sponsored a rally in Washington, attended by at least sixty thousand—supporters claimed the number was much higher—calling for Congress to "kill the bill."[21] Then, in early November, Republicans won two new governorships, one in New Jersey and one in Virginia, in campaigns that were interpreted as being at least partially about Obama and health care reform. It was becoming clear that life in Washington was not going to be the same as life on the campaign trail. In the fight over health care, Obama's rhetoric—he made fifty-four speeches on the topic through the spring of 2010[22]—failed to move the needle of public opinion. If he was going to win at all, it would have to be the ugly way, in the back rooms of the Capitol, one vote at a time.

By the fall, it was clear that Obama could count on no Republican votes in either chamber. The House passed its version of health care reform on November 8, 2009, by a vote of 220–215; the Senate passed its own version over Christmas, with no votes to spare, after skeptical moderates like Ben Nelson of Nebraska and Mary Landrieu of Louisiana received special considerations in the bill. Just as the two sides sat down to negotiate a common bill, a special election threw the health care project into turmoil again.

Senator Edward Kennedy of Massachusetts had died the previous summer, leaving Obama a martyr to motivate the health care troops but also a vacant seat to defend. Political analysts had simply assumed that Democrats would hold the seat; Massachusetts is one of the most Democratic states in the union, having given 61 percent of its vote to Obama in 2008. The last Republican senator from the state, liberal Republican Edward Brooke, was defeated in November 1978. Not until about two weeks before the vacancy election between Democrat Martha Coakley and Republican Scott Brown in January 2010 did it begin to seem that Brown had a chance. On Election Day, Brown won by a comfortable margin, with the support of the Tea Party, based on a campaign promise to become "the 41st vote against Obamacare"—a number that would allow Republicans to filibuster a conference report.

Brown's election in the bluest of the blue states reverberated around the country. The depth and breadth of the popular revolt against Obamacare had been revealed in dramatic fashion, and Democratic leaders in Washington were temporarily stunned. At a leadership pow-wow, Obama, Pelosi, and Reid considered drafting a narrower, more moderate, bill. Instead, they decided to go forward with the Senate's version of health care reform, which, while very comprehensive, did not include the House's provisions for government-run "public option" insurance. Because the Senate was now vulnerable to a filibuster, Democrats had to abandon the search for a negotiated common bill. The House would have to simply vote to adopt the Senate version, on the promise that the Senate would use the reconciliation process, which is normally used for budget cuts and requires only fifty-one votes, to fix some of the smaller objections that House Democrats had toward the Senate bill.[23]

As usual, principle and politics comingled in this decision. The president and other top Democrats were philosophically committed to "go big." They had been given a brief window of opportunity to achieve a major policy change that had obtained near-theological status among progressives. They also believed that their political problems would only worsen if they backed off now. House Democrats were told that Obama's presidency would be ruined if they did not fall in line; optimistically, Bill Clinton promised that Obama's approval rating would go up by ten points immediately if health care reform passed.

So, with a hostile public to the right of them and a determined Obama and Pelosi to the left of them, House Democrats went into the valley and, one by one, announced their support. It took until mid-March to come within striking distance of the magic number of 218. The final holdouts were a small band of pro-life Democrats, mostly northeastern and Midwestern Catholics, who wanted stronger assurances that the bill would not fund abortions. When, at the final hour, Obama signed an executive order that satisfied them, Pelosi had the votes she needed.

Democrats celebrated the victory, which represented the greatest expansion of the federal government since the Great Society. Many hoped, with New York congressman Dan Maffei, that "now we can put this behind us." Like Clinton's prediction, Maffei's hope proved too optimistic. The Tea Party movement, far from retreating after the defeat, was invigorated by the fight and enraged by both the result and the seemingly corrupt manner in which the sausage got made. Republicans expressed a determination to fight for repeal. Constitutional challenges were announced by several states almost immediately. These challenges argued that the individual insurance mandate exceeded Congress's power under the Commerce Clause and that states were being improperly coerced to expand their Medicaid payments. Rather than gaining in the polls, Obama continued his slump. In November 2009, right around the initial House passage of Obamacare, the president's RCP average approval rating fell below 50 percent; by July 2010, his approval ratings were upside down, where they stayed through midterm election day. And Obamacare itself remained unpopular. From the time of its passage, in poll after poll, a majority or plurality indicated that their preference was for the program to be repealed.

As with the stimulus, the health care bill represented a major legislative victory for Obama. Much more than the stimulus, the health care victory was an emblem of the president's determination. But it was also representative of a rigid, highly partisan approach that pushed forward despite numerous warning signs and that provoked and fueled a backlash that would cost his party dearly in November. By midway through the battle, Gallup was measuring a significant increase in the percentage of Americans calling themselves conservative.[24] "What's really exceptional at this stage of Obama's presidency is the extent to which the public has moved in a conservative direction on a range of issues," wrote Andrew Kohut of the Pew Research Center in December 2009. "These trends have emanated as much from the middle of the electorate as from the highly energized conservative right."[25]

Although opposition to the stimulus and health care were rallying points for both Republicans and conservative independents, a number of other issues aggravated them. These issues included bailouts for General Motors and Chrysler automobile companies, a federal takeover of federally guaranteed student loans, and the proposed "cap and trade" bill (which passed the House but languished in the Senate). The 2,319-page Dodd-Frank financial regulation bill was more popular, but symbolized for some the regulatory overreach of the administration. The president's $1.5 trillion annual deficits tied together fears of an out-of-control government and declining economic prospects.[26] Job growth in the spring of 2010 had led Vice President Joe Biden to promise that the nation was about to embark on "recovery summer," but by September the economy had stalled again and the unemployment rate was stuck at 9.6 percent.

## MIDTERM SHELLACKING

Even without troubles over the economy and health care, astute observers could see that Obama might face an uphill climb in 2010. He had won

69 percent of first-time voters in 2008 but just 50 percent of those who had cast ballots before.[27] In a lower-turnout midterm election, the latter would be much more likely than the former to vote. Also, owing to large Democratic victories in 2006 and 2008, House Democrats were exposed: forty-nine came from congressional districts in which John McCain had beaten Barack Obama in 2008. Many had run as moderates or conservatives but would have to defend the liberal record of Nancy Pelosi's House.

When the votes were counted, Republicans had scored an impressive victory that promised to bring the Obama "change" to an abrupt halt. The contours of that victory included the following:

- A net gain of sixty-three House seats, the largest number the Republicans had picked up in any election since 1938. Altogether, Republican House gains were the third largest in any midterm in the last century, producing their largest House majority since 1948 (see table 2.1). Against dozens of losing Democratic House members, only two Republican incumbents in heavily Democratic districts went down. The GOP gained in every region, posting big wins in Ohio, Pennsylvania, and New York, advancing in Illinois and the upper Midwest, sweeping the Dakotas and New Hampshire, picking up strength in the Pacific Northwest, and gaining in states that were trending Democratic in 2008 such as Virginia, Florida, and Colorado. Some venerable committee chairs such as Ike Skelton (Armed Services) and John Spratt (Budget) were among the victims. An irony of the election was that the sins of the progressive Democrats in the House were often visited on more moderate Democrats. The moderate, "Blue Dog" wing of the House Democratic Party was decimated. Meanwhile, staunch progressives like Nancy Pelosi and Barney Frank, typically running in Democratic strongholds, held onto their seats.
- A pick-up of six seats in the Senate. This showing disappointed some Republicans who had hoped for outright control, which seemed within reach at varying points during the campaign. Indeed, Republicans probably threw away at least three winnable races (in Delaware, Nevada, and Colorado) where stronger candidates failed to win the party primary. Nevertheless, the Republican gain represented *nearly one-third* of the nineteen Democratic seats up for election in 2010 and a figure twice the average Senate loss in midterm elections since 1910. Republicans easily held open seats that analysts had once expected to be tough, such as New Hampshire, Florida, Ohio, Kentucky, and Missouri. Half of their gains came in red states, the other half in blue territory.
- In an important development that was overshadowed by gains in Congress, Republicans also racked up big wins at the state level.

> The GOP scored a net gain of six governorships and nearly seven hundred state legislative seats, attaining their highest total of legislative chambers since the 1920s.[28] This state-level success gave Republicans the upper hand in a number of congressional redistricting fights. In the aftermath of the midterms, more than a dozen Democratic state legislators nationwide switched parties.

When the 2010 campaign began, President Obama and the Republicans agreed on the question of what the election was all about. The contest, the president readily admitted, would be a verdict on his domestic agenda of stimulus policies, health care reform, and taxes on the wealthiest. Obama spoke of "guarding the change," with John Boehner responding, on behalf of Republicans everywhere, "Hell no!"

Consequently, the 2010 election was among the most nationalized midterm campaigns in American history, on par with elections such as 1858, 1946, and 1994. It also bears noting that every midterm since 1994 has been highly nationalized by historic standards, a result not only of huge events—the first health care reform proposal (1994), the looming impeachment (1998), the 9/11 attack and the prospect of the Iraq War (2002), the Iraq War (2006), and now Obama's "change" agenda (2010)—but also of sharpening party conflicts that draw clearer divisions on national issues. Nearly every Republican competing for national office, and many running for state office, ran against the Obama agenda and made it the centerpiece of the campaign. Only some Democrats, sensing national trouble, sought to "localize" their contests, a tactic that worked in some of the Senate contests with weaker Republican candidates. A postelection survey by Democracy Corps and Resurgent Republic found party control of Congress helped decide a congressional vote for 74 percent of Republicans, 57 percent of Democrats, and 51 percent of independents. Among those who backed a Republican candidate, 44 percent said their vote was a vote for the candidate, 34 percent said it was a vote to check the agenda

**Table 2.1. Five Largest Midterm Election Losses by President's Party, 1910–2010 (in order of House losses)**

| *Year* | *House* | *Senate* |
|---|---|---|
| 1922 | 75 | 8 |
| 1938 | 71 | 6 |
| 2010 | 63 | 6 |
| 1914* | 59 | (5) |
| 1910 | 57 | 10 |

* The 1914 midterm was the first after ratification of the Seventeenth Amendment, providing for direct election of senators. The Democratic pickup reflected the difference between legislative election and popular election.

of President Obama and Democrats, and 14 percent said it was a vote against the Democrat. Forty-three percent of independents who voted Republican said their vote reflected a desire to check President Obama and the Democrats, compared with 30 percent who voted for the Republican candidate and 19 percent who voted against the Democrat.[29]

Throughout the campaign, analysts pointed to the "enthusiasm gap" between Republicans and Democrats, with Republican voters clearly more motivated. In the end, the national House electorate was 35 percent Republican and 35 percent Democratic, in contrast with 2008, when Democrats held a 40–33 percent edge. What hurt Democrats even more was that independent voters swung heavily against them. In 2006, when Democrats gained control of Congress, independents favored Democrats by a 57–39 percent margin; in 2010, the situation was reversed, with independents (who accounted for a quarter of the electorate) supporting Republican candidates by a 56–37 percent margin.[30]

Other exit poll results showed Obama's 2008 coalition to be endangered. Republicans won the men's vote by a wide margin, while women (who supported Obama by a 56–43 margin in 2008) split their votes evenly. Those making $100,000 or more, voters who had been drifting toward the Democrats in recent years, moved back toward the Republicans. First-time voters—who overwhelmingly backed Obama in 2008—were much less numerous in 2010, and those who showed up gave Democrats only a slight edge. White Catholics and white working-class voters, two (overlapping) swing groups among whom Obama had struggled in 2008, gave Republicans huge margins in 2010. Racial minorities continued to back Democrats but by lower percentages than two years before (see table 2.2). These shifts worried Democrats and gave hope to Republicans. But the question remained: which electorate, 2010 or 2008, would show up in 2012? Much of the debate over polling that later played itself out on the editorial pages and political blogs regarding polling accuracy revolved around this question.

If special election and midterm election results seemed to prefigure a Republican victory in 2012, the midterm exit polls also contained warning signs for the GOP. Most voters, including a majority of Independents, blamed the ongoing economic difficulties on either Wall Street or George W. Bush, not on Obama. And, although the election results might have represented a Great Repudiation of Obama's stewardship and agenda, they did not indicate an equally enthusiastic embrace of the Republican Party. Exit polls showed that a majority of voters had an unfavorable opinion of the party. Republicans won because voters who viewed them unfavorably were more willing to hold their noses and vote for them anyway than were the roughly equal proportion of voters who viewed the Democrats unfavorably. As Haley Barbour, Republican governor of Mississippi and former Republican National Committee chair, commented, "It's a very important observation that this is a referendum on Oba-

**Table 2.2. Voting in US House Elections by Demographic Group and Region, 2008–2010 (in percentages)**

| | 2008 | | 2010 | |
|---|---|---|---|---|
| | D | R | D | R |
| Female | 56 | 42 | 48 | 49 |
| Male | 52 | 46 | 41 | 55 |
| White | 45 | 53 | 37 | 60 |
| Black | 93 | 5 | 89 | 9 |
| Latino | 68 | 29 | 60 | 38 |
| 18–29 years | 63 | 34 | 55 | 42 |
| 65+ years | 49 | 48 | 38 | 59 |
| >$100,000 | 56 | 41 | 49 | 48 |
| $100,000+ | 48 | 50 | 40 | 58 |
| Catholic | 55 | 42 | 44 | 54 |
| Independent | 51 | 43 | 37 | 56 |
| First-time vote | 63 | 35 | 45 | 43 |
| Northeast | 61 | 38 | 54 | 44 |
| South | 48 | 50 | 37 | 61 |
| Midwest | 53 | 45 | 44 | 53 |
| West | 58 | 39 | 49 | 48 |

*Sources*: www.cnn.com/ELECTION/2008/results/polls/#val=USH00p1; www.cnn.com/ELECTION/2010/results/polls/#val=USH00p1.

ma's policies, and the American people do not like Obama's policies. . . . We Republicans, we have to understand they're not saying, 'Hey, we love you, Republicans.'"[31]

Several alternative explanations of the Republican sweep were offered by analysts. Some suggested that the 2010 election was about generalized anger directed at incumbents. Some of this anger naturally fell on the party (the Democrats) with full responsibility for running the show in Washington. And in the Republican Party, too, there was substantial pressure exerted against incumbents early on by the "Tea Party" movement. Two Republican Senate incumbents, Robert Bennett of Utah and Lisa Murkowski of Alaska, lost primary contests, though a general-election write-in campaign enabled Murkowski to keep her seat after ethics issues doomed the GOP nominee. Florida governor Charlie Crist, the GOP establishment's choice for the US Senate, decided to run as an independent after it became clear that Marco Rubio would trounce him in the primary. (Rubio trounced him in the general election instead.) In Delaware, moderate Representative Mike Castle unexpectedly lost the Senate nomination to insurgent Christine O'Donnell. When it came to the final election, though, the story in the House was not one of incumbents losing, but of Democratic incumbents losing. Every Republican incumbent who was renominated won reelection, while two Democratic incumbents, Russ Feingold of Wisconsin and Blanche Lincoln of Arkansas, lost their seats.

Another explanation, favored by Democrats, was that Republicans had succeeded through a campaign of misinformation made possible not just by huge sums of money—Democrats overall spent as much as Republicans—but by a profusion of "outside" money flowing from the controversial *Citizens United* Supreme Court decision. That decision, announced in January 2010, declared any prohibition on direct campaign spending by corporations or labor unions to be an unconstitutional infringement on freedom of speech (though they could still be prohibited from contributing to candidates). However, postelection analyses showed that money did not tip the scales; at most, it leveled the playing field for viable challengers. Outside spending in 2010 went to races that were already saturating the airwaves.[32]

For his part, the president blamed the opposition's success on the enormity of the problems and the complexity of the policy responses. "It was a lot for the public to digest," Obama explained. "It was also a lot for me to be able to communicate effectively to the public in any coherent way."[33] However, if the president's message had failed to sink in, it was not for lack of effort or technological innovation. And, of course, this was the same president who had come to office having been widely praised for his communication skills. Insufficient quantity or quality of communication seemed an unlikely explanation for the Democratic defeat.

In the final analysis, Democrats could not admit that the election had been a referendum on Obama's first two years in office and then still press forward with the same policy agenda. Thus, most Democrats denied that the election ever had anything to do with "the change." It was instead all about Americans' reaction to economic conditions. Hendrik Hertzberg of the *New Yorker* explained, "the longest and deepest mass suffering" of the Great Recession "has occurred with Obama in the White House" (in contrast to the Great Depression, when the deepest suffering preceded FDR's accession to power).[34] Some analysts went so far as to suggest that, given the gravity of America's persistent financial woes, Republicans should have won more convincingly than they did.

This argument, too, seemed designed to serve a political purpose—defending the president's agenda—rather than offer a genuine explanation. Pre-election political science models, heavily influenced by economic conditions, predicted Republican House gains between twenty-two and fifty-two seats.[35] The actual pickup of sixty-three exceeded even the top forecast. Perhaps the standard models did not fully take account of the unusually bad unemployment picture in 2010. But compare 2010 to

1982, the one midterm since the Second World War when unemployment was even *higher* than in 2010. In 1982, the in-party Republicans lost 14 percent of their House seats. At that rate, only thirty-six seats would have changed hands in 2010—not enough for John Boehner to become Speaker. In 1982, the president's party had no net loss of Senate seats. In 2010, it lost six. Something more was going on than a reflex reaction to economic circumstances.

The Republicans' account of 2010 did not ignore the importance of the economy, but in their account the anemic recovery stemmed from the core elements of Obama's "change" and was inseparable from it. To Republicans, the problem in Obama's approach was his failure to appreciate the sources of productive wealth, which comes not from bigger government but from the activity of private business and entrepreneurs. Economic "philosophy" in this large sense was in fact the main voting issue. It was for this reason as well that Obama's appeal against the big banks, Wall Street, the insurance companies, and the wealthy gained so little traction. While most Americans, including many on the right, were angered at big business, many also became convinced that Obama's agenda struck squarely at the sources of wealth generation. For many Republicans, and especially for their allies in the Tea Party movement, economic issues also joined a deeper concern. To them, the size of government and the federal debt represented not only a burden on future generations and a threat to American power, but also a threat to the Constitution itself.

No matter the explanation, as the dust settled from the 2010 midterms, it was clear that the "Obama as FDR" storyline was dead. What would take its place was less certain. Recent history provided no clear answer. The nation over the previous two decades had lived through a period of its greatest partisan fluctuation. Since 1992 the presidential majority had changed party hands four times, control of the House three times, and the Senate twice. The question moving forward was whether 2010 would be overturned like the great Republican victory of 1946, would serve as the harbinger of a full party sweep like the Democratic midterm victories of 1930 and 2006, or would inaugurate a new era of divided government and stalemate like 1994.

## DEAD CAT BOUNCES

One of the key determinants of which narrative would unfold was Obama's own response to the 2010 electoral results. One of the immediate questions emerging from the 2010 elections was whether Obama would react by tacking to the center, as Bill Clinton did after 1994, or by digging in and doubling down on his agenda. Clearly, some things (such as cap and trade) were now off the table, but how far would Obama go to meet the new House majority in the middle?

Obama's first chance to rebuild his public standing came in the lame-duck session of the outgoing Congress. In an appeal to gays and social liberals, Democrats used their nearly expired strength in Congress to pass a legislative repeal of Bill Clinton's 1993 "Don't Ask, Don't Tell" policy that kept openly gay and lesbian recruits out of the armed forces. The Senate also passed an arms-control treaty with Russia that had been stalled. But these were merely predictable attempts to add liberal legislation before the clock ran out. What led some analysts to see the potential for an Obama move to the center was his decision to drop opposition to extension of the full Bush tax cuts, which were set to expire. He had previously called for extension only of the tax cuts for individuals making less than $200,000 or families making $250,000 per year, allowing taxes to rise on higher-income earners. Instead, he negotiated a two-year extension of all current income tax rates. In a Super Bowl interview with Bill O'Reilly of Fox News, he backed away from what he had told Joe the Plumber back in 2008:

> O'REILLY: Do you deny that you are a man who wants to redistribute wealth?
> OBAMA: Absolutely.
> O'REILLY: You deny that?
> OBAMA: Absolutely. I didn't raise taxes once. I lowered taxes over the last two years.[36]

Tragedy soon gave Obama another opportunity to burnish his centrist and postpartisan credentials. On January 8, 2011, Arizona's Democratic congresswoman Gabrielle Giffords and several others were shot at a speaking event in Tucson. Giffords survived—barely—but suffered serious brain damage. Although some commentators on the left immediately blamed the Tea Party, the shooter turned out to be an apolitical loner with a history of mental health problems. Although the tragic event apparently had nothing to do with the state of the nation's political discourse, Obama took the opportunity to call for greater civility. The president's role as national healer momentarily elevated him above the political fray, and lifted his approval rating past 50 percent for the first time since November 2009. However, the aftermath of the Giffords shooting was arguably the end of the president's brief postelection move toward the center.

Obama stayed over 50 percent in the RCP polling average for all of four days before slipping again, but another critical event gave him a more lasting boost. On May 1, the world heard the news that Osama bin Laden, founder of al-Qaeda and mastermind of the 9/11 attack that killed three thousand Americans and plunged the nation into a multifront war, had been killed in a US commando raid carried out by Navy SEALs. bin Laden had been hiding in a compound in Pakistan, but US intelligence had tracked him down and Obama had given the order to pull the trigger. One SEAL reportedly told another, "We just reelected [Obama]." It may have been true that bin Laden was found through a trail of intelligence that was originally developed in the Bush years, and that (as Mitt Romney would later suggest) any president with a clear shot at bin Laden in the post-9/11 world would have taken it, but to his credit, Obama *was* that president, and *did* take the shot. Unsurprisingly, Obama enjoyed a boost as a result of Bin Laden's death but the bounce was relatively small and short-lived. Indeed, the aftermath demonstrated how vulnerable Obama might be. The bin Laden bounce lasted only a month before the president's approval rating was back below 50 percent, after having topped out at 52.6 percent on May 24. This would be his highest average approval rating between the end of October 2009 and election day 2012.Though bin Laden would prove useful in a year, for the time being all that could be said was that Obama had enjoyed a couple of "dead cat bounces"—and things were about to get worse.

## THE DEBT DEBACLE

If Obama's post-honeymoon high point came in May 2011, his low point was soon to follow. Throughout his presidency, Obama had been dogged by criticism of his budget deficits and the meteoric increase in the overall national debt. While some of the increased deficit was the consequence of a slow economy and lagging tax receipts, much was also the result of the 2008 stimulus and other "pump-priming" policies. These developments were a major motivation behind the Tea Party movement, and the Republican midterm gains were largely won by candidates committed to attacking the nation's fiscal problems. As long as they remained true to their convictions, and Obama to his, a collision on fiscal policy was inevitable.

Preliminary skirmishing had yielded no clear advantage. The bipartisan Simpson-Bowles Commission, which Obama had appointed to provide advice regarding the mounting national debt, recommended a package of tax increases, spending cuts, and entitlement reforms in December 2010.[37] However, the commission recommendations did not have the two-thirds support needed for the recommendations to receive automatic consideration on the floor of Congress, and Obama made little effort to rally support. In the spring of 2011, Republicans negotiated a budget deal with Obama that purported to shave $38 billion off of future deficits, but Republican enthusiasm and Democratic anger was quickly tempered when it became clear that the vast majority of spending cuts were not set to occur for nearly a decade.

The real battle came over the debt-limit increase that Congress would need to pass when the federal government reached its legal borrowing limit in early August. Conservative Republicans hoped to use the debt-ceiling measure as leverage to force Obama and Senate Democrats to accept significant spending cuts. Although debt ceiling increases are usually routine, it is not unheard of to use them as a vehicle for attaching deficit reduction legislation. In the best example, the 1985 Gramm-Rudman-Hollings deficit reduction bill, which mandated declining deficits enforced by automatic spending cuts, was attached to a debt ceiling increase. As dire warnings circulated about what would happen if the debt ceiling was not increased, John Boehner and Barack Obama negotiated. According to journalist Bob Woodward's unflattering account in his book *The Price of Politics*, Boehner offered Obama $800 billion in increased revenue through tax reform in exchange for spending cuts. On the cusp of an agreement, Obama increased his revenue demands by half, causing Boehner to walk away. Ultimately, Boehner reached a deal with Harry Reid, with Obama largely a bystander. Obama did not get the tax increase on the "rich" that he had insisted on. On top of this, he had to swallow $1 trillion in cuts. He had never put his own detailed plan on the table, and he seemed ineffective to the point of near-irrelevance. The episode appeared to many Americans as a failure of presidential leadership on a question of crucial long-term importance to the nation. The fallout for Obama was long lasting. The debt-ceiling deal Democrats and Republicans finally arrived at was well short of the target of deficit-reduction goals widely believed to be appropriate and necessary. As a consequence, Moody's quickly downgraded the credit-worthiness of the United States, seemingly putting the United States on the trajectory of Greece or Spain.

Although Republicans and Democrats were unable to make much headway in 2011, they committed themselves to revisit the issue before the end of 2012. Negotiators established a congressional "supercommittee" to come back in the fall with a larger deficit-reduction package. Failure by the supercommittee would trigger, one year later, automatic spending cuts totaling $1.2 trillion over the next ten years divded between defense and domestic spending. The deadline came and went without the supercommittee having reached any agreement, a result that Obama exerted no visible energy to avoid. It was clear to all that resolution of the fiscal debate would have to await the 2012 election. The two sides were too far apart, and had resolved to leave the issue in the hands of the American people.

The debt-ceiling fight and its aftermath put Barack Obama in the most tenuous position of his presidency. The right remained angry at his policy direction, while the left quietly seethed at his ineffectiveness. His approval rating, which had already fallen below 50 percent by early June, went upside down again and reached its low point of the first term, an average of 42.8 percent on October 4 (Gallup had Obama as low as 39 percent around the same time). Moreover, the overall mood of the voters darkened, with larger percentages saying the country was going in the wrong direction. At one point in mid-October, only 17 percent said the nation was on the right track; 76.5 percent said it was not. For a brief moment, in head-to-head matchups with Mitt Romney, Obama was losing. Although it is difficult to make such a judgment in the absence of a campaign, a prudent person would not have bet on Barack Obama if the election had been held in October 2011. Fortunately for the president, it was not.

## THE LONG CLAW BACK

From the end of 2011 until the general election campaign commenced in earnest, Obama gradually clawed back to a stronger position, though never one that made his reelection unproblematic. He did so without the benefit of any single fortuitous event, but by a combination of smaller events and strategic choices.

His comeback began with another fight over taxes in December. As part of a drive to promote job creation, Congress and the president had passed a temporary reduction in the Social Security payroll tax from 6.2 percent to 4.2 percent. This tax cut was most beneficial to lower-income workers, who typically pay more in payroll tax than in income tax. Critics claimed that the cut had not actually done much to stimulate job creation, and hastened the day when the Social Security books would be in the red. When the tax cut was about to expire, Obama and Democrats called for an extension, a position Republicans opposed. Having reversed the parties' traditional image on tax cuts, Obama forced the Republicans to relent. He gained a twofer: he won a much-needed victory, reestablishing his leadership credentials, and he laid the groundwork for the coming campaign, in which he would emphasize Republican lack of concern for the common man.

Bolstering this theme would be the Occupy Wall Street movement, which sprung up in September of 2011 in Zuccotti Park in Manhattan's financial district and spread around the country. The Occupy movement repeated Obama's claim that the "top 1 percent" was largely responsible for the economic difficulties and was nevertheless benefitting more than anyone while others suffered. Although its platform remained cloudy, the Occupy movement gave Obama a sort of passionate counterweight on the left to the Tea Party movement on the right.

Then, in November 2011, the nation learned that the unemployment rate had fallen (barely) below 9 percent. Starting in December, Obama benefitted from a series of relatively strong job reports that gave reason for greater optimism about the economy. The Bureau of Labor Statistics reported that the number of new jobs increased by 223,000 in December, 275,000 in January, 259,000 in February, and 143,000 in March, which brought the unemployment rate down to 8.2 percent.[38] Key economic indicators now appeared to be moving in the right direction at long last.

If some observers had declared Obama unelectable in October, the jobs reports, juxtaposed against a muddied and sometimes-vicious Republican nomination race, led others to declare him unbeatable in February. Later in the spring, job growth slowed again to fewer than one hundred thousand a month, the unemployment rate remained high by historical standards, and the overall labor market remained depressed, with labor participation rates still well below their level before the onset of the Great Recession. Nevertheless, Obama had received a much-needed boost as the election year got underway.

Despite Main Street and Wall Street both showing signs of life, Pennsylvania Avenue remained hopelessly gridlocked. For the third year in a row, the Senate failed to pass a budget resolution as required by law. The House continued passing budgets that had no effect and no realistic chance of making it through the Senate. Whatever damage might have been done to Obama's capacity to lead legislatively, the 2010 elections, by giving Republicans the House and keeping the Senate in Democratic hands, had both blurred responsibility and prevented Republicans from using Congress to fashion a coherent alternative agenda or send Obama popular veto bait.

Like Harry S Truman, though, Obama was able to use the tools at his disposal to begin mobilizing key constituencies for the coming electoral fight. When Joe Biden slipped up and acknowledged what nearly everyone already knew, that Obama was a supporter of same-sex marriage, the president finally stepped forward and declared that his position had "evolved." When the Department of Health and Human Services began issuing regulations for the implementation of Obamacare, it required all employers, including religious institutions, to provide coverage for contraceptives and abortion-inducing drugs. When the Catholic Church and others objected on grounds of freedom of conscience, the administration "compromised" by excluding churches but continued to insist on the mandate for other religious organizations such as church-operated schools, hospitals, and social services agencies. A thirty-one-year-old Georgetown University student by the name of Sandra Fluke became a left-wing celebrity when she became a spokesperson for the HHS mandate and drew the ire of conservative radio talk-show host Rush Limbaugh, thus giving a face to the Obama campaign's "war on women" theme.[39] Environmentalists were courted when Obama indefinitely postponed consideration of the Keystone Pipeline meant to carry oil from Canada to the United States in January 2012.[40]

Slowly, Obama's job approval ratings began to climb back into the mid- to high 40-percent range. From January to July, his RCP average approval rating was steady at between 46 and 49 percent, alternating frequently between being upside down and not. As importantly, the percentage of Americans saying the country was going in the right direction roughly doubled, from 17 percent in October 2011 to around 35 percent throughout the first half of 2012. By no means was this an ideal place to be as an incumbent president running for reelection, and it is an indication of how far Obama had fallen in late 2011 that this significant recovery still left him with lower than 50 percent approval, with about three in five Americans saying the country was on the wrong track. Nevertheless, he had clawed back into contention, and led Romney by a small margin in most polls.

## LOOKING TO NOVEMBER

In sum, Barack Obama had been on something of a roller coaster, but not one that would have elicited much excitement at a theme park. His ups and downs, though real enough, were modulated by the equally real ceiling and floor that limned the outer limits of his popular support. After his honeymoon, Obama never exceeded 52.6 percent approval, which he won for a brief moment only after dispatching Americans' public enemy number one, never fell below 42 percent, and spent most of his time in a narrow range in the mid- to high 40s.

Obama had come to office promising "Hope and Change." In his first two years, he had delivered quite a bit of change, but many Americans remained unconvinced that they shared his vision for the country. Voters delivered a change of their own in 2010, forcing the president into a posture of defending his gains in trench warfare. The Obama administration's inability to overcome Washington's persistent partisan cleavages or adequately address the nation's persistent economic woes left hope in short supply as well. Surveys showed that substantial majorities of Americans felt the country was on the wrong track and that the American future was growing dimmer. In an October 2011 interview, he uncharacteristically stumbled over a question about his next campaign's theme:

> GEORGE STEPHANOPOULOS: We actually got a great question on Twitter about 2008. It's from Gale Glover, and he asks, "If hope and change define the 2008 campaign, what two words are going to make—are going to define 2012?"
> PRESIDENT OBAMA: I—you know, I haven't quite boiled it down to a bumper sticker yet. But I think what'll—define 2012 is—you know, our vision for the future. That's three words. Four.
> GEORGE STEPHANOPOULOS: It's five, actually.[41]

None of this meant that the president could not win reelection. Obama was in a worse position than almost anyone would have predicted in January 2009 but in a better position than he had found himself in late 2011. He was hanging on, as a Truman rather than a Roosevelt. He had a loyal enough base, a strong enough campaign apparatus, and just enough economic improvement to keep himself in the game. It was just a different game. Not basketball, with its graceful layups and beautiful three-point shots, but rugby.

## NOTES

1. See Mortimer B. Zuckerman, "The Great Jobs Recession Goes On," *U.S. News*, Feb. 11, 2011, www.usnews.com/opinion/mzuckerman/articles/2011/02/11/the-great-jobs-recession-goes-on.

2. Overall, taking into account the size of the labor market, private-sector job growth totaled 13 percent under Reagan compared to only 3 percent under Obama. Stephanie Cutter, "Barack Obama's Campaign Says His Recovery Has Outpaced Ronald Reagan's in Job Creation," The Truth-O-Meter, PolitiFact.com, Aug. 22, 2012, www.politifact.com/truth-o-meter/statements/2012/aug/27/stephanie-cutter/barack-obama-says-his-recovery-has-outpaced-ronald/.

3. Emi Kolawole, "U.S. Slips in World Economic Forum's Global Competitiveness Rankings," *Washington Post*, September 5, 2012, accessed December 30, 2012, www.washingtonpost.com/blogs/innovations/post/us-slips-in-world-economic-forums-competitiveness-rankings/2012/09/05/22eda50e-f77f-11e1-8398-0327ab83ab91_blog.html.

4. President Barack Obama, press conference, June 29, 2011, www.presidency.ucsb.edu/ws/?pid=90590.

5. Frank Newport and Lydia Saad, "Obama's Monthly Job Approval Edges Higher in March," Apr. 9, 2012, Gallup Poll, www.gallup.com/poll/153800/obama-monthly-approval-edges-higher-march.aspx.

6. "How President Obama Compares to Other Incumbents," American Presidency Project, accessed Jan. 10, 2013, www.presidency.ucsb.edu/.

7. See James Fallows, "Obama Explained," *The Atlantic*, March 2012, accessed Apr. 26, 2012, www.theatlantic.com/magazine/print/2012/03/obama-explained/8874. Ed Goeas and Brian Nienaber, "Republican Poll Analysis: 2012 Shaping Up to Be Truman 1948 or Carter 1980?," George Washington University/Politico Battleground Poll, accessed Jan. 1, 2012, http://research.gwu.edu/staticfile/Research/GMI/GW%20Battleground/Nov14/Republican_Analysis.pdf. Also Rich Lowry, "The Spirit of '48," *National Review* online, Nov. 29, 2011, accessed Nov. 30, 2011, http://nationalreview.com/articles/print/284272.

8. *Time* magazine covers, "The New New Deal," Nov. 24, 2008, www.time.com/time/covers/0,16641,20081124,00.html.

9. Gerald F. Seib, "In Crisis, Opportunity for Obama," *Wall Street Journal*, Nov. 21, 2008, http://online.wsj.com/article/SB122721278056345271.html.

10. Michael Gerson, "Political Honeymoon Over for President," *State Journal-Register*, Aug. 8, 2009, accessed June 29, 2010, www.sj-r.com/opinions_columnists/x1558731508/Michael-Gerson-Political-honeymoon-is-over-for-President.

11. Thomas E. Mann, "Whose Stimulus: President Obama's or the Democratic Congress'?," Brookings Institution, Aug. 18, 2009, accessed Aug. 18, 2009, www.brookings/opinions/2009/0807_obama_mann.aspx?p=1.

12. Peter Baker, "Education of a President," *New York Times Magazine*, Oct. 12, 2010, www.nytimes.com/2010/10/17/magazine/17obama-t.html?_r=3&ref=magazine&pagewanted=all%22. Also see John J. Pitney Jr., "Filling Gaps in the White House Website, Part 52: Shovel-Ready," *Epic Journey* blog, Oct. 13, 2010, www.epicjourney2008.com/2010/10/filling-gaps-in-white-house-website_13.html.

13. *Washington Post*/ABC News Poll, October 3, 2010, www.washingtonpost.com/wp-srv/politics/polls/postpoll_10052010.html.

14. Paul Ryan, Eric Cantor, and Kevin McCarthy, *Young Guns: A New Generation of Conservative Leaders* (New York: Simon and Schuster, Threshold Editions, 2010), 52.

15. "Obama Touts Single-Payer System for Health Care," *Wall Street Journal*, Aug. 19, 2008, http://blogs.wsj.com/washwire/2008/08/19/obama-touts-single-payer-system/.

16. See Timothy M. LaPira, "The Allure of Reform: The Increasing Demand for Health Care Lobbying, from Clinton's Task Force to Obama's Big [Expletive] Deal," *Interest Group Politics*, 8th ed., ed. Allen J. Cigler and Burdett A. Loomis (Washington, DC: CQ Press, 2012), 345–74.

17. Maryann Barakso, "Dissenting Doctors: The Internal Politics of the AMA during the Health Care Reform Debate," *Interest Group Politics*, 8th ed., ed. Allen J. Cigler and Burdett A. Loomis (Washington, DC: CQ Press, 2012), 97–109; Frederick R. Lynch, *One Nation Under AARP: The Fight over Medicare, Social Security, and America's Future* (Berkeley: University of California Press, 2011), 187.

18. For an overview of the Tea Party movement, see Scott Rasmussen and Douglas Schoen, *Mad as Hell: How the Tea Party Movement Is Fundamentally Remaking Our Two-Party System* (New York: HarperCollins, 2010); Andrew E. Busch, "Political Movements, Presidential Nominations, and the Tea Party," in *The Making of the Presidential Candidates 2012*, ed. William G. Mayer and Jonathan Bernstein (Lanham, MD: Rowman & Littlefield, 2012), 59–92.

19. John J. Pitney Jr., "The Tea Part Movement as a Starfish," *Epic Journey* blog, Sept. 15, 2010, www.epicjourney2008.com/2010/09/tea-party-movement-as-starfish.html.

20. Matt Kibbe and Dick Armey, *Give Us Liberty* (New York: HarperCollins, 2010), 65.

21. Russell Goldman, " Tea Party Protesters March on Washington," ABC News, Sept. 12, 2009, http://abcnews.go.com/Politics/tea-party-protesters-march-washington/story?id=8557120#.UN9sLG88B8E.

22. Mark Knoller, "Obama Has Given 54 Speeches on Health Care," CBS News, March 19, 2010, www.cbsnews.com/8301-503544_162-20000825-503544.html.

23. Ceci Connolly, "How Obama Revived His Health-Care Bill," *Washington Post*, March 23, 2010.

24. Lydia Saad, "Conservatives Finish 2009 as No. 1 Ideological Group," Gallup Poll, January 7, 2010, www.gallup.com/poll/124958/conservatives-finish-2009-no-1-ideological-group.aspx.

25. Andrew Kohut, "Obama's 2010 Challenge: Wake Up Liberals, Calm Down Independents," Pew Research Center for the People and the Press, Dec. 19, 2009, http://pewresearch.org/pubs/1444/obamas-challenge-december-approval-conservative-shift.

26. This shortfall was more than twice as large as the biggest deficits of World War II even after adjusting for inflation. As a proportion of the economy, the 2010 deficit was smaller than World War II deficits but twice as large as Depression-era deficits.

27. Edison Research exit poll, Nov. 4, 2008, www.cnn.com/ELECTION/2008/results/polls/#USP00p1.

28. See Tim Storey, "Legislature Landslide," Sabato's Crystal Ball, accessed Dec. 9, 2010, www.centerforpolitics.org/crystalball.

29. Resurgent Republic, "Post-Election Poll Highlights: Independents Propel Republican Victories in 2010," Resurgent Republic, Nov. 9, 2010, www.resurgentrepublic.com/research/polling-analysis/post-election-poll-highlights-independents-propel-republican-victories-in-2010.

30. See exit poll data at: www.cnn.com/ELECTION/2006/pages/results/states/US/H/00/epolls.0.html (2006); www.cnn.com/ELECTION/2008/results/polls/#val=USH00p1 (2008); www.cnn.com/ELECTION/2010/results/polls/#USH00p1 (2010).

31. Andy Barr, "Haley Barbour: Voters Not Saying 'We Love You,'" *Politico*, Nov. 1, 2010, www.politico.com/news/stories/1110/44488.html.

32. Eric McGhee, Brendan Nyhan, and John Sides, "Midterm Postmortem," *Boston Review*, Nov. 11, 2010, http://bostonreview.net/BR35.6/sides.php. "The median amount of money raised by Democrats who faced more than $50,000 in independent spending was $1.7 million. The same number for Republican candidates was $1.3 million. This wasn't David vs. Goliath. It was two Goliaths, beating each other to a pulp." Hendrik

Hertzberg, "Recession Election," *New Yorker*, Nov. 1, 2010, www.newyorker.com/talk/comment/2010/11/01/101101taco_talk_hertzberg.

33. Ron Fournier and Ronald Brownstein, interview with President Obama, *National Journal*, Oct. 24, 2010, http://nationaljournal.com/whitehouse/complete-transcript-of-obama-interview-20101024?page=3.

34. Hertzberg, "Recession Election."

35. James E. Campbell, "Forecasts of the 2010 Midterm Elections," *PS: Political Science and Politics* 43 (October 2010): 625–26.

36. "Transcript of President Obama's Super Bowl Interview with Bill OvReilly," *Politics Daily*, www.politicsdaily.com/2011/02/06/transcript-of-president-obamas-pre-super-bowl-interview-with-bi/.

37. The National Commission on Fiscal Responsibility and Reform, *The Moment of Truth: Report of the National Commission on Fiscal Responsibility and Reform*, Dec. 2010, www.fiscalcommission.gov/sites/fiscalcommission.gov/files/documents/TheMomentofTruth12_1_2010.pdf.

38. "Employment, Hours, and Earnings," from the Current Employment Statistics survey (National), accessed Dec. 28, 2012, http://data.bls.gov/cgi-bin/surveymost.

39. Bart Stupak, the Michigan Democrat who led most pro-life House Democrats to support for Obamacare, considered the HHS mandate a betrayal of the promise Obama made to secure his support. By then, he had already retired from the House and Obamacare was law.

40. Barack Obama, "Statement on the Keystone XL Pipeline," Jan. 18, 2012, online by Gerhard Peters and John T. Woolley, The American Presidency Project, www.presidency.ucsb.edu/ws/?pid=98935.

41. "Transcript: George Stephanopoulos' ABC News/Yahoo! News Exclusive Interview with President Obama," ABC News, http://abcnews.go.com/Politics/transcript-george-stephanopoulos-abc-news-yahoo-news-exclusive/story?id=14659193#.UN947288B8E.

# THREE

# The Republican Nomination Contest

Why did Mitt Romney win the 2012 Republican nomination? One possible explanation is that his showing in 2008 made him the inevitable choice in 2012. Though he lost the nomination to John McCain, he got 4.7 million votes, and won eleven primaries and caucuses. One theory holds that when a GOP president is running, the party turns to "the next in line," someone who has already sought the nomination or been on the party's ticket. Examples include Richard Nixon in 1960 and 1968, Ronald Reagan in 1980, George H. W. Bush in 1988, Bob Dole in 1996, and McCain in 2008.

"Next-in-line" candidates may have experience and name identification, but not a lock. Half a dozen examples hardly make an iron law, especially when there are counterexamples. Steve Forbes, who won 1.8 million votes in the 1996 Republican primaries, was arguably the "next in line" for the 2000 nomination, but lost to George W. Bush. In 2012, two other Republicans had as much claim as Romney to be "next in line."

Romney was an uncomfortable fit for the contemporary GOP. The party has three major factions, of roughly equal size.[1] With his corporate background, he did appeal to old-school Republicans, who favor business interests and shun social issues. But he had major problems with the other two factions. Social and religious conservatives care about abortion, same-sex marriage, and other concerns that fluster the old school. Although he had moved their way, they knew that he had supported legal abortion and gay rights in the not-too-distant past. The Tea Party Republicans want to cut spending and believe that the Constitution puts strict limits on federal power. They had fought President Obama's health care legislation, which resembled the Massachusetts law that was the crowning accomplishment of Mitt Romney's governorship.

One might have expected that he would face a strong field of rivals. After their 2010 midterm victories, Republicans thought that they could win back the White House. The Democrats not only seemed to be leaking public support but were also losing their material advantages. In the wake of *Citizens United* and other decisions, outside spending groups could now counterbalance the president's fundraising ability. Such conditions would normally draw blue-chip candidates. But by the start of 2012, most of the contenders faced questions about their electability. Mitt Romney, the one who seemed most plausible both as a nominee and potential president, stirred little enthusiasm in the ranks. He clinched the nomination only after the others had stumbled. Republicans did so much not *choose* Romney as *settle* for him. What happened?

To understand the contest, we have to look at the political history that shaped the party's talent pool as well as the individual decisions that determined who would and would not run. If these decisions had turned out differently, the nomination might have gone to someone else.

## THE EMPTY CHAIRS

After leaving office on January 20, 2009, George W. Bush was the president who wasn't there. He appeared at few political events, and Republican politicians seldom uttered his name. No wonder. Voters expect their president to foster peace and prosperity, but Bush left amid two wars and a financial disaster. At the end of his term, just 17 percent of respondents told Gallup that he would go down as an "outstanding" or "above average" president, compared with 56 percent who called him "below average" or "poor."[2]

Besides the natural tendency of politicians to shun unpopular figures, Republicans had special reason to consign Bush to nonperson status. Far from ushering in an era of conservative governance, Bush presided over an expansion of federal power. In a 2010 book, Paul Ryan talked about GOP principles of limited government and added: "I admit that in recent years Republicans abandoned these principles. We lost the true path and suffered electoral defeats."[3]

The Bush years left the Republican Party with a thin roster of potential presidential candidates. Few stars rose from the administration's ashes. Former OMB directors Mitch Daniels and Rob Portman managed to win statewide elections, but the Bush connection was a mixed blessing for them at best. Others found themselves tainted by ethics controversies, Iraq, or the economic crash.

Republicans lost their House and Senate majorities in the 2006 midterm and suffered further erosion with the Obama victory. Between 2004 and 2008, they went from 232 to 178 seats in the House and from 55 to 41 senators. Senators George Allen (R-VA) and Bill Frist (R-TN) were once the subject of presidential speculation but Allen went down to defeat and Frist retired after scathing reviews for his time as majority leader. Most of the Republican survivors were obscure to the general public, and many were objects of scorn among Tea Party activists. The Troubled Asset Relief Program—the bailout of financial institutions—was particularly unpopular at the GOP grassroots. "A lot of the senators that stood up and voted for TARP paid a huge price for it," said former Senate Republican leader Trent Lott (R-MS). "That last couple of years of the Bush administration were a real drag."[4]

Not one sitting member of the Senate would seek the 2012 nomination.

Governorships have long been another source of presidential candidates, and the Bush years took their toll here, too. In 2006 alone, the GOP went from twenty-eight governors to twenty-two, mostly in smaller states. Even if California's Arnold Schwarzenegger had not been ineligible because of his Austrian birth, the state's fiscal woes had wrecked his political standing. In Florida, Charles Crist generated some presidential whispers, but he undercut his chances by literally embracing President Obama early in 2009. He opted for a Senate race, which he lost to Marco Rubio after pulling out of the primary and running as an independent. Crist's immediate predecessor—a successful, Spanish-speaking conservative—would have been an ideal candidate except for one thing: his name was Jeb Bush.

The 2010 midterm suddenly brought the Republicans back up to strength on Capitol Hill and in the statehouses, but most of the new senators and governors were not yet ready for a presidential race. One big winner, however, had served in office for nearly a decade. By a surprisingly wide margin, Texas governor Rick Perry beat back a primary challenge from Senator Kay Bailey Hutchison. Though Perry had served as Bush's lieutenant governor, their relationship had long been frosty: in fact, most of the Bush camp backed Hutchison in the 2010 primary. Perry's conservatism, fundraising ability, and big-state executive experience all made him a highly plausible candidate. And his estrangement from Bush was a bonus.

For months after the midterm, however, Perry denied any interest in a presidential race. Meanwhile, several other major public figures considered running, only to back out in the end. They are worth a look here because their choices had consequences for those who did run. These noncontenders fall into three rough categories: the other "next-in-line" Republicans who had come to prominence in 2008; the Washington insiders who had become effective governors; and the "Hudson River longshots," northeasterners more famous for brash personalities than for any accomplishments in public policy.

*The "Next-in-Line" Republicans*

Besides Mitt Romney, two other Republicans had become potential 2012 contenders as a result of the 2008 campaign. One was John McCain's running mate, Sarah Palin. Even after poor performances in television interviews hurt her among independent voters, she maintained the enthusiastic support of a portion of the GOP base.

In 2009, Palin abruptly resigned the governorship of Alaska. The move stemmed at least in part from financial pressures. Political enemies had exploited a state law that had made it easy to lodge ethics complaints against her, resulting in big legal bills that she would have to pay out of her own pocket.[5] While the resignation cut short her executive experience and opened her to the criticism that she was a "quitter," it freed her to become a full-time celebrity. She took advantage of this opportunity with television appearances, book tours, and an extensive presence on social media. Following in the path of other potential presidential contenders, she campaigned for Republican congressional candidates and established her own PAC, which spent $4.4 million in the 2010 cycle.[6]

Visibility did not translate into electability. Many voters doubted her qualifications, and moderates were leery of her hardline rhetoric. In five AP polls during 2011, her favorability rating never topped 39 percent and her unfavorability never went below 55 percent.[7] Within the GOP, her core of followers competed with a growing chorus of naysayers who worried that her nomination would blow an otherwise-winnable election. In September 2011, a survey for Fox News found that 72 percent of conservatives and 71 percent of Republicans wanted her to stay out.[8] In October, she announced that she would not run.

The other "next-in-line" Republican was former Arkansas governor Mike Huckabee, who had sought the nomination in 2008. While Romney got the second-highest aggregate popular vote in the GOP primaries and caucuses that year, Huckabee was close behind—and actually won a few more delegates than Romney.[9]

Like Palin, Huckabee was a favorite of religious and social conservatives. Also like Palin, he had a background in broadcasting and had become a regular on Fox News. Unlike Palin, he had a strong public image. In a January 2011 Gallup survey of Republicans, he had the highest net favorable score.[10] In March, Gallup found that he was Republicans' top choice for the party's nomination, with 19 percent. Next were Romney (15 percent), Palin (12 percent), and Gingrich (10 percent.) Without Palin in the race, he had a 23–16 percent advantage over Romney.[11] Reviewing his own trial-heat surveys in swing states, Democratic pollster Tom Jensen noted that Huckabee ran about as well against Obama as Romney.[12]

Such findings were not flukes: Huckabee was a good politician. In 2008, he had held his own against Romney despite raising less than one-sixth as much money. During debates and other public appearances, he displayed great poise and a disarming sense of humor. Perhaps no conservative Republican since Reagan could speak directly to the television camera with so much conviction and apparent ease.

In May 2011, he opted out.[13] His previous campaign had given him invaluable experience and high name identification, but it had shown him how tough a presidential race can be. A 2012 campaign would have meant economic sacrifice, because he was earning a high income for the first time. For much of his tenure in Arkansas, he had been the nation's lowest-salaried governor, and he had to take time out from the 2008 campaign to make paid speeches.[14] In an interview with Howard Kurtz of *The Daily Beast*, Huckabee also revealed an attitude that set him apart from many politicians. "I'm not a megalomaniac. I don't think I'm the only person who can save America."[15]

It is impossible to know how good Huckabee's fundraising and organization would have been if he had run in 2012. But given his showing in 2008 and his polling numbers in 2011, one can imagine that he could have emerged as Romney's main rival.

### *The Insiders*

Governors Mitch Daniels of Indiana and Haley Barbour of Mississippi were hardly household names, but both commanded respect among Republican elites. Daniels had wide-ranging experience in government and business, and had won reelection in 2008 with 58 percent even as Barack Obama was carrying the state. Barbour had chaired the Republican National Committee in 1994 and the Republican Governors Association in 2010, helping engineer two of the GOP's greatest midterm victories. As governor of Mississippi, he had earned praise for his effective leadership in the aftermath of Hurricane Katrina.

The two had been friends since serving as aides in the Reagan White House, and they did not want to compete against each other. But both explored the possibility of running. Early in 2011, Barbour hired well-regarded professionals for his political action committee.[16] At the 2011 Conservative Political Action Conference banquet, Daniels got high marks for a substantive speech on economic policy.[17] A "Draft Daniels" movement enlisted students at three dozen campuses and made some clever YouTube videos.[18]

Both got into trouble because of interviews with Andrew Ferguson of *The Weekly Standard*. When Ferguson asked Barbour about his youth in the Deep South, he referred to the local Citizens Council as "an organization of town leaders."[19] Critics pointed out that the Citizens Councils fought for segregation. Barbour pulled out in mid-2011, saying that he lacked the necessary "fire in the belly." Electability might have influenced his decision. Particularly after the dust-up over his remarks, it was clear that Mississippi's racial history would be a big drawback in a race against an African American incumbent. With Barbour's full frame and deep drawl, a debate with the president would have resembled a scene from *In the Heat of the Night*.

Daniels wanted the party to focus on economics, and in his interview with Ferguson, he said that next president should "call a truce on the so-called social issues."[20] The remark upset some leaders on the right.[21] And Daniels had an even bigger problem: in the 1990s, his wife had left him and their children for a doctor, who in turn divorced his wife to marry her. A few years later, she broke with the doctor and remarried Daniels. In a presidential campaign, she would have been chum for tabloid-media sharks.[22] Daniels withdrew, saying: "In the end, I was able to resolve every competing consideration but one, but that, the interests and wishes of my family, is the most important consideration of all."[23]

Neither Daniels nor Barbour would have been a front-runner, but either could have cut into Romney's base of old-school Republicans.

*The Hudson River Longshots*

Donald Trump, the television personality and real estate developer, flirted with a presidential bid early in 2011. Famously averse to handshakes, he told the *Des Moines Register* how far he was willing to go: "If I decide to run, I will be shaking hands with everybody."[24]

In an April poll by the Pew Research Center, 39 percent of Republicans named him as the possible GOP candidate that they had heard the most about lately—more than all other possible candidates combined.[25] Trump's challenge was that his fame had come from his colorful personal life and controversial business deals. In 2004, he had tried to trademark his reality-show catchphrase, "You're fired!"[26]

Trump latched onto the "birther" movement, demanding that the president prove that he was born in the United States. Though there was no doubt about the question—the Honolulu papers carried his birth announcement in 1961—Trump whipped up enough interest that the president persuaded Hawaii to release his "long form" birth certificate. Trump took credit, and soon afterward, he said that he would not enter the race. It is hard to say whether his proto-candidacy was a serious move or just a stunt. Either way, his wealth would have enabled a Trump campaign to have some effect, if only to cause mischief.

In 2009, Chris Christie won the governorship of New Jersey, an impressive feat in light of the state's Democratic leanings. YouTube made him a hero among Republicans, who loved watching him tell off hecklers and union activists. In 2011, he gave a speech at the American Enterprise Institute, which a bipartisan panel of observers acclaimed for its substance and style.[27] In the fall of 2011, GOP donors and fundraisers urged him to get into the race. After giving the matter some very public consideration, he finally said no and instead endorsed Romney.

With just over two years on the job, Christie would have faced questions about lack of experience. Nevertheless, he could have raised a fair amount of money and siphoned some of Romney's support in the Northeast.

Although they were potentially the strongest, these noncandidates were not the only plausible contenders to consider making a run and then decline to do so. The list of noncandidates also included former U.S. ambassador to the United Nations John Bolton, U.S. senators Jim DeMint (SC) and John Thune (SD), former New York governor George Pataki, former New York City mayor Rudy Giuliani, and Indiana congressman Mike Pence. Some had considerable strength.

## ROMNEY AND THE REST

With several formidable (and some not-so-formidable) opponents out of the way, Mitt Romney had a clearer path to 2012. His formal announcement of candidacy in June 2011 was anticlimactic because he had stayed in the national political arena after losing the 2008 nomination to John McCain. In 2009 and 2010, he maintained his PAC and stumped for Republican candidates. He also published a book that combined reflections on his life with conservative prescriptions for public policy.[28]

By conventional standards, he had good qualifications. With a JD and an MBA from Harvard, he built a highly successful career and become CEO of Bain Capital, a private-equity firm. He had a grounding in international affairs. He lived in France for two years as a Mormon missionary, rescued the 2002 Winter Olympics in Salt Lake City, and had done business for Bain all over the world. As governor of heavily Democratic Massachusetts, he showed that he could work across the aisle on a variety of issues.

The 2008 campaign was a disappointment for him, but as a trained executive, he set about to learn from it. Before Barack Obama took office, he was already meeting with aides to review the last race and assess the next.[29] One lesson was that he should stick to a consistent message. "He would try to talk social issues with a church hall crowd, he would talk foreign policy issues with a think tank crowd, and he would talk business with a chamber of commerce crowd," said Kevin Madden, his 2008 press secretary.[30] In 2008, he spoke to reporters often and in detail. He also put huge sums into advertising long before primaries and caucuses began. As a result, he handed ammunition to his opponents and drained his own resources. In the next campaign, he would be stingy with both press comments and early TV spots. Mark McKinnon, a former aide to Bush and McCain, summed it up: "Nothing teaches you about winning like losing."[31] He may have over-learned the lesson, but that would not become evident until later.

Opposition to the Obama agenda had become a motivational force in the GOP, and Romney sought to tap it. The title of his book *No Apology* alluded to the oft-repeated GOP charge that the president had been overly apologetic about America's history. The paperback, which came out in 2011, was even harsher on Obama than the hardcover. The new introduction adopted Tea Party rhetoric to criticize Democrats: "Like the monarch the revolutionaries rejected, they have no limit on the amount they would tax the people and their enterprises."[32] Yet Romney had only limited appeal to the Tea Party Republicans. The Massachusetts health care law was one stumbling block. Another was his corporate career: many Tea Party supporters suspected collusion between big business and big government. Romney's support for TARP fed these suspicions, although he faulted the program's implementation.

Some problems from 2008 carried over into 2012. Now as then, he often came across as programmed and passionless. Though he was forgoing neckties during many campaign events, his clothes still looked expensive. Even worse, he committed gaffes that made him sound like a clueless rich person, such as his odd joke to jobless Floridians: "I'm also unemployed."[33] As noted earlier, social conservatives wondered whether his rightward shift was a conversion of convenience. Another source of trouble lurked beneath the surface, as it had before. In June 2011, Gallup found that 20 percent of Republicans would not vote for their party's nominee if that person happened to be a Mormon.[34] Although the figure was even higher among Democrats (27 percent), the bias of one in five Republicans appeared to be a significant burden for Romney.

So for all of his experience, name recognition, and fundraising ability, Romney did not start the campaign as a prohibitive frontrunner. In July 2011, Gallup used an open-ended format to ask Republicans and Republican-leaning independents about their choice for the nomination. More than half expressed no preference and only 13 percent picked Romney.[35] He did only a bit better in closed-ended surveys. In the RealClearPolitics polling averages throughout 2011, his support among Republicans never topped 25 percent.[36] This situation was unusual. Between 1952 and 2008, there were ten competitive races for the GOP nomination: nine without an incumbent Republican president seeking reelection, plus the 1976 race between President Gerald Ford and Ronald Reagan. In eight of those ten campaigns, the eventual nominee was the front-runner by March of the year before the election.[37]

Clearly, another Republican could snatch the nomination from Romney. Two former governors, both having something in common with him, thought that they might have a chance.

*St. Paul and the Frenemy*

Tim Pawlenty had twice won gubernatorial elections in Minnesota (2002 and 2006), enabling him to say that he, too, could win blue-state voters. Compared with Romney, his upbringing had been more modest and his personality was warmer. To overcome his obscurity and limited campaign budget, he followed St. Paul's admonition to "become all things to all people"[38] —or more precisely, all factions of the party. To old-school Republicans, he stressed his record as a pragmatic problem-solver.[39] To social and religious conservatives, he emphasized that he was a born-again Christian.[40] And to Tea Party audiences, he came across as a born-again constitutionalist.[41] He was, as some put it, a "full-spectrum conservative," with the potential to build a broad coalition. After the general election, Romney's campaign manager said that Pawlenty was the rival who most worried the Romney campaign in the early stages of the race.[42] The question was whether the St. Paul approach would actually enable Pawlenty to build a broad coalition or whether it would blur his identity.

Jon Huntsman Jr. had recently won his second term as governor of Utah when President Obama named him as ambassador to China in 2009. He was well suited for the job. He had learned Chinese during his Mormon mission in Taiwan and had previously served as ambassador to Singapore. There was speculation that Obama also had an ulterior motive: to neuter him as a potential opponent.[43] Nevertheless, Huntsman left his post in 2011 to run for the nomination.

As a former businessman, Huntsman potentially appealed to the same old-school faction as Romney. In fact, they were distant cousins, both descended from a Mormon pioneer. Their families had long known each other, and the two men had been on friendly terms until they both sought to head the Salt Lake City Olympics. Romney won, and in the 2008 Republican nomination contest, Huntsman returned the favor by endorsing McCain.[44] To topple his old frenemy in 2012, Huntsman would have to surmount some tall hurdles. First, although his father was a billionaire, his own wealth was not enough for self-financing. Second, his two-year absence from the country meant that his public profile was low and his GOP ties had atrophied. He would struggle for money and grassroots support. Third, his foreign policy credentials carried only modest political weight at a time when voters cared more about economics.[45] And fourth, he had just been an Obama appointee, no asset in the anti-Obama party.

In 2008, Mitt Romney faltered when he lost many old-school Republicans to McCain. In 2012, his strategic posture was different. Unless Pawlenty or Huntsman could gain traction, he would have this vote largely to himself.[46]

*Candidates with Limited Potential*

Several candidates would vie with one another (and with Romney, to some extent) for the support of other Republicans. All had handicaps.

Representative Ron Paul of Texas was making his third run for president. In his first (1988), he was the Libertarian Party nominee and received less than one-half of 1 percent of the popular vote. Twenty years later, he ran for the Republican nomination. He gained a zealous following, raised $34 million (twice as much as Huckabee), and took part in televised debates. Though he broke into double-digit support in several states, he did not win a single primary or caucus. His showings demonstrated that the party had a libertarian niche—but also that it was a small niche. Republicans were uneasy with his isolationism and fondness for conspiracy theories, and they took offense at his suggestion that American foreign policy had provoked the 9/11 attacks. Paul was not going to gain the nomination. He did have a chance to win a bloc of delegates, thereby gaining leverage in the unlikely event that no one entered the GOP convention with a majority.

Herman Cain, former CEO of Godfather's Pizza and the National Restaurant Association, became a conservative hero in 1994 when he confronted President Clinton over health care reform at a town hall meeting.[47] Cain lost Georgia's 2004 GOP Senate primary, but the 2012 election gave him an opportunity to become the Tea Party Republicans' champion. Health care was one of their main concerns, and his long record on that issue gave him credibility in their eyes. He also offered them poetic justice. Liberals liked to accuse them of racism, and one way to discredit that charge would be to support a conservative African American for president.

Cain had a charismatic personality, but he lacked crucial elements of a serious candidacy. He had little campaign money or organization. Aside from part-time advisory posts with the Federal Reserve, he had never held public office. He had no background in foreign policy and national security, and gave no hint that he had studied these issues. One more deficiency would prove fateful: he had never endured intense scrutiny from the national media or top-level opposition researchers.

Representative Michele Bachmann of Minnesota had become a bogeywoman to liberals by making incendiary remarks on cable television. In 2008, for instance, she told Chris Matthews that she was concerned that Barack Obama "may have anti-American views."[48] Her 2008 and 2010 congressional campaigns drew money nationally from those on the left who despised her and from those on the right who liked her for the enemies that she had made. Bachmann hoped that she could parlay her media prominence into a top-tier candidacy. She gained some attention when she hired veteran consultant Ed Rollins, who had managed Ronald Reagan's 1984 reelection and Mike Huckabee's 2008 nomination campaign. In June of 2011, Rollins compared her with Sarah Palin, who was still pondering a run: "People are going to say, 'I gotta make a choice and go with the intelligent woman who's every bit as attractive.'"[49] His remark not only gave a whiff of sexism, but it also needlessly alienated Republicans who liked Palin. It was an omen that his time with Bachmann would be neither long nor happy.

Coming from a broken home and having cared for twenty-three foster children, Bachmann had a compelling life story. She had legal experience and could make focused arguments, but her wild rhetoric repelled as many as it attracted. Her Capitol Hill reputation was bad. A survey of congressional aides ranked her among the "least eloquent" and most "clueless" members of the House.[50] Her chaotic management style led to high staff turnover. As one of her House GOP colleagues put it: "When your captain's crazy, it's time to find a new ship."[51]

Compared with Bachmann, former Pennsylvania senator Rick Santorum had a weightier legislative résumé, including work on the Combating Autism Act of 2006 and the momentous welfare reform of 1996. He could also point to a record of cross-party electoral appeal. Whereas she had underperformed in a Republican district, he had twice won Senate elections in the swing state of Pennsylvania. (He lost badly, however, amid the Bush downdraft of the 2006 midterm.)

In one important respect, he did resemble Bachmann: his rhetoric on social issues engendered ferocious liberal hostility. In a 2003 interview with the Associated Press, he discussed *Griswold v. Connecticut*, a 1965 Supreme Court case that struck down a ban on contraceptives. The case recognized a constitutional right to privacy, which Santorum said "destroys the basic unit of our society because it condones behavior that's antithetical to strong healthy families. Whether it's polygamy, whether it's adultery, where it's sodomy, all of those things, are antithetical to a healthy, stable, traditional family."[52]

Santorum's supporters would say that such statements were not gaffes, just bold assertions of controversial positions. Other Santorum comments were clearly unforced errors. Asked why Sarah Palin was not at the 2011 Conservative Political Action Conference, he implied that she was greedy: "I have a feeling that she has some demands on her time, and a lot of them have financial benefit attached to them." He added that she had "all these kids" to look after—an odd comment from a father of seven. "I will not call him the knuckle-dragging Neanderthal," Palin responded in an interview. "I'll let his wife call him that instead."[53]

The candidate most associated with unforced errors was former House Speaker Newt Gingrich. After leading House Republicans to their takeover of the chamber in 1994, he became notorious for self-destructive bombast. Amid a tense 1995 confrontation over the budget, House Republicans heard a constant refrain from their own core supporters: "Tell Newt to shut up!"[54]

During his speakership, his image got mostly unfavorable ratings in national surveys, and he got low approval ratings for the job he had done in office.[55] An ethics investigation of his finances led to an official reprimand, and prompted nine GOP colleagues to take the unusual step of not voting to reelect him as speaker in 1997. After the drive to impeach President Clinton nearly cost them their majority in the 1998 midterm, House Republicans made clear to Gingrich that he was no longer welcome, and he resigned.[56] Most of them were aware of something that was not yet public knowledge: during a national controversy about President Clinton's sexual behavior, Gingrich was carrying on an extramarital affair with a House staffer. Within two years, Gingrich divorced his then-wife and married the staffer, Callista Bisek.

For all of his daunting liabilities, Gingrich still had impressive assets. A former college professor, he could speak with fluency (if not depth) on nearly any topic. He was peerless at getting media attention and arousing the passions of conservative audiences. As the 2012 campaign got under way, more than a decade had passed since his departure from Congress. Many Republicans had gradually come to see him less as a politically radioactive former House Speaker than as a fascinating orator.

Once he got in the race, he soon reminded people how he had gotten into so much trouble in the 1990s. During a May 15 appearance on *Meet the Press*, he criticized Representative Paul Ryan's plan to reform Medicare. "I don't think right-wing social engineering is any more desirable than left-wing social engineering. . . . I'm against Obamacare, which is imposing radical change, and I would be against a conservative imposing radical change."[57] The comments angered conservatives, and Gingrich quickly backtracked.

Gingrich's approach to management had always been erratic, and this campaign was no different. He exasperated his top aides by following his wife's advice to limit his campaign activities. After the Ryan flap, when they wanted him to spend his time mending fences and raising money, he decided to go off on a two-week Mediterranean cruise. When he got back, they quit en masse. Gingrich vowed to stay in the race and wage a different kind of campaign based on social media and debate appearances. Conservative activists were dubious of this approach and looked for another horse to ride.

At the bottom of the heap of announced candidates were the erratic Michigan congressman Thaddeus McCotter, former Louisiana governor Buddy Roemer (who had not held office since 1992), and political consultant and gay rights activist Fred Karger. The trio posed no threat to any serious candidate, and rarely made the news.

*Boston, We Have a Problem*

Two of Gingrich's departing staffers, Dave Carney and Rob Johnson, had previously worked for Texas governor Rick Perry. Their earlier decision to sign with Gingrich had seemed to signal that Perry really was not a candidate.[58] Now, these trusted aides could be available to a Perry presidential campaign. And over the previous several months, the weakness of the field had prompted Perry to think about running.

Perry appealed to the same Tea Party Republicans and social conservatives that Gingrich was courting. (Gingrich had contributed a foreword to Perry's recent book, titled *Fed Up!*[59]) For these factions, Perry was the superior choice. Gingrich's long congressional experience and lucrative special-interest connections made him unconvincing as a political outsider. Perry had started as a cotton farmer and had spent his entire career in Texas. Perry was also an evangelical Christian who had been married to his childhood sweetheart for twenty-nine years, whereas Gingrich was a Lutheran-turned-Baptist who had converted to his third wife's Catholicism.

In contrast to most of the field, Perry was credible as a general-election candidate. As the longest-serving governor in Texas history, Perry had more experience as a government executive than any of the others, including Romney. In his 2010 primary race against Hutchison, he had assembled a top-flight campaign staff, which applied the kind of rigorous research methods that had worked so well for President Obama.[60] Texas had weathered the Great Recession better than most states, and its economy was growing. Whether or not Perry's policies had much to do with this success, it still gave him bragging rights.

As he edged toward an announcement in the summer of 2011, his name identification and support were rising fast. In July, Gallup found that he was the preferred candidate of 18 percent of Republican identifiers and leaners, just behind Romney, with 23 percent. After he announced his candidacy in mid-August, he jumped to the front, with 29 percent to Romney's 17 percent.[61] At Romney headquarters in Boston, such numbers must have been a concern. Equally challenging was Perry's likely financial strength. As the chief executive of a large, prosperous state with many rich Republicans, he could gather a great deal of money. In a conversation with blogger Rich Galen, one Texan spoke for many: "We are a Texas business. Perry is either going to be President of the United States or he's going to be Governor of Texas for the next three years. In either case, our name is going to be on that first finance report."[62]

Perry nonetheless had a couple of problems, only one of which was evident.

First, he was off to a late start. He had to fill his war chest, build state organizations, and prepare for televised debates, which were already under way. His rivals had been doing these things for months or years. There was little time for settling the turf battles and organizational hitches that plague any presidential campaign. The extended nomination calendar, which we shall discuss shortly, could buy him a little space, but not much. Given his vertical ascent in the polls, he could expect attacks from the other candidates almost at once. The old air force pilot was soaring into a dogfight.

The second problem seemed like a minor one at first. On July 1, Perry had surgery to fix an old back ailment. Apart from having to wear orthopedic shoes instead of his usual cowboy boots, he gave no outward sign of any lingering effects. But a year later, *Texas Tribune* journalist Jay Root reported that the procedure had forced him to suspend his rigorous workouts, and that the lack of exercise aggravated an undiagnosed case of sleep apnea.[63] Perry quibbled with the account, saying that the surgery instead caused a painful nerve condition that kept him up at night.[64] Either way, he was suffering from serious sleep deprivation just as he was launching the toughest campaign of his life. "It had a big impact," Dave Carney told a post-election conference. "The whole campaign was built upon a very aggressive, arduous schedule of travel in order to make up for lost time."[65]

## THE STRUCTURAL ENVIRONMENT

In the four years since Romney had lost to McCain, the rules and practices of the nomination process had changed in some important ways.

Party conservatives were unhappy with McCain, and thought the front-loaded calendar of primaries and caucuses enabled him to secure the nomination before Republican voters had a chance to deliberate on their choice. More generally, analysts had long criticized front-loading for short-circuiting the process, disenfranchising later-voting states, and posing huge obstacles to entry by lesser-known candidates. The 2008 convention empowered the Republican National Committee (RNC) to set up a special committee to propose changes in the process. In August 2010, following the report of the special committee, the RNC voted to forbid states from choosing delegates before March 6, with four exceptions: Iowa, New Hampshire, South Carolina, and Nevada. These states could vote as early as February 1. To encourage other states to hold primaries and caucuses later in the year, and to make it more likely that the race would be extended in any case, the RNC forbade winner-take-all primaries before April 1. States that violated any of these dates would forfeit half their delegates.[66]

The rule change did not work out quite as its advocates had hoped. Florida scheduled its primary on January 31. In response, Iowa moved its caucuses to January 3, while New Hampshire and South Carolina moved their primaries to January 10 and January 21. In addition, Arizona and Michigan set their primaries for February 28. All five states accepted the delegate penalty for going early. Arizona and Florida broke the rules a *second* time by holding winner-take-all primaries, but the rules did not provide for any additional penalty beyond what they had already taken for jumping the March 6 starting date.

In any event, the ban on winner-take-all primaries before April 1 was not as far-reaching as some media accounts suggested. Each state had a certain number of statewide or at-large delegates, plus three delegates for every U.S. House district. According to the RNC counsel, a state voting before April 1 had to allocate at-large delegates in proportion to the vote for the candidates, but could still allocate congressional district delegates on a winner-take-all basis (win the district, win all the delegates from that district).[67]

Had the 2012 nomination contest remained open all the way to the convention, the details of the allocation rules would deserve a lengthier discussion here. Much more significant was the impact of the procedural change on the nomination calendar. In spite of the few states that broke the rules, a number did decide to hold their delegate selection events later than in 2008. It would now take longer for any candidate to get a majority.

Some Republicans hoped that a prolonged nomination process would help the party by sustaining grassroots interest and media attention, just as the Obama-Clinton fight had done for the Democrats in 2008. Others were doubtful. Massachusetts RNC member Ron Kaufman said that 2012 was different: "This cycle we are running against an incumbent Democrat raising a billion dollars. And to elongate the process—for whoever the nominee was going to be—makes no sense."[68] Chris Christie was even blunter, referring to the rule changes as "the dumbest idea anybody ever had." Like Kaufman, he noted that it was not 2008 anymore: "[Y]ou're running against an incumbent president who will not have a primary. So your ideas make ours longer, so that we can beat each other up even longer."[69]

Romney adapted. In 2008, he had hoped to win a quick victory by storming the early primaries and caucuses. That approach failed when Huckabee won Iowa and McCain won New Hampshire. In 2012, the early blitz strategy would be even less feasible, so Romney's advisers worked on the assumptions that no single state would settle the race and that delegate arithmetic would matter.[70]

The other structural changes came in the field of campaign finance. In the early 1970s, Congress set up partial public financing of presidential nomination campaigns. Eligible candidates could get federal funds to match small individual contributions, so long as they abided by national and state spending caps. From 1976 to 2000, most major contenders took part in the system. Candidates then increasingly concluded that its constraints were too onerous, especially since they could now raise large sums via the Internet. In the 2012 race, all of the major GOP candidates opted out.[71]

An even bigger development involved outside spending.

In the 2010 case of *Citizens United v. Federal Election Commission*, the US Supreme Court ruled that political spending is protected speech under the First Amendment, and the government may not bar corporations or unions from spending money to support or oppose political candidates.[72] The decision built on findings in *Buckley v. Valeo* (1976) and *Wisconsin Right-to-Life Committee v. Federal Election Commission* (2007). Together with subsequent legal and regulatory action, *Citizens United* led to the creation of a new kind of political organization, the independent-expenditure-only political action committee, better known as the super PAC. Whereas a regular PAC receives contributions and gives to candidates under strict limits, a super PAC may accept unlimited contributions from individuals, corporations, and unions, and may make unlimited expenditures during campaigns, provided that it does not directly coordinate with candidates or parties.

Though political professionals have found loopholes, the ban on coordination affects the kind of ads that super PACs tend to run. Candidates may not speak directly for themselves in these ads, nor may they privately provide super PACs with advance texts of their speeches and issue statements. It is thus easier for these groups to run attacks against the opposition than positive messages for their favored candidates. Candidates and party organizations are more than willing to let the super PACs take responsibility for negative advertising, which is often controversial. Super PACs played a leading role in the 2010 midterm election, and they would emerge as major forces in the 2012 Republican nomination campaign.

The rise of super PACs guaranteed a barrage of televised attacks. The extension of the primary season meant that this barrage would last a long time. One thing was certain, therefore: during the early months of 2012, a lot of television viewers would hear a lot of bad things about Republican candidates.

## DEBATES AND AFFAIRS

In the race for the 2000 Republican nomination, there were thirteen debates, starting in October of the previous year.[73] In the 2012 context, there would be twenty, starting in May 2011.[74] These debates would have an outsized influence, elevating some candidates and hurting others. Republicans would have brief affairs with Romney rivals, only to ditch them when their flaws became too glaring. They kept working their way back to Romney, without a burning love inside.

*Minnesotan Farewell*

The first debate took place in Greenville, South Carolina, on May 5. Pawlenty, Santorum, Cain, and Paul were there, along with former New Mexico governor Gary Johnson, who would later switch to the Libertarian Party. Lacking the marquee names of Romney and Gingrich (Perry was not yet in), the event got only a modicum of attention. In hindsight, though, it did foreshadow key developments. Journalist Byron York wrote that one candidate missed a chance: "When it was over, Pawlenty had underwhelmed the audience, doing what many felt was an OK job—passable answers, no gaffes—but also not taking full advantage of the opportunity he had to distinguish himself from the others." By contrast, he wrote, Cain "thrilled" participants in a focus group. At the same time, Cain seemed oddly unprepared to discuss the war in Afghanistan, saying only that he would consult military experts once he got in office.[75]

Romney and Gingrich attended a June 13 debate in Goffstown, New Hampshire. Bachmann was there, too, and she used the occasion to announce that she had filed candidacy papers with the Federal Election Commission. Pawlenty made the biggest news, and for the wrong reason. He had recently linked the president's health care policy to the Massachusetts law, calling it "Obamneycare." When the debate moderator asked him to elaborate, he declined. Trying not to look aggressive, he instead looked passive, botching another chance at the top tier.

In mid-August, Pawlenty tried to come back in the Ames Straw Poll, a nonbinding event designed to raise money for the Iowa GOP. Although it had nothing to do with delegate selection and was even not a good predictor of what would happen in the Iowa caucuses, candidates had often treated it as a test of organizational strength. Pawlenty flunked, finishing a distant third behind Bachmann and Paul. (Perry, Romney, Gingrich, and Huntsman did not actively campaign there.) Pawlenty quickly withdrew from the race, and endorsed Romney a month later.

Bachmann did not get much of a boost from Ames. Perry upstaged her by announcing his candidacy in the same news cycle. At a GOP dinner the next day in Bachmann's hometown of Waterloo, Iowa, Perry worked the crowd and gave an energetic speech. Bachmann stayed in her bus until it was her turn to speak, and failed to come out after a local official introduced her. Only after a second introduction did she belatedly appear.[76]

As Perry's poll numbers shot up, Bachmann's campaign fell to the same organizational turmoil that had plagued her congressional office. Ed Rollins quit as manager, and his old friend Rich Galen observed in his blog: "I am willing to bet heavy money that Rep. Bachmann—or Rep. Bachmann's husband—decided they knew more about how to run a Presidential campaign than Ed did and he told them he was perfectly happy to let them prove it."[77] Subsequent reporting confirmed Galen's speculation. Bachmann would stay in the race until January, but it was already clear that she would not be the conservative finalist against Romney. That distinction apparently belonged to Perry.

*Oops*

Despite having to deal with wildfires in Texas, Perry was able to make a September 7 debate at the Reagan Presidential Library in Simi Valley, California. He got generally good reviews. Five days later, at a debate in Tampa, he came under heavy fire from the other candidates. Romney asked him if he still wanted to end Social Security as a federal program, as he had written in his book. "I think we ought to have a conversation," Perry replied. "We're having that right now, governor," said Romney. "We're running for president."[78] Bachmann attacked him for a Texas executive order requiring young girls to get a vaccination against cervical cancer. The audience seemed to side with her, but then she stepped on her own story. In a post-debate interview, she claimed that a mother had told her that the vaccine had damaged her daughter's brain. There was no evidence that the vaccine had ever done any such thing to anyone, and even some sympathetic conservatives gave up on her at this point.[79]

The cuts that Perry sustained in Tampa were nothing compared with the gashes that he inflicted on himself in Orlando on September 22. Romney pressed him on why Texas gave in-state tuition discounts to undocumented aliens. Perry replied that "if you say that we should not educate children who have come into our state for no other reason than they've been brought there by no fault of their own, I don't think you have a heart."[80] Reporter Jay Root later wrote: "As Romney's spokesman Ryan Williams said later that night at the bar, it was like poking a stick in the eyes of the vast number of Republican primary voters who oppose this. It wasn't enough for Perry to disagree with his critics. He had to insult them, too."[81] His problems went beyond that one moment. Conservative columnist Michael Medved said that Perry "looked and sounded ill prepared, uncertain, dull, vacuous and embarrassingly out of his depth. Even the Texan's top admirers (and I like him personally and greatly respect his achievements as governor) must cringe at the chilling prospect of a Perry-Obama debate."[82]

Perry's fatigue was catching up with him. So was his late start, as Byron York shrewdly observed: "For Romney, debate preparation involves taking all the things he has already thought through and finding the most effective way to present them in one-minute answers. For Perry, debate preparation is trying to learn new stuff about national issues that he should have been thinking about a long time ago."[83] Between mid-September and early October, Gallup found that his support among Republicans had plunged from 31 percent to 15 percent.[84]

In an October 26 speech in New Hampshire, Perry turned in a strange, uncharacteristic performance. A YouTube video showed him mugging and giggling like a teenager. On *The Daily Show*, Jon Stewart joked that he had either been drinking or had just returned from the dentist.[85] A more likely explanation was sleep deprivation. In any case, doubts about his fitness were harming his candidacy, and it would take just one more big mistake to ruin it for good.

He made that mistake during a debate on November 9. Returning to his anti-Washington theme, he said that he would scrap federal three agencies: "Commerce, Education, and the—what's the third one there? Let's see." Over a period of fifty-three seconds he tried to remember the third. Following a suggestion from Romney, moderator John Harwood asked if it was the Environmental Protection Agency.

> PERRY: No, sir, no, sir. We were talking about the agencies of government—the EPA needs to be rebuilt. There's no doubt about that.
> HARWOOD: But you can't—but you can't name the third one?
> PERRY: The third agency of government I would—I would do away with, Education, the . . .
> (UNKNOWN): Commerce.
> PERRY: Commerce and, let's see. I can't. The third one, I can't. Sorry. Oops.[86]

A few minutes afterward, he remembered that the third agency was the Department of Energy. Too late. Twenty years earlier, it might have taken a while for such a gaffe to sink into public consciousness. In 2011, it was instantly the subject of countless OMGs and LOLs on Twitter. YouTube made it available anytime—in high definition, no less—to the 99 percent of Americans who had not seen it live on CNBC. Right after the debate, Perry knew he was in trouble and tried to salvage his campaign through self-deprecating humor, including an appearance on David Letterman. The effort was futile. In a matter of weeks, he had gone from front-runner to national laughingstock, and there was no way back.

### *Up and Down with Cain and Gingrich*

As Rick Perry was falling, Herman Cain was rising. By early November, Gallup found him in a tie with Romney, and other polls put him ahead.[87] Audiences initially applauded his "9-9-9" tax-reform plan, which would replace the current tax code with a 9 percent flat-rate personal income tax, a 9 percent corporate income tax, and a 9 percent national sales tax. Cain got the idea not from an economist but from an investment advisor in Pepper Pike, Ohio. It did not stand up to scrutiny. Liberals pointed out that it would be regressive, conservatives worried that the sales tax would give Washington a new source of revenue, and more neutral economists estimated that it would blow up the deficit.[88]

Cain's surge in the polls subjected him to close attention from opponents and the media. The surge lost strength when it became clear that he was ill prepared to be a serious candidate. He made contradictory statements about abortion and border security and mocked the idea that he should be able to name the president of "Ubeki-beki-beki-beki-stan-stan." When a reporter asked about the uprising in Libya, Cain paused and then asked if Obama had supported the uprising. He paused again, saying he had "all of this stuff twirling around in my head."[89] Coming off his own bad experience with Bachmann, Ed Rollins said of Cain: "You can't ad lib your way through a presidential campaign. If you're at the back of the pack, maybe you can do that, but when you're a front-runner, and people are judging you, it can be very detrimental."[90]

Professional campaigns conduct vulnerability studies to find anything in their candidates' backgrounds that could cause trouble. Cain's organization failed to do so. In late October, the media revealed that the National Restaurant Association had settled sexual harassment claims against him during his tenure there. His campaign had known that the story was coming, but did nothing to prepare for it.[91] The final blow was the revelation that he had given financial support to a woman with whom he had had a thirteen-year affair. He soon withdrew.

Newt Gingrich was the immediate beneficiary of Cain's collapse. Although many journalists had assumed that he would withdraw soon after his staff implosion in June, he did exactly what he said he would do: make his case in social media and televised debates. After one debate in October, Brian Montopoli and his CBS colleagues wrote:

> Yes, he sometimes seemed condescending, and yes, he once again attacked debate moderators for wanting to spur . . . debate. But Gingrich's campaign is in the midst of a surprising resurrection from a series of early missteps, and he kept doing what has been working for him on Tuesday. The former speaker was professorial, making historical references left and right and casting himself as an ideas man who is someone above the fray. It's probably not going to lead him to the nomination, but it's turning what had been a catastrophic campaign into a respectable one.[92]

A New Hampshire poll registered growing support for Gingrich, and when asked why he was moving up, 44 percent of respondents cited his depth of knowledge, 10 percent mentioned strong debate performances, while another 6 percent said they liked his efforts to challenge the media in the debates.[93] On November 21, Gallup found that Gingrich and Romney were in a statistical tie among Republicans nationwide.[94]

At some point, gravity was bound to take hold. His controversial past had left him with more baggage than just about anyone else in national politics. For all his self-assurance in the current race, moreover, he had been getting away with gaffes that would have hobbled a front-runner. In one debate, he suggested that Representative Barney Frank (D-MA) and former senator Chris Dodd (D-CT) should go to prison for their role in the financial crisis.[95] In another debate, he hinted that nonbelievers were unfit for high office: "How can you have judgment if you have no faith? And how can I trust you with power if you don't pray?"[96]

Once Gingrich moved into the top tier, other candidates piled on. During a debate in Iowa, Romney took advantage of Gingrich's more unorthodox ideas: "What, places where we disagree? Let's see: we can start with his idea to have a lunar colony that would mine minerals from the moon. I'm not in favor of spending that kind of money to do that."[97]

Gingrich was also absorbing hits off the debate stage. Ron Paul ran web videos seeking to define him as a corrupt Washington insider who got rich by "selling access."[98] In Iowa, 45 percent of political ads were attacks on Gingrich, many coming from Restore Our Future, a pro-Romney super PAC.[99] The mainstream media were suddenly full of detailed stories casting a harsh light on Gingrich's background. A *Politico* summary by James Hohmann suggested that the negative information was coming from GOP opposition researchers.[100] The influential conservative magazine *National Review* issued a unique editorial anti-endorsement. In a winnable election, the editors wrote, they feared "that to nominate former Speaker Newt Gingrich, the frontrunner in the polls, would be to blow this opportunity." They emphasized his record in office:

> His character flaws—his impulsiveness, his grandiosity, his weakness for half-baked (and not especially conservative) ideas—made him a poor Speaker of the House. Again and again he combined incendiary rhetoric with irresolute action, bringing Republicans all the political costs of a hardline position without actually taking one. Again and again he put his own interests above those of the causes he championed in public.[101]

The siege had an effect. In early December, Gallup put Gingrich at the head of the field with 37 percent support, compared with Romney's 22 percent and single digits for all the others. By month's end, he was behind Romney, 23 percent to 27 percent.[102] And on Christmas Eve, the Virginia Republican Party put some more coal in his stocking when it announced that he had failed to submit enough valid signatures to qualify for the state's March 6 primary.

### *The State of Play on New Year's Day*

Even without the benefit of alcohol, Mitt Romney had reason to be cheerful as he rang in the new year. A respected study of presidential nomination politics found that the nomination goes to the candidate who takes the lead before the primaries.[103] Mitt Romney was now that candidate.

On the right, either Huckabee or Perry might have galvanized social conservatives and Tea Party Republicans. But Huckabee chose to remain in broadcasting, and Perry self-destructed. A year earlier, Romney had faced the prospect of splitting the old-school Republican vote with several other contenders. The threat faded away. Barbour, Daniels, and Christie chose not to run, Pawlenty pulled out, and Huntsman never found his niche. In debates, Huntsman tried to display his foreign-policy expertise by saying some occasional words in Mandarin. Most viewers did not care, and a small number of people fluent in Chinese noticed that he did not actually speak the language very well.[104]

Overall, as table 3.1 shows, Romney's material advantages were daunting. Only Ron Paul had raised half as much money, and he had hit his very low ceiling of Republican voter support. Jon Huntsman Sr. could have exploited his network of business contacts to raise millions for his son, but did not do so. Though he did contribute a substantial sum to a pro-Huntsman super PAC, he could have given much more.[105]

Romney did well in most debates, which reassured Republicans who worried about how he would hold up in a televised confrontation with President Obama. (He did err when he offered to bet Perry $10,000 that the Texas governor had misstated Romney's health care position, which made him sound like one of the rich golfers in *Caddyshack*.) Comparing him with the field, Republicans increasingly acknowledged that he could be their best bet to win a general election. "Romney's not conservative enough for me," one GOP insider told *National Journal*, "but [I'm] not sure anyone else is capable or can beat him." Said another: "Republicans are beginning to realize that this is a choice between Romney and the unelectable."[106]

Yet for Romney, there were clouds on the horizon. Polls showed that at least two-thirds of Republicans nationwide were either undecided or backing somebody else. In addition to the well-funded pro-Romney su-

**Table 3.1. Campaign Receipts through December 31, 2011**

| | |
|---|---|
| Romney | $56,073,108 |
| Paul | 25,901,305 |
| Perry | 19,775,136 |
| Gingrich | 12,648,565 |
| Bachmann | 10,100,742 |
| Huntsman | 5,882,409 |
| Santorum | 2,178,703 |

*Source*: Federal Election Commission, "Presidential Pre-nomination Campaign Receipts Through December 31, 2011," www.fec.gov/press/bkgnd/pres_cf/pres_cf_odd_doc/presreceiptsye2011.pdf.

per PAC, there were super PACs supporting Gingrich (Winning Our Future) and Santorum (Red, White, and Blue Fund). Over the now-extended primary season, Romney could expect to be on the receiving end of attack ads by the latter groups.

The odds-on favorite was still Mitt Romney. But it was uncertain how long it would take him to clinch the nomination and how much damage he would suffer along the way.

## THE IMPERFECT TIE

The Iowa caucuses are an odd feature of the nomination process. Because they are the first "official" contest, they can help or destroy candidates. But they do not actually choose any national convention delegates; instead they choose delegates to county conventions, which in turn choose delegates to later meetings that actually pick the people who attend the national convention. On the GOP side, each precinct takes a separate straw poll of the attendees' presidential preferences. These straw poll results—which have only an indirect relationship to the delegate count—become the main focus of media coverage. Turnout tends to be much lower than in primaries because caucuses require more time from participants and do not allow for mail ballots. And unlike primaries, which are subject to state election laws and fairly strict vote-counting rules, caucus procedures tend to be informal.

In 2008, Romney had counted on an Iowa victory to get the momentum that he needed. But the caucuses drew many social and religious conservatives, who gave an upset victory to Huckabee and dealt a blow to Romney's hopes. In 2012, Romney spent less time in the state, and was careful to avoid raising public expectations. Outside the media spotlight, however, the Romney campaign was working hard to identify sympathetic Republican voters and get them to caucus sites.[107]

Meanwhile, Rick Santorum was crisscrossing the state in a pickup truck belonging to supporter Chuck Laudner, a prominent conservative in Iowa politics. The "Chuck Truck" took him to more than 370 town hall meetings in all of the state's 99 counties.[108] Santorum's lack of funds necessitated the low-tech approach, but by New Year's Eve, it began to pay off when a *Des Moines Register* poll of likely caucus participants showed a late surge for him.[109]

On caucus night, January 3, the Iowa contest ended in a virtual dead heat, with Romney and Santorum each getting about 25 percent. The vote count put Romney just eight votes ahead, and most news stories described the outcome as a narrow victory for him. Two weeks later—after the New Hampshire primary—a recount showed Santorum with a lead of thirty-four votes. It was a statistically trivial difference in a tally that had no legal significance to begin with, but the initial reports of a "victory" gave Romney a psychological boost. Had the caucus night vote count put Santorum ahead, the media would have called it a defeat for Romney. Even as it was, the outcome marked a sudden advance for Santorum, who had spent most of 2011 with national poll numbers in low single digits. In the first two nights after Iowa, the Gallup tracking poll put his support at 21 percent.[110] He was now in second place, just eight points behind Romney.

Santorum soon had other reasons to feel good. In the weeks ahead, he would get more than $4 million in contributions. The Red, White, and Blue Fund, the super PAC that had spent about $289,000 on ads to help him in Iowa, was planning to spend a good deal more in the upcoming primaries.[111] There would now be less competition for social conservatives and Tea Party Republicans: after running far behind Santorum in Iowa, Michele Bachmann withdrew from the race and Rick Perry said that he would reassess his candidacy.

Santorum's chances of nomination were still remote. In Iowa, he got a plurality among evangelical Christians, who made up 57 percent of caucus participants.[112] In most primary states, the evangelical share of the GOP vote would be smaller. Though the influx of money was welcome, he was still raising less than Romney, and had only a skeletal organization. The campaign did without any internal polling at all, leaving it blind to information and trends that the public polls were not covering.[113] He would now get more attention and airtime in debates, but because he had so little staff, his debate preparation was weaker than Romney's.

Most important of all, Santorum did not have a clean shot at the front-runner. Newt Gingrich got only 13 percent in Iowa, but he was still in the race.

## DOWN TO FOUR

Just before the January 10 New Hampshire primary, Romney had another of his "rich guy" moments when he told the Nashua Chamber of Commerce about the joys of termination. Arguing in favor of competition among health insurance companies, he said: "I like being able to fire people who provide services to me. You know, if someone doesn't give me the good service I need, I want to say, you know, I'm going to go get someone else to provide that service to me."[114] In context, the remark was reasonable enough, but it was easy to take out of context. Huntsman and Gingrich criticized Romney, though it was too late to change many votes in the primary. Looking ahead to the fall campaign, Democrats saved the line in their opposition research files.

For a long time, it had been clear that Mitt Romney would win New Hampshire. He had a home in the state, had served as governor of neighboring Massachusetts, and was running a stronger New Hampshire operation than any other Republican. The only real questions were whether he would gain a "big" victory in the eyes of the media and whether Huntsman could run at least a decent second in a state that had often favored moderates and mavericks.

The answer to the first question was yes. Romney got 39 percent, far head of Ron Paul's 23 percent. Huntsman ran third, with 17 percent, so the answer to the second question was a resounding "no." Huntsman soon withdrew from the race, wiped anti-Romney material from his website and YouTube channel, and offered a tepid endorsement of his frenemy.[115] Romney would have no more competition for the old-school GOP vote.

Gingrich ran a disappointing fourth in New Hampshire, but he was about to enter friendlier territory. The January 21 South Carolina primary was the one major contest where he had a ground advantage, with a dozen paid staffers and five offices. No other candidate had more than one office.[116] Myrtle Beach was the site of the next debate, where reporter Juan Williams challenged Gingrich for calling President Obama a "food stamp president" and suggesting that poor children might learn work habits by janitorial work at schools. Gingrich hit back hard, defending his work proposal by saying, "Only the elites despise earning money." At the end of his answer, he got a standing ovation.[117] Liberals saw the exchange as raw race-baiting. In the days ahead, they would accuse Gingrich of sneering at an African American journalist and an African American president in order to rile up South Carolina whites. Conservatives saw Gingrich's remarks as an affirmation of opportunity and an overdue smackdown of liberal media bias.

Three days later, CNN reporter John King gave Gingrich another gift. He opened a debate by asking Gingrich about his ex-wife's recent accusation that he had once asked her for an "open marriage." Gingrich responded: "I think the destructive, vicious, negative nature of much of the news media makes it harder to govern this country, harder to attract decent people to run for public office. And I am appalled that you would begin a presidential debate on a topic like that. . . . I am tired of the elite media protecting Barack Obama by attacking Republicans."[118] It was another smackdown, another standing ovation, and another shot of political adrenaline. On January 19, Gingrich got a further lift when Perry formally withdrew from the race and gave him a strong endorsement. In the three weeks before the two South Carolina debates and the Perry endorsement, every major public poll showed Romney ahead in the state. In the final days, Gingrich took the lead.[119]

On January 21, Gingrich's air victories and ground advantages enabled him to defeat Romney in South Carolina, 40 percent to 28 percent, with Santorum at 17 percent. He seemed to be back in the fight. In the next couple of weeks, some national polls showed him resuming his lead over Romney. But this moment at the top would be brief. He had little ground organization in the upcoming primaries, and with only three debates left, he would have few additional chances to shine onstage.

Super PACs were very active in the South Carolina primary campaign. Restore Our Future spent millions on ads attacking Gingrich. Thanks to an infusion of money from billionaire casino magnate Sheldon Adelson, Winning Our Future was able to flood the state with anti-Romney spots. In one ad, sad-looking people said that they had lost jobs at companies that Bain Capital took over during Romney's tenure. A narrator began: "A group of corporate raiders led by Mitt Romney. The company was Bain Capital. More ruthless than Wall Street." One elderly man said that Bain "pulled the rug out from under our plant" while an elderly woman said of Romney: "I feel that is a man that destroyed us." The ad then directed viewers to an online documentary trashing Bain.[120] Media fact-checkers questioned the accuracy of the documentary and the ads, which were probably not decisive in moving South Carolina into the Gingrich column. But as attacks on Romney's business record continued throughout the primaries, they planted some doubts about Romney in the minds of millions of voters.

The Obama campaign nudged this process along. It made sure that laid-off workers from Bain-owned companies went to Republican primary states to tell their stories. Obama aides were puzzled that the Bain attacks did not start in a big way until South Carolina. But when they did, said Deputy Campaign Manager Stephanie Cutter, "We were surprised at [their] vehemence . . . and also just slightly concerned that by potentially going overboard that would spoil the issue going forward."[121]

Now, as the big Florida primary loomed on January 31, only four candidates were left: Romney, Gingrich, Santorum, and Paul.

## THE PENALTY STATES AND THE SANTORUM SURGE

As mentioned earlier, Florida, Arizona. and Michigan all accepted delegate penalties for holding primaries before March 6. If they wanted attention from candidates and the media, however, it was a price worth paying. All three would have a major influence on the race.

Romney's campaign was confident about Florida because of its sophisticated effort to identify and mobilize early voters. Hundreds of thousands of mail ballots were insurance against a Gingrich resurgence. But after Romney's surprisingly big loss in South Carolina, his campaign took a tougher approach. In mailings and on the air, it went after Gingrich's record, while Restore Our Future followed the campaign's lead with negative ads of its own. Some of these ads claimed that Gingrich supported funding for "China's brutal one-child policy" even though the bill in question barred the use of funds for "involuntary sterilization or abortion."[122] Romney kept up the offensive during a debate in Tampa, where he twice said that Gingrich had resigned from the House "in disgrace." In Jacksonville a few days later, Romney delivered what the Associated Press called "a surprisingly commanding and aggressive performance."[123]

One defining moment involved the candidates' personal finances. Romney attack ads had criticized Gingrich's consulting fees from Freddie Mac, the government-sponsored enterprise that had been part of the 2008 financial meltdown. Gingrich had recently responded that Romney had invested in the company as well as the other mortgage giant, Fannie Mae. Romney's opposition researchers went to work, and when Gingrich raised the issue during the debate, Romney was ready.[124] "And Mr. Speaker, I know that sounds like an enormous revelation, but have you checked your own investments? You also have investments through mutual funds that also invest in Fannie Mae and Freddie Mac."[125] Gingrich had no effective comeback, and was wobbly for the rest of the debate.

In both Florida debates, Romney said that he did not want mass deportations, and that the answer was instead "self-deportation." He explained that a verification system would keep undocumented immigrants from finding work, so they would leave on their own. When Gingrich suggested that he was anti-immigrant, Romney struck back: "Mr. Speaker, I'm not anti-immigrant. The idea that I'm anti-immigrant is repulsive. Don't use a term like that."[126] Romney may have won this exchange, but the "self-deportation" line would later help Democrats argue that he was indeed anti-immigrant. (During the second general election debate, President Obama said of Romney: "His main strategy during the Republican primary was to say, we're going to encourage self-deportation: making life so miserable on folks that they'll leave."[127])

On January 31, Romney won the Florida primary with 46 percent to Gingrich's 32 percent. In a big state with several media markets, Romney's financial advantage was important. His campaign and the pro-Romney super PAC outspent their Gingrich counterparts by about four to one. And among Republicans who said that the debates were important to their vote, Romney won by eight points.[128] Florida killed Gingrich's comeback. It showed that he did not have momentum, that he could botch debates, and that Romney could win in a Southern state. Gingrich's national poll numbers started to drop as fast as they had gone up after South Carolina. Though Adelson's super PAC money could keep him in the race for a while longer, his own campaign's resources were too skimpy for the big contests ahead.

A February 4 victory in the Nevada caucuses—where fellow Mormons showed up in large numbers—gave Romney another reason to smile. But if he thought he was starting to wrap up the nomination, he got a rude surprise on February 7, when Santorum won caucuses in Minnesota and Colorado, as well as a nonbinding primary in Missouri.

(Santorum benefited in Missouri from the Gingrich campaign's earlier failure to meet the filing deadline.) All three contests were low-turnout affairs, where conservatives cast a disproportionate share of the vote. While the Santorum campaign itself was low on funds, the pro-Santorum Red, White, and Blue Fund spent about a quarter-million dollars just before the February 7 contests, with most of the money going to fund television ads in Minnesota. The super PAC also bought spots in Missouri and paid for phone banks in Missouri and Colorado.[129]

In all three states, delegate selection would take place later, but the contests had an impact. According to the Project for Excellence in Journalism, those victories marked the peak of Santorum's media coverage, as reporters depicted him as the underdog beating the odds. During the week of February 6–12, his positive coverage spiked to 48 percent and negative dropped to 23 percent.[130] He also started to lead Romney in national polls of Republicans. More important, several polls put Santorum ahead in Michigan, where Romney had grown up and where his father had served as governor. "If Romney loses Michigan, all hell breaks loose," one senior GOP strategist told CNN.[131] Not only did Santorum appeal to working-class voters in the state, but he also had some help from the other side of the ideological divide. Four years earlier, Rush Limbaugh had tried to prolong the Democratic nomination campaign—and thereby hurt the party—though "Operation Chaos," an effort to get his supporters to vote in Democratic contests for Hillary Clinton. In 2012, liberal blogger Markos Moulitsas mounted "Operation Hilarity" to do the same for Santorum.[132] With an open primary process in Michigan and no real contest on the Democratic side, it was possible for Democratic identifiers to cross over.

In mid-February, Romney seemed to be stumbling. During an appearance at the Conservative Political Action Conference, he said: "I was a severely conservative Republican governor." The remark put off many of his listeners, as journalist Byron York explained: "To conservative ears, the word sounded odd. 'Severe' is a word liberals use to describe conservatism, not a word conservatives use to describe themselves."[133] Others thought of the old joke about being a lady: if you have to say you are, you ain't.

By the end of the month, though, Romney's material advantages came into play. Restore Our Future ran ads depicting Santorum as a big-spending Washington insider. The onslaught was so severe that Santorum ran a response ad depicting a Romney lookalike shooting mud at Santorum cutouts. And Santorum's Michigan organization was no match for Romney's. "Mitt has a great advantage as far as having boots on the ground," said Jim Thienel, the Republican chair in Oakland County, where the party apparatus backed Romney.[134]

At the same time, the top-tier spotlight exposed Santorum's flaws. The last debate of the primary campaign took place on February 22, and he did poorly. He was defensive about inconsistencies in his voting record as well as his past support for his Pennsylvania colleague Arlen Specter, a liberal Republican who later switched to the Democrats. In an interview on the weekend before the primary, Santorum criticized John F. Kennedy's famous 1960 speech to the Baptist ministers in Houston. "To say that people of faith have no role in the public square?" he said of Kennedy's view of the separation of church and state. "You bet that makes you throw up."[135] The comment was a double-barreled shot at his own foot. First, by more than a two-to-one margin, Republicans had a favorable view of JFK.[136] Second, Catholics made up 30 percent of Michigan's Republican primary electorate.

Romney won Michigan with 41 percent to 38 percent for Santorum. Though Democrats voting in the contest did back Santorum, Romney won self-identified Republicans. And as in most other states, Catholic primary voters backed Romney over their co-religionist. Romney might not have enjoyed this narrow victory at all if Gingrich had not taken 7 percent, thereby splitting the conservative vote. But Santorum's showings in Michigan polls had drastically reduced expectations for Romney, so a win was a win.

On the same night, Romney also took Arizona by a twenty-point margin. Arizona's primary had received less publicity than Michigan's, but from the standpoint of delegate arithmetic, it was a bigger victory for Romney. Whereas he got only sixteen of Michigan's thirty delegates, he received all of Arizona's twenty-nine delegates in its winner-take-all contest.

## THE TRIUMPH OF ARITHMETIC

As we explained in our previous book, Barack Obama won the 2008 Democratic nomination by building an early lead in the delegate count and preventing Hillary Clinton from catching up.[137] "The task for the Clinton campaign yesterday was clear," wrote Obama campaign manager David Plouffe in a memo the day after the 2008 Texas primary. "In order to have a plausible path to the nomination, they needed to score huge delegate victories and cut into our lead. They failed." Four years later, Romney political director Rick Beeson said, "We've read those same memos."[138] Though there were differences between the two parties' nomination processes, the underlying logic was the same: if the leading candidate kept getting more delegates, the other candidate would eventually find it impossible to get a majority at the convention.

In the March 6 "Super Tuesday" contests, Romney won six states while Santorum won three and Gingrich took his home state of Georgia. The biggest prize was Ohio, where Romney's statewide vote margin was less than 1 percent. Romney won in more Ohio congressional districts than Santorum, and because the winner in each district got all of its delegates, Romney got thirty-eight of the sixty-three delegates at stake.

Gingrich's 15 percent share of the Ohio vote earned him no delegates, but the Santorum campaign thought that it changed the outcome. "We'd never ask anybody to get out of this race," said Santorum spokesperson Hogan Gidley on primary night. "But you look at the numbers: If Newt were out of this race, we'd be winning these states by ten points."[139] National poll data, however, were not so clear-cut. According to a mid-March Gallup poll, 40 percent of Gingrich voters picked Romney as their second choice, compared with 39 percent for Santorum and 12 percent for Paul.[140]

Week by week, the math kept adding up for Romney, and he drew strength from places that normally get little attention. On Saturday, March 10, Santorum won the Kansas caucuses while Romney won caucuses in the Virgin Islands, Guam, and the Northern Mariana Islands. Together with delegates from Wyoming county conventions, these victories put Romney ahead in delegates for the weekend. (Again, Romney was following the Obama playbook. In 2008, David Plouffe puzzled reporters by saying that Obama was "organizing heavily in Guam,"[141] but his victory there helped extend his lead over Clinton.) The following Tuesday, Santorum finished first in the Alabama and Mississippi primaries, but had to split their delegates with Romney and Gingrich. Meanwhile, Romney took enough delegates in the Hawaii and American Samoa caucuses to come out on top for the night.

Santorum went to Puerto Rico in hopes of scoring an upset win in the commonwealth's primary, but made things worse for himself. To become a state, he said, Puerto Rico should adopt English as its "main language." The suggestion angered Puerto Ricans, and caused one of his leading supporters on the island to take back his endorsement.[142] Romney crushed him there by a margin of more than eight to one. The defeat was humiliating enough, but Santorum also burnished his credentials for being gaffe-prone, raising further questions about his political judgment. The time he spent in Puerto Rico was time away from Illinois or some other place where he might actually have won some delegates.

Santorum tried to stay afloat by raising the Bain issue and calling Romney a "Wall Street financier."[143] He also argued that Romney would have a hard time in November. "I'd love to be able to get one-on-one with Gov. Romney and expose the record that would be the weakest record we could possibly put up against Barack Obama. . . . [We] can't nominate such a weak candidate." Referring to Romney's positions on health care, the environment, and financial bailouts, he said: "Governor Romney is on the same page as Barack Obama on all of these issues. . . . We can't be out there nominating someone who gives away the most important issues that conservatives care about in this election when it comes to the economy."[144]

On March 20, however, Romney defeated Santorum in the Illinois primary by 47–35 percent, a victory that padded his delegate advantage and finally started to create an aura of inevitability around his nomination. Jeb Bush said that it was time for Republicans to unite around Romney, and the Tea Party group FreedomWorks withdrew its opposition to him. "It is a statistical fact that the numbers favor Mitt Romney," said FreedomWorks vice president Russ Walker. "We are dedicated to defeating Obama and electing a conservative Senate that will help Romney repeal Obamacare and address the nation's economic and spending challenges."[145]

Santorum won a late victory in Louisiana, but Romney now had just over half of the 1,144 delegates he needed to win the nomination. Santorum's total was less than half of Romney's. He was trailing Romney by double digits in national polls, and was rapidly losing support even in his home state of Pennsylvania. After Romney won primaries in Maryland, Wisconsin, and the District of Columbia, the math became even more daunting. On April 10, Santorum suspended his candidacy. Although it would still be more than a month before Romney would have enough delegates in hand to clinch the nomination formally, Republican National Committee chairman Reince Priebus declared Romney to be the party's presumptive nominee on April 25. Gingrich withdrew a week later, but by this time, hardly anybody noticed.

## CONSEQUENCES

One way to compare the length of primary campaigns is to look at the dates on which the nominees secured a majority of delegates (table 3.2). By this measure, the 2012 campaign was lengthy indeed.

The "long slog," as the Romney campaign staff called it, did benefit the GOP in a couple of ways. First, it bolstered the nominee's legitimacy in the eyes of the party base. In 2008, many conservatives thought that the front-loaded calendar enabled John McCain to seize the nomination before the rank and file could appraise him fully. In 2012, the party got a chance to give Romney a long, hard look and weigh the alternatives. Second, it honed Romney's campaign skills. He had always known the issues, but twenty debates gave him plenty of practice at making points forcefully and putting opponents on the defensive. This experience paid off in his first general-election debate with President Obama.

But if the nomination race was an education for Mitt Romney, the tuition was expensive. It cost his campaign about $87 million and kept him from focusing on the general election until well into the spring of 2012. In the meantime, the Obama campaign had been methodically building its general-election machinery, and by April, it had dozens of field offices in key states.[146] Still, it worried about anti-Obama attacks

**Table 3.2. Dates on Which GOP Candidates Secured a Majority of Delegates**

| | |
|---|---|
| 1976 | August 16 |
| 1980 | May 24 |
| 1988 | April 26 |
| 1992 | May 5 |
| 1996 | March 26 |
| 2000 | March 14 |
| 2004 | March 10 |
| 2008 | March 4 |
| 2012 | May 29 |

*Source*: For 1976–2000: William G. Mayer and Andrew E. Busch, *The Front-Loading Problem in Presidential Nominations* (Washington, DC: Brookings, 2004), 50.

from Romney and GOP super PACs. "Our air defenses weren't ready," said Obama strategist David Axelrod. "They gave us a pass, for whatever reason."[147] The reason, of course, was that Romney did not have the nomination in hand and had to concentrate on beating his GOP rivals.

Some commentators have claimed that the GOP nomination process hurt Romney by pulling him too far to the right. But Romney's conservative journey took place mostly before 2008, which is why he won the endorsement of *National Review* in that nomination campaign. His basic positions for 2012 were in place by the start of the race, and changed little through the end of the primary season. But the "long slog" did create many opportunities for verbal missteps, and Romney made his share, from "severely conservative" to "self-deportation." Romney had won running a campaign with few substantive positive themes, relying on superior resources to batter at his opponents' weaknesses with largely unanswered negative barrages—an approach with obvious limitations in the upcoming general election fight against a well-funded incumbent. In the end, Republicans settled for Romney, gambling that everything should ride on an economic referendum.

Most of all, the race showed that Romney lacked the party's full-throated enthusiasm. In spite of their obvious weaknesses, several candidates—Perry, Cain, Gingrich (twice), and Santorum—were all able to outpoll Romney nationally at various points in the campaign. The highly decentralized Tea Party movement, which had the potential to be a kingmaker, never warmed to Romney but failed to unite behind an alternative. After Perry and Cain imploded in the fall of 2011, comedian Jon Stewart declared that Romney must be the "luckiest [expletive deleted] on earth."

It turned out that he was only the second-luckiest. And his luck was going to expire.

## NOTES

1. The key word is *roughly*. Surveys employing different kinds of categories have varied somewhat in their results. See: Peter Wallsten, "Tea Party Already Shapes '12 Race," *Wall Street Journal*, Oct. 24, 2010, http://online.wsj.com/article/SB10001424052702304354104575568730326784138.html; Peyton Craighill, "The Many Faces of the Republican Party," *Washington Post*, Aug. 20, 2012, www.washingtonpost.com/blogs/the-fix/wp/2012/08/20/the-many-faces-of-the-republican-party.

2. Lydia Saad, "Americans Expect History to Judge Bush Worse than Nixon," Gallup Poll, Jan. 16, 2009, www.gallup.com/poll/113806/Americans-Expect-History-Judge-Bush-Worse-Than-Nixon.aspx.

3. Paul Ryan, Eric Cantor, and Kevin McCarthy, *Young Guns: A New Generation of Conservative Leaders* (New York: Simon and Schuster, Threshold Editions, 2010), 129.

4. Jonathan Martin, "Absent from 2012 Race: Congressmen," *Politico*, Feb. 23, 2011, www.politico.com/news/stories/0211/50023.html.

5. Lisa Demer, "Palin's Legal Debts Pile Up," *Anchorage Daily News*, March 20, 2009, www.adn.com/2009/03/20/731157/palins-legal-debts-pile-up.html.

6. Center for Responsive Politics, "SarahPAC Summary," May 20, 2011, www.opensecrets.org/pacs/lookup2.php?strID=C00458588&cycle=2010.

7. The AP-GfK Poll, Oct. 2011, http://surveys.ap.org/data/GfK/AP-GfK%20Poll%20October%202011%20Topline%20FINAL_2012.pdf.

8. Dana Blanton, "Fox News Poll: Perry Overtakes Romney as Top GOP 2012 Pick; Most Say Palin Should Stay Out of Race," Fox News, Sept. 1, 2011, www.foxnews.com/politics/2011/09/01/fox-news-poll-perry-overtakes-romney-as-top-gop-2012-pick-most-say-palin-should-1905707772/.

9. "2008 Republican Popular Vote," RealClearPolitics, www.realclearpolitics.com/epolls/2008/president/republican_vote_count.html; "2008 Republican Delegates," RealClearPolitics, www.realclearpolitics.com/epolls/2008/president/republican_delegate_count.html.

10. Frank Newport, "Within GOP, Huckabee Most Liked, Palin Best Known" Gallup Poll, Jan. 20, 2011, www.gallup.com/poll/145508/Within-GOP-Huckabee-Liked-Palin-Best-Known.aspx.

11. Jeffrey M. Jones, "Huckabee Has Slight Edge, Palin Down, in GOP '12 Preferences," Gallup Poll, March 25, 2011, www.gallup.com/poll/146792/Huckabee-Slight-Edge-Palin-Down-GOP-Preferences.aspx.

12. Tom Jensen, "Huckabee's the Best Bet for Now," Public Policy Polling, Jan. 4, 2011, http://publicpolicypolling.blogspot.com/2011/01/huckabees-best-bet-for-now.html.

13. Serafin Gomez and L. A. Holmes, "Huckabee Opts against 2012 White House Bid," Fox News, May 14, 2011, www.foxnews.com/politics/2011/05/14/huckabee-opts-2012-white-house-bid/.

14. Byron York, "Huckabee Decision Will Shape GOP Presidential Race," *Washington Examiner*, Apr. 11, 2011, http://washingtonexaminer.com/article/113416.

15. Howard Kurtz, "Huckabee: 'I'm Not a Megalomaniac,'" *The Daily Beast*, Feb. 23, 2011, www.thedailybeast.com/articles/2011/02/23/five-reasons-mike-huckabee-isnt-running-for-president.html.

16. Chris Cillizza and Aaron Blake, "Haley Barbour's Inside Game," *Washington Post*, March 21, 2011, www.washingtonpost.com/blogs/the-fix/post/haley-barbours-inside-game/2011/03/20/ABd3Cw5_blog.html.

17. Tom Beaumont, "Daniels at CPAC Calls for Broad, Civil, Conservative Coalition," *Des Moines Register*, Feb. 11, 2011, http://blogs.desmoinesregister.com/dmr/index.php/2011/02/11/daniels-at-cpac-calls-for-broad-civil-conservative-coalition.

18. Neil King Jr., "Mitch Daniels Gets 2012 Plug—from Students," *Wall Street Journal*, Jan. 27, 2011, http://blogs.wsj.com/washwire/2011/01/27/mitch-daniels-gets-2012-plug-from-students.

19. Andrew Ferguson, "The Boy from Yazoo City," *The Weekly Standard*, Dec. 27, 2010, www.weeklystandard.com/articles/boy-yazoo-city_523551.html.
20. Andrew Ferguson, "Ride Along with Mitch," *The Weekly Standard*, June 14, 2010, www.weeklystandard.com/articles/ride-along-mitch.
21. David Paul Kuhn, "Mitch Daniels' Moment, and Dilemmas," RealClearPolitics, Feb. 16, 2011, www.realclearpolitics.com/articles/2011/02/16/mitch_daniels_moment_and_dilemmas_social_conservative_truce_cpac_obama_108918.html.
22. Erin McPike, "Why Mitch Daniels Said No," RealClearPolitics, May 22, 2011, www.realclearpolitics.com/articles/2011/05/22/why_mitch_daniels_said_no_109948.html.
23. Erin McPike, "Daniels Will Not Run for President," RealClearPolitics, May 22, 2011, www.realclearpolitics.com/articles/2011/05/22/daniels_will_not_run_for_presidency_109947.html.
24. Tom Beaumont, "Trump Says He Would Play in Iowa, Aides to Visit," *Des Moines Register*, March 3, 2011, http://blogs.desmoinesregister.com/dmr/index.php/2011/03/03/register-exclusive-trump-says-he-would-play-in-iowa-aides-to-visit-Monday.
25. "Trump Most Visible among Possible GOP Contenders," Pew Research Center for the People and the Press, Apr. 20, 2011, www.people-press.org/2011/04/20/trump-most-visible-among-possible-gop-contenders/.
26. "Donald Seeks to Trump 'You're Fired' Market," The Smoking Gun, March 18, 2004, www.thesmokinggun.com/documents/crime/donald-seeks-trump-youre-fired-market.
27. Kendra Marr, "Experts: Chris Christie's Moment Is Now," *Politico*, Feb. 16, 2011, www.politico.com/news/stories/0211/49701.html.
28. Mitt Romney, *No Apology: The Case for American Greatness* (New York: St. Martin's, 2010).
29. Sasha Issenberg, "The Long-Distance Runner," *Boston Globe Magazine*, Aug. 30, 2009, www.boston.com/bostonglobe/magazine/articles/2009/08/30/the_long_distance_runner/.
30. Michael D. Shear and Ashley Parker, "Lectern Gone, Romney Finds More Success," *New York Times*, Oct. 24, 2011, www.nytimes.com/2011/10/25/us/politics/for-romney-lesson-of-2008-is-fewer-lessons.html.
31. Erin McPike and Carl M. Cannon, "Romney Applies Lessons of 2008 to 2012 Run," RealClearPolitics, July 15, 2011, www.realclearpolitics.com/articles/2011/07/15/romney_applies_lessons_of_2008_to_2012_run_110582.html.
32. Matt Viser, "Romney Rips Obama in New Paperback," *Boston Globe*, Feb. 1, 2011, www.boston.com/news/nation/washington/articles/2011/02/01/romney_rips_obama_in_new_paperback.
33. PBS NewsHour, "Romney Tells Floridians, 'I'm Also Unemployed,'" YouTube, June 16, 2011, http://youtu.be/TgGXKA43WY4.
34. Lydia Saad, "In U.S., 22% Are Hesitant to Support a Mormon in 2012," Gallup Poll, June 20, 2011, www.gallup.com/poll/148100/Hesitant-Support-Mormon-2012.aspx.
35. Jeffrey M. Jones, "Majority of Republicans Can't Name a 2012 Favorite," Gallup Poll, July 15, 2011, www.gallup.com/poll/148526/majority-republicans-name-2012-favorite.aspx.
36. "2012 Republican Presidential Nomination," RealClearPolitics, www.realclearpolitics.com/epolls/2012/president/us/republican_presidential_nomination-1452.html.
37. Lydia Saad, "Lack of GOP Front-Runner for 2012 Is Atypical," Gallup Poll, March 7, 2011, www.gallup.com/poll/146489/Lack-GOP-Front-Runner-2012-Atypical.aspx.
38. 1 Corinthians 9:22.

39. Christopher Rowland, "Pawlenty Takes on 'Problem-Solver' Mantle in N.H.," *Boston Globe*, March 10, 2011, www.boston.com/news/politics/politicalintelligence/2011/03/pawlenty_takes_1.html.

40. Sarah Pulliam Bailey, "Q&A: Tim Pawlenty on Evangelicals and the Issues," *Christianity Today*, Jan. 27, 2011, www.christianitytoday.com/ct/2011/januaryweb-only/qatimpawlenty.html.

41. Scott Conroy, "Pawlenty Builds Tea Party Support," RealClearPolitics, May 3, 2011, www.realclearpolitics.com/articles/2011/05/03/pawlenty_builds_tea_party_support_109724.html.

42. Jill Lawrence, "Four Ways Campaign 2012 Might Have Led to a Different President," *National Journal*, Dec. 3, 2012, www.nationaljournal.com/politics/four-ways-campaign-2012-might-have-led-to-a-different-president-20121203.

43. Carrie Budoff Brown and Mike Allen, "Obama Naming Huntsman Ambassador to China," *Politico*, May 16, 2009, www.politico.com/news/stories/0509/22589.html.

44. Jason Horowitz, "Presidential Hopefuls Huntsman, Romney Share Mormonism and Belief in Themselves," *Washington Post*, March 4, 2011, www.washingtonpost.com/wp-dyn/content/article/2011/03/03/AR2011030305195.html.

45. Frank Newport, "Republicans Remain Focused on Government Power, Spending," Gallup Poll, March 28, 2011, www.gallup.com/poll/146831/republicans-remain-focused-government-power-spending.aspx.

46. Jay Cost, "Morning Jay: Romney's Strategic Advantages," *The Weekly Standard*, Oct. 26, 2011, www.weeklystandard.com/blogs/morning-jay-romneys-strategic-advantages_604015.html.

47. Bob Cohn and Eleanor Clift, "The Lost Chance," *Newsweek*, Sept. 18, 1994, www.thedailybeast.com/newsweek/1994/09/18/the-lost-chance.html.

48. Andy Barr, "GOP Rep on Obama's 'Anti-American' Views," *Politico*, Oct. 17, 2008, www.politico.com/news/stories/1008/14684.html.

49. Ben Smith and Maggie Haberman, "Stars Collide: Michele Bachmann and Sarah Palin," *Politico*, June 8, 2011, www.politico.com/news/stories/0611/56480.html.

50. "Best and Worst of Congress 2012," *Washingtonian*, Aug. 29, 2012, www.washingtonian.com/articles/people/best-and-worst-of-congress-2012/indexp2.php.

51. Jonathan Allen, "Bachmann Aide No Longer Taking Care of Business," *Politico*, Nov. 4, 2009, www.politico.com/news/stories/1109/29141.html.

52. Associated Press, "Excerpt from the Santorum Interview," *USA Today*, Apr. 23, 2003, http://usatoday30.usatoday.com/news/washington/2003-04-23-santorum-excerpt_x.htm.

53. Andy Barr, "Republicans Learn the Cost of Attacking Sarah Palin," *Politico*, Feb. 12, 2011, www.politico.com/news/stories/0211/49394.html.

54. David Maraniss and Michael Weisskopf, *Tell Newt to Shut Up!* (New York: Simon and Schuster, Touchstone Books, 1996), 156.

55. Frank Newport, "Gingrich an Unpopular Figure during His Tenure as Speaker," Gallup Poll, Nov. 11, 1998, www.gallup.com/poll/4141/gingrich-unpopular-figure-during-tenure-speaker.aspx.

56. Francis X. Clines, "Big Collective Push Preceded Gingrich's Big Fall, Some Republicans Recall," *New York Times*, Nov. 8, 1998, www.nytimes.com/1998/11/08/us/speaker-steps-down-speaker-big-collective-push-preceded-gingrich-s-big-fall-some.htm.

57. *Meet the Press* transcript for May 15, 2011, MSNBC, www.msnbc.msn.com/id/43022759/ns/meet_the_press-transcripts/#.UGtlSE2HJ8E.

58. Jan Crawford, "Newt Out, Perry In?," CBS News, June 9, 2011, www.cbsnews.com/8301-504564_162-20070377-504564.html.

59. Rick Perry, *Fed Up! Our Fight to Save America from Washington* (New York: Little, Brown, 2010).

60. James G. Gimpel, "Inside Rick Perry's Outside-the-Box Campaign," *National Review Online*, March 8, 2010, www.nationalreview.com/corner/195911/inside-rick-perrys-outside-box-campaign/james-g-gimpel.

61. Jeffrey M. Jones, "Perry Zooms to Front of Pack for 2012 GOP Nomination," Gallup Poll, Aug. 24, 2011, www.gallup.com/poll/149180/Perry-Zooms-Front-Pack-2012-GOP-Nomination.aspx.

62. Rich Galen, "The Money Chase," Mullings, Oct. 17, 2011, www.mullings.com/10-17-11.htm.

63. Jay Root, *Oops! A Diary from the 2012 Campaign Trail* (San Francisco: Byliner Digital, 2012).

64. Jay Root, "Perry Downplays Sleep Apnea That Office Confirmed," *Texas Tribune*, Sept. 27, 2012, www.texastribune.org/texas-people/rick-perry/perry-downplays-sleep-apnea-office-confirmed.

65. Lawrence, "Four Ways."

66. *The Rules of the Republican Party*, as amended by the Republican National Committee, Aug. 6, 2010, www.gop.com/images/legal/2008_RULES_Adopted.pdf.

67. Josh Putnam, "An Update on 2012 Republican Delegate Selection Rules," *Frontloading HQ*, Feb. 27, 2011, http://frontloading.blogspot.com/2011/02/update-on-2012-republican-delegate.html.

68. John Avlon, "How Republicans Screwed Themselves with Their Own Proportional-Delegate Trap," *The Daily Beast*, March 13, 2012, www.thedailybeast.com/articles/2012/03/13/how-republicans-screwed-themselves-with-their-own-proportional-delegate-trap.html.

69. Amanda Terkel, "Chris Christie on RNC Proportional Delegate Rules: 'Dumbest Idea Anybody Ever Had,'" *Huffington Post*, Feb. 23, 2012, www.huffingtonpost.com/2012/02/23/chris-christie-rnc-delegate-dumbest-idea_n_1296571.html.

70. Dan Balz, "After 2008, Romney Works a Very Different Campaign," *Washington Post*, Nov. 29, 2011, www.washingtonpost.com/politics/after-2008-romney-works-a-very-different-campaign/2011/11/29/gIQAd2e58N_story.html.

71. Stephen Dinan, "No Major Takers for Federal Campaign Funds," *Washington Times*, Jan. 8, 2012, www.washingtontimes.com/news/2012/jan/8/federal-campaign-funds-find-no-candidate-takers.

72. *Citizens United v. Federal Election Commission*, 558 U.S. 310 (2010).

73. Eric M. Appleman, "Candidates Engaged in Many Debates but Relatively Few People Watched," Democracy in Action, March 24, 2000, www.gwu.edu/~action/primdeb/primdeb.html.

74. American Presidency Project, "Presidential Debates 1960–2012," www.presidency.ucsb.edu/debates.php.

75. Byron York, "Inside the GOP Debate: Pawlenty Underwhelms, Cain Struggles, Santorum Scores," *Washington Examiner*, May 6, 2011, http://washingtonexaminer.com/article/113709.

76. Kevin Hall, "Bachmann Fails While Trying to Upstage Perry in Her Hometown," *Iowa Republican*, Aug. 15, 2011, http://theiowarepublican.com/2011/bachmann-fails-while-trying-to-upstage-perry-in-her-hometown/.

77. Rich Galen, "A Very Important Week," Mullings, Sept. 7, 2011, www.mullings.com/09-07-11.htm.

78. Full transcript of CNN-Tea Party Republican debate, Sept. 12, 2011, http://transcripts.cnn.com/TRANSCRIPTS/1109/12/se.06.html.

79. Steven Hayward, "Giving Up on Bachmann," *Powerline* blog, Sept. 14, 2011, www.powerlineblog.com/archives/2011/09/giving-up-on-bachmann.php.

80. "Transcript: Fox News–Google GOP Debate," Fox News, Sept. 22, 2011, www.foxnews.com/politics/2011/09/22/fox-news-google-gop-2012-presidential-debate/.

81. Root, *Oops!*

82. Michael Medved, "Rick Perry, Beginning of the End?," *The Daily Beast*, Sept. 23, 2011, www.thedailybeast.com/articles/2011/09/23/rick-perry-in-gop-debate-beginning-of-the-end.html.

83. Byron York, "Lesson of Perry's Candidacy: Think Before You Run," *Washington Examiner*, Oct. 13, 2011, http://washingtonexaminer.com/article/912976.

84. Lydia Saad, "Cain Surges, Nearly Ties Romney for Lead in GOP," Gallup Poll, Oct. 10, 2011, www.gallup.com/poll/149990/Cain-Surges-Nearly-Ties-Romney-Lead-GOP-Preferences.aspx.

85. "Indecision 2012—Ruh Roh Edition," *The Daily Show*, Oct. 31, 2011, www.thedailyshow.com/watch/mon-october-31-2011/indecision-2012---ruh-roh-edition.

86. "Your Money, Your Vote: The Republican Presidential Debate," CNBC, live from Oakland University in Rochester, MI, Nov. 9, 2011, www.cnbc.com/id/45074943/FULL_TRANSCRIPT.

87. Frank Newport, "Cain Ties Romney atop GOP Field," Gallup Poll, Nov. 7, 2011, www.gallup.com/poll/150617/Cain-Ties-Romney-Atop-GOP-Field.aspx; Corbett B. Daly, "Herman Cain Tops Mitt Romney in Latest CBS/NYT Poll," CBS News, Oct. 25, 2011, www.cbsnews.com/8301-503544_162-20125120-503544/herman-cain-tops-mitt-romney-in-latest-cbs-nyt-poll.

88. "Herman Cain's 9-9-9 Tax Plan: 5 Reasons to Reject It," *The Week*, Oct. 13, 2011, http://theweek.com/article/index/220244/herman-cains-9-9-9-tax-plan-5-reasons-to-reject-it; Jennifer Rubin, "Herman Cain's Math Is Wrong," *Washington Post*, Oct. 13, 2011, www.washingtonpost.com/blogs/right-turn/post/herman-cains-math-is-wrong/2011/03/29/gIQAf1YZgL_blog.html.

89. Don Walker and Craig Gilbert, "Cain Stumbles on Libya Question," *Milwaukee Journal Sentinel*, Nov. 14, 2011, www.jsonline.com/news/statepolitics/cain-backs-collective-bargaining-for-public-employees-l931tg4-133828808.html.

90. Robin Abcarian, "Herman Cain Losing Some Steam," *Los Angeles Times*, Oct. 28, 2011, http://articles.latimes.com/2011/oct/28/nation/la-na-cain-20111029.

91. Chris Stirewalt, "Cain Campaign Gets Smoked on Harassment," Fox News, Oct. 31, 2011, www.foxnews.com/politics/2011/10/31/cain-campaign-gets-smoked-on-harassment.

92. Brian Montopoli Corbett B. Daly and Lucy Madison, "GOP Debate in Vegas: Winners and Losers," CBS News, Oct. 18, 2011, www.cbsnews.com/8301-503544_162-20122333-503544.html.

93. Shawn Millerick, "Poll: Romney, Gingrich in Statistical Dead Heat in N.H.," *NH Journal*, Nov. 18, 2011, http://nhjournal.com/2011/11/18/poll-romney-gingrich-in-statistical-dead-heat-in-n-h.

94. Jeffrey M. Jones, "Romney, Gingrich Now Top Choices for GOP Nomination," Gallup Poll, Nov. 21, 2011, www.gallup.com/poll/150845/Romney-Gingrich-Top-Choices-GOP-Nomination.aspx.

95. Joshua Miller, "Newt Gingrich Suggests Prison for Barney Frank, Chris Dodd Over Wall Street Crisis," *Roll Call*, Oct. 22, 2011, www.rollcall.com/news/newt_gingrich_suggests_prison_barney_frank_chris_dodd_wall_street_crisis-209389-1.html.

96. "Full Transcript CNN Western Republican Presidential Debate," CNN, Oct. 18, 2011, http://transcripts.cnn.com/TRANSCRIPTS/1110/18/se.05.html.

97. "Full Transcript: ABC News Iowa Republican Debate," ABC News, Dec. 11, 2011, http://abcnews.go.com/Politics/full-transcript-abc-news-iowa-republican-debate/story?id=15134849.

98. James Hohmann, "Morning Score: Paul Hits Gingrich for 'Selling Access,'" *Politico*, Dec. 12, 2011, www.politico.com/morningscore/1211/morningscore477.html.

99. Kevin Liptak, "Nearly Half of Iowa Ads Attack Gingrich," CNN, Dec. 30, 2011, http://politicalticker.blogs.cnn.com/2011/12/30/nearly-half-of-iowa-ads-attack-gingrich/.

100. Hohmann, "Morning Score: Paul Hits Gingrich."

101. "Winnowing the Field," *National Review Online*, Dec. 14, 2011, www.nationalreview.com/articles/285787/winnowing-field-editors.

102. Frank Newport, "Romney Edges Gingrich, 27% to 23%, for National GOP Lead," Gallup Poll, Dec. 29, 2011, www.gallup.com/poll/151823/Romney-Edges-Gingrich-National-GOP-Lead.aspx.

103. R. Lawrence Butler, *Claiming the Mantle: How Presidential Nominations Are Won and Lost Before the Votes Are Cast* (Cambridge: Westview, 2004).

104. Geoffrey Sant, "'I Really Want You to Do My Vice-America President,'" *Slate*, Oct. 31, 2011, www.slate.com/articles/news_and_politics/explainer/2011/10/is_jon_huntsman_fluent_in_chinese_.html.

105. Jim Rutenberg, "Huntsman, Out of Options, Bets It All on New Hampshire," *New York Times*, Jan. 7, 2012, www.nytimes.com/2012/01/08/us/politics/ready-or-not-huntsman-faces-his-moment-in-new-hampshire.html.

106. Taylor West and Peter Bell, "GOP Insiders Near-Unanimous in Predicting Romney Nomination," *National Journal*, Oct. 28, 2011, http://hotlineoncall.nationaljournal.com/archives/2011/10/gop-insiders-ne.php.

107. Sasha Issenberg, "Anatomy of a Narrow Victory," *Slate*, Jan. 4, 2012, www.slate.com/articles/news_and_politics/victory_lab/2012/01/romney_s_iowa_win_it_took_a_lot_more_than_money_.single.html.

108. Robin Abcarian, "Rick Santorum's Work in Iowa Paying Off," *Los Angeles Times*, Jan. 2, 2012, http://articles.latimes.com/2012/jan/02/nation/la-na-santorum-iowa-20120103.

109. "Romney Leads Paul in New Des Moines Register Iowa Poll; Santorum Surges," *Des Moines Register*, Dec. 31, 2011, http://caucuses.desmoinesregister.com/2011/12/31/romney-leads-paul-in-new-des-moines-register-iowa-poll-santorum-surging.

110. Frank Newport, "Romney, Santorum Rising Nationally after Iowa," Gallup Poll, Jan. 6, 2012, www.gallup.com/poll/151931/Romney-Santorum-Rising-Nationally-Iowa.aspx.

111. Kevin Bohn, "Super PAC Supporting Santorum to Become More Active," CNN, Jan. 5, 2012, http://politicalticker.blogs.cnn.com/2012/01/05/super-pac-supporting-santorum-to-become-more-active.

112. "Entrance Polls: Iowa Republicans," CNN, Jan. 3, 2012, www.cnn.com/election/2012/primaries/epolls/ia.

113. Sasha Issenberg, "Can You Win a Campaign Without Conducting Polls?," *Slate*, March 20, 2012, www.slate.com/articles/news_and_politics/victory_lab/2012/03/rick_santorum_can_the_former_pennsylvania_senator_win_a_campaign_without_conducting_a_single_poll_.html.

114. Maeve Reston, "Mitt Romney: 'Fire People' Remark Taken Out of Context," *Los Angeles Times*, Jan. 9, 2012, http://articles.latimes.com/2012/jan/09/news/la-pn-mitt-romney-fire-people-remark-taken-out-of-context-20120109.

115. Michael D. Shear, "Huntsman Campaign Tries to Wipe Romney Slate Clean," *New York Times*, Jan. 16, 2012, http://thecaucus.blogs.nytimes.com/2012/01/16/huntsman-campaign-tries-to-wipe-romney-slate-clean.

116. Molly Ball, "Newt's Secret Campaign: How Gingrich Really Won S.C.," *The Atlantic*, Jan. 22, 2012, www.theatlantic.com/politics/archive/2012/01/newts-secret-campaign-how-gingrich-really-won-sc/251783/.

117. Rich Lowry, "Gingrich Comes Out Swinging in South Carolina Debate," Fox News, Jan. 17, 2012, www.foxnews.com/opinion/2012/01/17/gingrich-spars-with-moderators-gop-rivals-in-fox-news-debate/.

118. "Republican Candidates Debate in Charleston, South Carolina," Jan. 19, 2012, www.presidency.ucsb.edu/ws/?pid=98936.

119. "South Carolina Republican Presidential Primary," RealClearPolitics, www.realclearpolitics.com/epolls/2012/president/sc/south_carolina_republican_presidential_primary-1590.html#polls.

120. Trip Gabriel, "PAC Deluges South Carolina Airwaves with Anti-Romney Ads," *New York Times*, Jan. 12, 2012, http://thecaucus.blogs.nytimes.com/2012/01/12/pac-deluges-south-carolina-airwaves-with-anti-romney-ads/.

121. Robert Schlesinger, "Obama's Operation Chaos," *US News and World Report*, Dec. 5, 2012, www.usnews.com/opinion/blogs/robert-schlesinger/2012/12/05/how-the-obama-campaign-sabotaged-romney-in-the-2012-gop-primary.

122. "Florida Ad War: Mitt Pounds Newt," FactCheck.Org, Jan. 26, 2012, www.factcheck.org/2012/01/florida-ad-war-mitt-pounds-newt/.
123. Jocelyn Noveck, "Romney's Forceful Body Language Scores in Debate," Associated Press, Jan. 27, 2012, http://m.startribune.com/politics/?id=138225544.
124. Jim Rutenberg and Jeff Zeleny, "Facing Second Loss to Gingrich, Romney Went on Warpath," *New York Times*, Jan. 28, 2012, www.nytimes.com/2012/01/29/us/politics/the-calculations-that-led-romney-to-the-warpath.html.
125. "Republican Candidates Debate in Jacksonville, Florida," The American Presidency Project, Jan. 26, 2012, www.presidency.ucsb.edu/ws/?pid=99075.
126. "Republican Candidates Debate."
127. "Presidential Debate in Hempstead, New York," The American Presidency Project, Oct. 16, 2012, www.presidency.ucsb.edu/ws/?pid=102343.
128. Chuck Todd et al., "First Thoughts: Why Florida Differed from South Carolina," NBC, Feb. 1, 2012, http://firstread.nbcnews.com/_news/2012/02/01/10288050-first-thoughts-why-florida-differed-from-south-carolina.
129. Dan Hartranft, "Super PAC Spending Boosts Santorum," Center for Responsive Politics, Feb. 16, 2012, www.opensecrets.org/news/2012/02/super-pac-spending-boosts-santorum.html.
130. "How the Media Covered the 2012 Primary Campaign: Rick Santorum," Project for Excellence in Journalism, April 23, 2012, www.journalism.org/analysis_report/rick_santorum.
131. Gloria Borger and Kevin Bohn, "Some Republicans Whisper about a Plan B," CNN, Feb. 20, 2012, http://politicalticker.blogs.cnn.com/2012/02/20/some-republicans-whisper-about-a-plan-b.
132. Michael D. Shear, "A Chance for Mischief in the Michigan Primary," *New York Times*, Feb. 27, 2012, http://thecaucus.blogs.nytimes.com/2012/02/27/a-chance-for-mischief-in-the-michigan-primary.
133. Byron York, "Did Romney Quell Conservative Doubts?," *Washington Examiner*, Feb. 11, 2012, http://washingtonexaminer.com/article/1120471#.UMJQPuRjuSo.
134. Kathy Banks Hoffman, "Mitt Romney Campaign's Organizational Strength Helps Ahead of 2012 Michigan Primary," Associated Press, Feb. 26, 2012, www.huffingtonpost.com/2012/02/26/mitt-romney-michigan_n_1302206.html.
135. George Stephanopoulos, "Rick Santorum: JFK's 1960 Speech Made Me Want to Throw Up," ABC News, Feb. 26, 2012, http://abcnews.go.com/blogs/politics/2012/02/rick-santorum-jfks-1960-speech-made-me-want-to-throw-up.
136. Dustin Ingalls, "JFK, Reagan, Clinton Most Popular Recent Ex-Presidents," Public Policy Polling, Sept. 15, 2011, www.publicpolicypolling.com/main/2011/09/jfk-reagan-clinton-most-popular-recent-ex-presidents.html.
137. James W. Ceaser, Andrew E. Busch, and John J. Pitney Jr., *Epic Journey: The 2008 Elections and American Politics* (Lanham, MD: Rowman and Littlefield, 2009), 118–21.
138. Michael D. Shear, "Romney Traces Obama's Path on Delegates," *New York Times*, March 3, 2012, www.nytimes.com/2012/03/04/us/politics/mitt-romney-focuses-on-delegate-tally-in-race-with-santorum.html.
139. Byron York, "A Weak Win for Romney in Key Ohio Race," *Washington Examiner*, March 7, 2012, http://washingtonexaminer.com/article/1164756#.UMenioM8B8E.
140. Jeffrey M. Jones, "Romney, Santorum Tie as Gingrich Voters' Second Choice," Gallup Poll, March 16, 2012, www.gallup.com/poll/153308/Romney-Santorum-Tie-Gingrich-Voters-Second-Choice.aspx.
141. Lynn Sweet, "Plouffe on Conference Call Says Obama within 300 Delegates of Clinching Democratic Nomination. 'Organizing Heavily in Guam,'" *Chicago Sun-Times*, Apr. 23, 2008, http://blogs.suntimes.com/sweet/2008/04/plouffe_on_wednesday_conference.html.
142. Matthew Jaffe and Shushannah Walshe, "Rick Santorum Defends Call for Puerto Rico to Adopt English after Delegate Defection," ABC News, March 15, 2012, http://abcnews.go.com/blogs/politics/2012/03/rick-santorum-defends-call-for-puerto-rico-to-adopt-english-after-delegate-defection.

143. Felicia Sonmez, "Rick Santorum's Camp Hits Mitt Romney on Bain Tenure," *Washington Post*, March 19, 2012, www.washingtonpost.com/blogs/post-politics/post/rick-santorums-camp-hits-mitt-romney-on-bain-tenure/2012/03/19/gIQAodCONS_blog.html.

144. "'This Week' Transcript: GOP Candidate Rick Santorum," ABC News, March 18, 2012, http://abcnews.go.com/Politics/week-transcript-gop-candidate-rick-santorum/story?id=15944142.

145. Ralph Z. Hallow, "Finally, Romney Gets Tea Party Support," *Washington Times*, March 20, 2012, www.washingtontimes.com/news/2012/mar/20/romney-gets-tepid-tea-party-support/.

146. Micah Cohen, "The General Election Ground Game: A First Look," *New York Times*, Apr. 17, 2012, http://fivethirtyeight.blogs.nytimes.com/2012/04/17/the-general-election-ground-game-a-first-look.

147. James Warren, "David Axelrod Surprised by Romney Campaign's Missed Opportunities," *The Daily Beast*, Nov. 27, 2012, www.thedailybeast.com/articles/2012/11/27/david-axelrod-surprised-by-romney-campaign-s-missed-opportunities.html.

# FOUR

# The Presidential Campaign

The 2012 contest offered a momentous choice wrapped inside of a forgettable campaign. President Obama and the Democrats stood for a major expansion of new federal entitlements and programs, higher taxes on the wealthy, greater regulation of the financial sector, and public-directed investment in energy. Republicans sought to hold the share of the size of government expenditures relative to the economy to previous levels (which, given built-in increases, meant altering and paring down existing entitlement programs), maintain or lower tax rates, ensure a lighter hand on regulations, and rely on market approaches to determine investments. For leading Democrats, the 2012 election was about protecting and expanding the Progressive agenda enacted in Obama's first term. For Republicans, it was about reversing much of this change and restoring limited government. The significance of this choice was evident to leaders on both sides, even if people disagreed on the terms to describe it. To some it was a decision between "big government" and constitutional government, to others between social democracy and a free enterprise system, and to others still between social justice and entrenched wealth.

The magnitude of the choice was more muted, though perhaps no less significant, in foreign affairs. While carrying out a tough clandestine war on terror through drone strikes, President Obama in his first term sought a reduced profile, or a smaller footprint, for the United States in the world, and favored cuts in military spending. American assertiveness and efforts to control events were to be less prominent than in the Bush era. Republicans spoke of strength, of maintaining current military spending, and of "American exceptionalism," a term suggesting a more active posture in world affairs. Finally, in the domain of social issues, the divide between conservatives and liberals continued on many value questions from marriage to abortion, intensified in some cases by the expansion of government that brought health insurance coverage for birth control services into the public realm. In the background also hung the possible appointment of two or three Supreme Court justices, enough to alter the court's balance for the next era.

Given these huge differences, the great clash of ideas and principles that might have been expected never quite took place. Both candidates acknowledged from time to time the importance of the choice, but the campaign's focus, if it had one, lay elsewhere. The thrust of the Obama campaign, especially of its ads, was an attack on Mitt Romney.[1] The president's main "positive" pitch was to raise taxes on the wealthy, backed up by a rhetoric of class division that bore in on "the breathtaking greed of a few."[2] As for Mitt Romney, though he carried the banner of conservative ideas during the campaign, by personal temperament and approach he has never been the kind of leader to stress basic principles or public philosophy. Described often as a problem solver, or more pejoratively as a technocrat, Romney did not enter politics as a movement conservative. In fact, he was more of a moderate, which left parts of his own record at odds with current Republican philosophy. Although he had moved piecemeal to embrace most conservative doctrines, the language was not natural to him. For much of the campaign he preferred to frame the decision as a referendum on President Obama's economic record and to tout his skills and competence at addressing economic underperformance. For reasons of political strategy, and of the focus of the public, he also decided not to press too much in the general election campaign on foreign affairs and cultural issues.

The profiles of the candidates also failed to measure up to the momentousness of the choice. Barack Obama was nothing like the figure he had been in the 2008 campaign, a beacon of hope possessed with "charisma" or the gift of grace. He campaigned this time by dividing rather than unifying, spending stature rather than building it. When the video clips are assembled at some point in the future to celebrate Barack Obama's presidency, it is unlikely that any will be taken from his 2012 campaign. As for Mitt Romney, whatever his qualities of steadiness and intelligence, no one has ever accused him of being an overly exciting figure. He has been characterized alternately as a private person who had difficulty connecting with others or as someone who lacked a political gene. No greater proof of this limitation is needed than to remember that much of the Republican convention was devoted to trying to make Mitt more human and accessible. Only in the last month of the campaign did Romney, for perhaps the first and only time in his political career, begin to instill deep enthusiasm into swelling crowds. The reaction buoyed him and his campaign, though only to contribute in the end to their surprise and disappointment at the outcome.

The campaign did have its rare admirable moments. Notwithstanding Obama's out-of-character poor performance in the first presidential debate, the other two debates were conducted on a high level. Both men impressed by their ability to express themselves with command, clarity, and coherence, qualities often in short supply in past presidential debates. Long-time columnist and political analyst George Will observed after the second debate: "I have seen every presidential debate in American history since the floor of Nixon and Kennedy in 1960. This was immeasurably the best."[3]

A final sign of the forgettable character of this campaign is that once it ended, no one much sought to dwell on it. This reaction was admittedly partly one of sheer exhaustion and overdose. After all the coverage, ads, and analysis, most Americans were relieved simply that it was over and took some satisfaction in flipping the channel whenever an expert or pundit dared to appear. But it was more than this. Besides his victory (no small thing), Obama drew little from the campaign in terms of added stature or new energy for an agenda, other than taxing the wealthy and immigration reform. There was no reason for him to dwell much on the campaign, and he did not. A number of Republicans sought to use the loss to derive a political advantage, arguing that Romney's defeat proved once again the disastrous consequences of allowing a moderate Republican to be foisted on the party by the establishment. Yet Romney had never been foisted on anyone, and he for the most part hewed to the conservative line. He never claimed to lead a "moderate" current within the Republican Party. Nor does Romney offer any prospect of doing so in the future. For the most part, though, Republicans accepted that Romney had performed credibly, though certainly not impeccably. There was, however, considerable criticism of the Romney campaign's tactical and technical side. Whatever lessons the elections might hold, it did not require revisiting every strategic decision or tearing the candidate to shreds.

By mutual consent, then, both sides found no reason to dwell on the campaign. Probably the statements most to be remembered about it are the gaffes that each candidate would prefer to have forgotten: Obama's claim, "If you've got a business, you didn't build that," and, especially, Mitt Romney's dismissal of the "47 percent . . . who believe that they are victims."

## ON STUDYING CAMPAIGNS

Do political campaigns matter in deciding the outcome of presidential elections? The answer to this question has divided students of elections, probably more than it should. One approach emphasizes what happens in the campaign, in the belief that what the candidates say and do, what strategies the campaign organizations follow, and what events occur during this period will often determine the result of the election. The author

Theodore White made this method famous in his *The Making of the President* series, which began with the election of 1960 and continued up through the election of 1972. Interestingly, White chanced to have written about the two closest races of the post-war period (1960 and 1968) and the two greatest landslides (1964 and 1972). His first book on the Kennedy-Nixon race, which won the Pulitzer Prize, established the model for the series. No wonder that it focused on the campaign. This contest was so close—till this day there are still disputes about who really won—that almost anything that happened could arguably be said to have determined the result. White's riveting narrative account captured the drama of this campaign, including the reactions to the first-ever presidential debate, in which John Kennedy prevailed in part by looking fitter than his rival. Kennedy chose to use make-up, while Nixon, who had been ill and appeared haggard, refused. Did powder on the face change the course of American history?

An alternative approach to studying elections ignores the campaign altogether. It focuses on predicting the outcome, well in advance of the election—indeed before the final campaign even begins—by presenting models based on various measures or "keys" that have been discovered to correlate with election outcomes. Economic indicators of one sort or another invariably form the basis of one of the keys. Leaving the pure mechanics aside, the underlying premise of these models is that certain conditions or fundamentals in place largely determine the result. If things are going well in the country, especially in the economic realm, the incumbent party wins, and if things are going poorly, it loses. Narratives of the campaign, such as White wrote, may be entertaining, but they do not add anything to the explanation of who wins. If queried about the role of the campaign, those using this approach would probably not deny that the campaign could, theoretically, be decisive—say, if one candidate acted in a truly aberrant way. But as things go, the candidates are professional politicians, and the campaigns are run by competent people. If there are campaign effects, they tend to cancel themselves out. In addition, after all the noise and diversions, campaigns often tend to make clear the fundamentals that prevail in the country.

Our approach in this series, which began in 1992, has been to consider first the fundamentals, though without recourse to technical models. Where the fundamentals point strongly in one direction, it is a matter of common sense that the campaign is most unlikely to decide the event. Interesting as Theodore White's narrative accounts were for the landslide elections in 1964 and 1972, they lacked drama on the main point. Nearly everyone—excepting, it seems, the candidates Lyndon Johnson and Richard Nixon—was certain of the outcome. Still, even in these cases, the campaign remains an important object of study for what the candidates say and for how the victor frames the choice, which can influence the course of American politics. Presidential campaigns can have significance well beyond the matter of who wins.

Scholars who employ models have continued over the years to fiddle with the best measures that predict the outcome. These efforts can provide helpful forecasts only within a certain range. There always remains the influence of the campaign, which we judge to be fairly significant. While campaigns produce effects that often tend to cancel out any net advantage, this is not always the case. Two candidates are contesting, and, as in any match, one may be better than the other. Or things may just happen to break in one way more than another. When the fundamentals in place in the nation do not allow a forecast of the outcome beyond the range of what the campaign can reasonably influence, or what we call "the campaign effect," it makes sense to proceed on the basis that the campaign may very well decide the result. In such elections, no one can know the outcome in advance for the simple reason that it is unknowable. It depends on the campaign. In the six presidential elections beginning in 1992, there have been no electoral landslides, and in only one or two (1996 and perhaps 2008) did the fundamentals approach forecasting a safe margin. For the others, conditions or fundamentals placed the election within the range being decided by the campaign effect.[4]

The 2012 election was clearly a could-win election for either candidate. The forecasts of the fourteen major models, released by the late summer of 2012, indicated how close the fundamentals placed the two candidates. Eight of the models predicted an Obama win and six a Romney win. In the average of these models, Obama is the predicted victor with 50.1 percent of the two-party national popular vote.[5] A similar kind of result emerges from surveying some of the less formal "rules of thumb" that were bandied about before the election to forecast the result. According to one rule, no incumbent in more than half a century had won with unemployment this high or disposable personal income this low; according to another rule, no incumbent had lost with second quarter GDP growth this high or a Gallup approval rating of at least 49 percent. The conclusion? Depending on which rule one follows, either President Obama couldn't lose in November, or he couldn't win.[6] One thing is certain: both the models and the rules of thumb are always adjusted after each election, in light of the results, in preparation for the next one.

Many in social science resist the idea of could-win elections because it leaves so much to events and to chance. They prefer instead to celebrate the pre-election model that comes closest to forecasting the actual result, contending that its accuracy proves that it is a correct model. There are certainly better and worse models, but in our view the fact that one forecast turns out to state the result is hardly proof that it is accurate or even that it is the best model. It more likely stated the result because the campaign effect this time happened to land in its favor. Or social scientists look at the exit polls and seek explanations for why the election turned out as it did. This approach is both sensible and helpful, as long as it does not forget the campaign effect. The problem is that many tend to reify their explanations, arguing more and more as time goes on that the result that occurred derived from certain measurable factors and is the only result that could have been. History always looks more predictable once the outcome is known.

Since we have spoken of the importance of the campaign effect, it will help briefly to restate what are the textbook features and elements of a campaign. The campaign is defined, partly for convenience sake, as taking place during a certain period of time. For the general election campaign today, this period begins from the point when the two major candidates are finally settled upon, which is in the spring. Only a couple of decades ago, a widely accepted formality held that the public campaign began "officially" on Labor Day. Now the public campaign gets into swing earlier, and the official start date passes with hardly a notice. What does remain a question—and professionals differ on this point—is the time when the bulk of the voters actually begin to focus on the campaign and give it their attention.

The campaign refers conceptually to two different things: (a) politically relevant events or trends that may occur during this time period, like the financial collapse that struck during the 2008 presidential campaign, and (b) the actions of the candidates, the campaign organizations, and other actors (e.g., the media and interest groups) that aim to influence the outcome, such as strategies and tactics, or unintended acts that have that effect, such as blunders and errors. The actors in turn are engaged in two basic activities (a) trying to persuade citizens to vote in a certain way and (b) planning and working to mobilize as many of their potential voters as possible to cast a ballot, especially in the states where it matters. Persuasion involves appeals to general ideas or public philosophies; arguments and positions on the basic areas of economic management, domestic welfare policy, social and cultural issues, and foreign affairs; and efforts to present one's qualities as a leader and president, such as competence, prudence, and empathy.

## STAGE ONE: THE SUMMER CAMPAIGN, APRIL 25–AUGUST 27

On April 25, the day after winning five northeastern state primaries, Mitt Romney became the Republican Party's presumptive nominee. For most of the spring and summer, the Obama campaign held the initiative and was successful in dominating the airwaves. The main objective was to define the opponent. The Obama campaign kept up a steady barrage of attack ads that painted Romney as an uncaring plutocrat whose callous vulture capitalism resulted in layoffs, heartache, and even a woman's death. Senior Obama aides claimed that Romney was a dog abuser, a schoolhouse bully, and even a felon.

Romney by and large held his powder, a response that many found baffling. Part of the reason was financial. The hard-fought nomination contest depleted most of the Romney campaign's resources for the preconvention period, and the vast majority of the funds left in the campaign's coffers were earmarked for the general election campaign, which by federal law cannot be used until after the conventions. Romney depended for his funding on the Republican National Committee and on pro-Republican PACs, such as Restore Our Future. These expenditures could not fully close the gap with Obama's outlays, which came mainly from his own organization. Nor could the Romney team control the messaging of the independent PACs. In the words of a Romney aide after the election, "It was very frustrating that the only message we could have any impact on whatsoever or could control at all is what we were doing."[7]

Many were nevertheless surprised that Romney did not tap into his own bank account to close the early funding gap. It may be that after fruitlessly spending $42 million of his own money in 2008, Romney was reluctant to go down this path again. But there was a more important reason. Spending his own capital would have opened Romney up to criticisms of attempting to buy the election, in effect vindicating the charges of the Obama ads. Here Romney faced one of his main vulnerabilities. He was a rich man defending capitalism, an uphill challenge in any democracy. Not only this, but he could not plausibly bill himself as a fully self-made man, in the mold of the Horatio Alger myth, who had risen from a hard-scrabble beginning to attain his position. True, most of his money was self-earned, not inherited, and Romney could—and did—claim the mantle of entrepreneur. But he could not deny benefitting from his father's fortune (won as president of American Motors Corporation) and prominence (George Romney had also served two terms as Michigan's governor). Adding to Mitt Romney's difficulty was how he had made his own fortune, through venture capital financing. It is difficult to trumpet the virtues of capitalism and the free-market system when you cannot display the particular good that you created. An auto executive can point to a car, a pizza chain owner to his pie crust, but the product of Romney's labor—though arguably no less real or necessary to the functioning of the nation's economy—is not as immediately understood. Venture capital destroys and rebuilds, closes down and refinances, but it does not by itself build a particular product or produce a service. Of all the emblems of capitalism, especially in the wake of the financial crisis of 2008, Mitt Romney, as the founder of a company named Bain Capital, had one of the toughest rows to hoe. Obama understood the difficulty when he praised "folks working with their hands, creating value, not just shuffling paper."[8]

Finally, the Romney campaign resisted large expenditures at this time because they believed most Americans, including the bulk of undecided or persuadable voters, would only begin paying concerted attention to the campaign in the final few months.[9] Like Muhammad Ali's "rope-a-dope" strategy, Romney would hunker down against the onslaught of an overeager opponent who would inevitably punch himself out in the early rounds. Then, right before the final bell, Romney would mount his own assault.[10]

Polling during the summer offered some evidence to vindicate Romney's strategy. The RealClearPolitics average of polls between April and the end of August showed Obama's support fluctuating between 45.7 and 48.9 percent, while Romney's stayed between 42.6 and 44.3 percent.[11] The Obama campaign, with its substantial spending advantage, seemed to be getting very little bang for its buck. The inelasticity of the polls was not the only bad news for the Obama Campaign. In May, Romney and the RNC outraised Obama and the DNC by $16 million.[12] Their fundraising edge would persist throughout the summer, which meant that Obama's spending advantage would not last.[13] Obama would not be able to rely for long on the overwhelming financial advantage that he had enjoyed in 2008, and, to this point, in 2012.

Another view of the Obama ad blitz, however, holds that these initial salvos had a potent effect. While voter intent did not shift markedly during the spring and summer, perhaps this was the time, after a divisive primary fight, that it should have been moving in Romney's favor. More importantly, Romney's favorability ratings began to decline. According to CNN/ORC polling, Romney's favorability went "under water" in the late summer, falling from a June favorability/unfavorability split of 48/42 percent to a 47/48 split in July.[14] Obama's campaign team was determined that by spending money early, they could define Romney on their terms, as a vulture capitalist, much as George Bush had defined John Kerry early in 2004.

Was the early Obama ad campaign one reason why Obama won? The experts and campaign strategists have continued to debate the issue. Exit polls, some say, show that the ads succeeded. Voters did not doubt that Romney was competent or could be a successful president, but they found him wanting in one quality: empathy. Perhaps voters thought that Romney would lead the country as Obama asserted he led Bain: cutting expenses for the benefit of the wealthy and at the expense of the less fortunate. Yet it is not clear whether the advertising blitz accounted for this judgment. His difficulty may have had much more to do with his own biography than any supposed masterstroke from David Axelrod. But in politics, as in sports, genius is rarely required. If a boxer's brow is bleeding, hit it again. If a horse is two hands taller, bet on him. If your opponent is very wealthy, request his tax returns.

Besides its attacks on Romney and, more broadly, on the wealthy, the Obama campaign sought to bolster support with key constituencies within the Democratic coalition by particularistic appeals and policy initiatives. Taking a cue from the Bush playbook of 2004, the Obama team concluded that this election could be won in large part by holding onto one's base. The organization of Obama's website neatly illustrates this strategy. Visitors to the site were presented nineteen links, each leading to a separate list of pledges and promises for a particular group. There was a link for women, for the elderly, for Native Americans, for "LGBT Americans," and so on. Obama engaged in the same sort of micro-targeting on the campaign trail. At each stop he pitched a series of initiatives aimed at the particular constituency. On a college campus in Ohio, Obama touted a student loan forgiveness program, at a meeting of National Association of Latino Elected Officials conference in Orlando, he highlighted his support for the DREAM Act, and at a speech in Ohio's manufacturing core, he trumpeted his role in the GM auto bailout. This was interest-group politicking, progressive style.

One group the Obama campaign courted with special zeal was women, especially unmarried women, whom Obama carried by the massive margin of 41 percent (seventy to twenty-nine) in 2008. This effort produced one of the strangest ads in electoral history: a short Internet slideshow titled "The Life of Julia." Like the sensible suitor in a Jane Austen novel, the key actor here—the government—sets out for the single woman the comfortable life it is prepared to offer her, if only she will commit. Each slide describes what government programs will greet the faceless cartoon everywoman as she ages. From the time Julia is three and happily enrolled in a Head Start program, to the point that she acquires a son along the way, until she retires as a sixty-seven-year-old Social Security recipient, Julia is well provided for: till death do us part. Even as it pursued the "Julia" strategy, the Obama campaign did not neglect the canonical women's issue: birth control. When the Catholic Church demanded an exemption from a provision of Obamacare that required employer health insurance policies to provide for birth control measures (including abortifacients), the Obama administration refused, leading to law suits.[15] Some commentators, on the left as well as on the right, viewed this controversy as dangerous for Obama. But team Obama seemed to have welcomed the fight, calculating its strong appeal to many women.

While Obama pursued a defensive strategy of holding on to its own, Romney knew that he would have to win over many voters who had gone for Obama in 2008. Fortifying the base would not be enough. By what means could he swing an additional 3 or 4 percent to the GOP column? The initial plan was to run a referendum on Obama's economic performance, presenting Romney as a reasonable alternative and giving no one a reason to vote against him. But with Romney trailing in the polls, many conservatives began to criticize the strategy as both ideologically unsatisfactory and politically insufficient. It was all caution, no boldness. Now began the drumbeat urging Mitt Romney to draw a stark distinction between his proposed agenda and the policies of the last four years, presenting Americans with "the big choice" between capitalism and limited government and continued centralization of control in Washington.

Further complicating this strategic debate was the long-awaited Supreme Court ruling on the constitutionality of Obamacare, which was handed down on June 28 in the case *National Federation of Independent Business v. Sebelius*. Obamacare had been challenged in the courts in a series of lawsuits beginning in 2010, brought mainly by some of the state attorneys general. Their claim was that the law contained provisions going beyond any legitimate power granted to Congress under Article I section 8 of the Constitution—in particular, in what became the crux of many of the arguments, that the requirement that all adults be required to purchase health insurance (or be subject to a penalty) could not be justified under the commerce clause, which was the constitutional power cited by defenders of the law. The opponents of the law argued that the commerce clause gave Congress the power to regulate interstate commerce, not to compel individuals to engage in commerce. Although liberal legal scholars scoffed at the suits and some appellate courts dismissed them, other appellate courts accepted the plaintiffs' reasoning and invalidated all or part of the law. This disagreement set up a showdown in the Supreme Court.

When oral arguments before the court were heard in March, which were followed by millions of Americans with the rare release of same-day audio recordings, court watchers strained to detect how various justices would finally vote. Of particular interest was Justice Anthony M. Kennedy, whom many thought might hold the swing vote between the four more liberal justices (Breyer, Ginsburg, Sotomayor, and Kagan) and the four more conservative justices (Scalia, Thomas, Roberts, and Alito). The stumbling performance of the government's lead attorney, Solicitor General Donald Verrilli, along with some of Kennedy's questions and comments led to widespread speculation that Kennedy might vote with the conservatives. When the decision was announced, Kennedy had indeed lined up with opponents of the bill. But it survived anyway, as Chief Justice John G. Roberts Jr. joined the court's four liberal justices to endorse the constitutionality of the individual mandate. The chief justice did so, however, on grounds that almost no one expected. Along with the opponents, he repudiated the administration's central argument and denied that the commerce clause extended to the point of compelling individuals to engage in commerce. But he found that the mandate was nevertheless constitutional as a tax, which, he contended, Congress clearly possesses the right to impose. Congress might not have deemed the mandate a tax, but the court could.

The ruling had huge political implications. In the wake of the decision, Romney and the Republicans continued to press for repeal of Obamacare, only now on policy, not constitutional, grounds. As Romney framed the issue after the decision: "What the court did today was say that 'Obamacare' does not violate the Constitution. What they did not do was say that 'Obamacare' is good law or that it's good policy." Obama could and did claim a general kind of vindication for the law. Although many polls indicated that a majority opposed the law, the court decision on constitutionality took some of the intensity out of the opposition. For better or worse, the Supreme Court in modern America has obtained the status as the definitive expositor of constitutionality. Once the court ruled Obamacare constitutional, though by the narrowest of margins and on technical grounds that few understood, the "great" public constitutional debate was over, and Obama had won.

All else is speculation. What would the political implications have been if the court had gone the other way, as so many anticipated? The nexus of issues revolving around the Supreme Court, judicial philosophy, and judicial appointments would have become a much larger issue in the campaign. Democrats could have used the ruling to stir up their base, though how far President Obama was prepared to take this issue is anyone's guess. For the Republicans, it is plausible that a ruling that Obamacare was unconstitutional would have given their opposition to the law greater credibility outside the Democrats' base, saddling Obama with the charge that he had wasted his term on an unpopular measure that could not even withstand constitutional scrutiny. Even more interesting is the question of how the campaign might have differed if the Supreme Court had found a way, as it certainly could have, to put a definitive ruling off until after the election. This scenario would have invited the candidates, in addition to debating the merits of the national health care law, to have confronted the general question of the limits of the federal government's constitutional authority to regulate all aspects of the American economy. If, as many surmised, Chief Justice Roberts sought to take the Supreme Court out of the campaign, he did so by taking the Constitution out of it as well.

The debate on strategy within the Republican Party between a campaign based on referendum and a campaign of choice came into focus on the question of whom Romney would select as his running mate. The choice of a vice presidential candidate is one of the set pieces in a campaign that indicates much about the nominee's values, in terms of both the personal qualities he esteems and the policy direction he will pursue. It is known, of course, that many nominees have looked to "balance" the ticket by choosing a vice presidential candidate known to represent a different current within the party than themselves. But the clear understanding in the lead-up to Romney's choice was that he would not be balancing, but sending a signal of where he wished to go. The final list of "likely picks" to emerge as August approached contained five names: Rob Portman, Tim Pawlenty, Marco Rubio, Chris Christie, and Paul Ryan. All were known to Romney, and all had previewed by stumping alongside with him during the summer. Commentators generally divided the list into two groups. First was the "safe choice" category made up of Pawlenty and Portman. These men were considered more moderate in their policy prescriptions and tone and therefore unlikely to scare off persuadable independents. They were most compatible with the referendum strategy. Second was the "bold choice" category made up of Rubio, Christie, and Ryan. All were favorites of movement conservatives—though Christie not to social conservatives—and all would energize the base. They were also clearly riskier candidates, as they might draw the focus of the campaign away from Obama's past failures and center it more on the conservatives' own plans for the future.

The betting was that Mitt Romney, a cautious man, would make the cautious choice. His selection of Paul Ryan came as a surprise, and it was taken as an indication that he was prepared to modify his referendum strategy. While Romney would continue to make the shortcomings of the Obama recovery the centerpiece, he was at least open to the "choice" idea. Call it cautious boldness. Ryan in some ways posed the greatest risk within this category, since, as chair of the House Budget Committee, he had prepared the Republican blueprint—the Ryan Plan—for how to deal with the budget and spending. It included some important changes in entitlement programs that Democrats had already branded as radical, and many of them now relished the opportunity to open a new line of attack against the Republican ticket.

Ryan broadened the scope of the election by making it about two competing sets of ideas about the role of government. Besides helping to ignite the Republican base and stimulate fundraising efforts, Ryan also energized Romney. One Romney staffer later characterized the relationship between them as a "bro-mance"; the two got along famously, and Ryan's presence seemed to focus and sharpen Romney's campaign speeches.[16]

Estimates of the importance of a vice presidential choice are usually at their height at the moment of selection, after which all come to realize that the significance of the selection has been exaggerated. In Ryan's case, he influenced the campaign, but he did not change it. Romney remained the cautious figure he had always been. Democrats attacked parts of Ryan's plan, particularly the transformation of Medicare into a voucher program, but Ryan ably defended it, avoiding any harm to Republicans. From the standpoint of a purely political calculation, Ryan did not end up bringing the sort of tangible benefits that vice presidential candidates are often, and perhaps unfairly, expected to. He did not deliver his home state of Wisconsin, nor did he help Romney in the Midwest generally. Ryan also did not seem to make the Republican ticket more appealing to blue-collar voters, as some said Christie might have, or chip into Obama's advantage among Hispanics, as Rubio might have. But Ryan's reputation as a devout Catholic may have shored up support among Evangelicals, who, some suspected, still had concerns about Romney's Mormon faith. While the selection of Paul Ryan was only a part of a concerted effort to win over Evangelicals—Romney's commencement speech at Liberty University, where he emphasized the Christian values he and his audience held in common, was clearly motivated by this same end—it seemed to help.

On July 13 at a campaign stop in Roanoke, Virginia, while referring to government-built infrastructure, Obama said, "If you've got a business—you didn't build that. Somebody else made that happen." Romney quickly seized on the quote, claiming, "It wasn't a gaffe. It was instead his ideology."[17] Democrats claimed that the quote was taken out of context; but even for the few persuadable voters who took the time to track down the full quote, proper contextualization may not have made Obama appear any more moderate. The similarities between the president's Roanoke speech and a speech eleven months earlier by Obama's confidant Elizabeth Warren were striking. Now a candidate for the senate seat in Massachusetts, Warren had fumed: "You built a factory out there? Good for you. But I want to be clear. You moved your goods to market on the roads *the rest of us* paid for." The implication was that wealth was in the first instance socially generated and thus in a sense socially owned, not the product of efforts of successful people and therefore by right their own.

Obama's comments initially received little attention in the mainstream media. ABC, NBC, and CBS did not run a single story on Obama's "you didn't build that comment" until Romney began emphasizing it on the campaign trail four days later.[18] The stories and editorials that were sprinkled into the news portrayed the gaffe as an innocuous point taken out of context. The major media's protective tone toward Obama was emblematic of a larger trend in the campaign. When Obama claimed during a June 8 press conference that the "the private sector is doing fine," it received one night's coverage and two passing references on mainstream evening news programs. Coverage of Romney was not quite so forgiving. Following Romney's trip to Europe in June, which began with the Romney gaffe of questioning whether the Brits' handling of security planning for the Olympic Games was up to snuff, the Media Research Center found that 86 percent of the stories about Romney's trip emphasized diplomatic blunders. But the gaffe during the summer that, arguably, hurt Romney the most was not even uttered by him. On August 19, the Republican Senate candidate from Missouri, Todd Akin, defended his position that abortions not be allowed in instances of rape by claiming that pregnancies rarely result from "legitimate" rape. The Democrats and mainstream media quickly picked up this quote and argued it was symptomatic of the current Republican Party's extreme position on social issues.

The major media's partisanship is certainly an important part of the story of this election, but it is not a new one. Along with the academy, unions, and the entertainment industry, the mainstream media has for many years been an institutional component in the Democratic power structure.[19] (Republicans have their power structure, too, which includes corporate boardrooms in the Midwest and certain white churches.) While it is true that network television stations, the *New York Times*, and the *Washington Post* are no longer the only stars in the media's firmament, they still shine the brightest. Fox News and talk radio do not have the same capacity to set the agenda of a campaign. When Rush Limbaugh speaks, Obama does not have to listen; but if the old Gray Lady raises her quivering voice, the candidates must respond. The mainstream media still have the capacity to turn an event into a potential "crisis" or "scandal." They decide what has to be addressed, and it can go a long way toward determining what can be ignored. They do so simply by ignoring it. When the mainstream press decided to focus on Romney's European trip or his unwillingness to release all the financial records Democrats demanded of him, these things made it into the public consciousness and demanded timely (and repeated) responses. When the mainstream press largely ignored the possibility of something fishy in the Obama administration's response to the Benghazi attacks, this story, for a while at least, never received anything like the attention that some believe it merited.

## STAGE TWO: THE CONVENTION PERIOD, AUGUST 27–SEPTEMBER 6

As the Convention period approached, something happened in the national polls. Stuck a few points behind Obama for most of the summer, Romney in mid-August began to climb and to approach parity. It may have been the bounce from the Ryan nomination, or it may have been that Obama's negative campaign began to produce a reaction. Whatever the reason, the opening of the convention season found the Republicans on the upswing and the Obama forces worried—worried enough to consider giving center stage at their convention to none other than William Jefferson Clinton.

By a kind of tradition now, the out party, meaning the party that does not control the White House, holds its convention first. Because of the television schedule for the Olympic Games, the Republicans set their convention at the end of August (26–30), with the Democrats following the next week. Strangely for this election, two hurricanes bracketed the contest: Hurricane Isaac came ashore as the Republican Convention opened and Hurricane Sandy made landfall in the last week of October.

Neither smiled on the Republicans' fortunes. Although Hurricane Isaac's cancellation of the first day of an excessive four-day convention schedule probably didn't hurt the Republicans that much, Sandy would be another story.

The script for the convention featured three major themes. First, speakers repeatedly highlighted Obama's "You didn't build that" gaffe with the response "We built it." This slogan became a rallying cry of the event, providing Republicans the chance to express a full-throated defense of limited government, free enterprise, and property rights. Knowing that Romney, because of his biography, was not the ideal pitchman for the "democratic" ideal of achievement, the Republican Party brought a platoon of self-made men and women to the stage to make the case for free-market capitalism. Each speaker gave an account of how he or she, or a loved one, had acquired a piece of the American Dream. The message was clear: Obama's economy represented a policy of managed decline, but, with Romney, America can once again be on the ascent.

Second, the convention was intent on trying to show that the Republican Party was open and diverse, not the caricature of the old white men's club that Democrats and much of the media were eager to draw. The roster of speakers included a large number with a Latin flavor, including Manny Pacquiao and rising political stars Susana Martinez, governor of New Mexico, and Marco Rubio, senator from Florida. Also at the podium were Indian Americans Nikki Haley, governor of South Carolina, and California congressional candidate Ricky Gill, along with African American Republicans such as Representative Tim Scott of South Carolina, former secretary of state Condoleezza Rice, and Utah congressional candidate Mia Love. The display of diversity might have hoped to win over some Hispanic voters, but its target was probably just as much white moderate voters seeking assurance that the party was not anti-minority.

Women were also prominently featured. To combat the charge that the GOP was waging a "war on women," the convention showcased the Republican bench of female political leaders, adding Governor Mary Fallin and Senator Kelly Ayotte to the list above. The most notable appeal to women, however, came from Ann Romney herself, who proclaimed, "I love you, women!" during her speech on the second day of the convention.

Lastly, the Romney campaign sought to use the convention to introduce, or, more accurately, to reintroduce, Mitt Romney to the American people. The convention would be his opportunity to show the American people, firsthand, that he was not the person portrayed in Obama's attack ads. After vigorous argument within the Romney camp, and the preparation of two drafts, a decision was made to use Romney's speech to emphasize his personal qualities over the ideological choice. The Democratic attack ads had already succeeded in one of their aims, putting Romney on the defensive and pushing him to use precious convention time to counteract them rather than make the case against Obama or for his own policies. The need to "humanize" Mitt was not in dispute, but the idea of using a speech to do so may have been asking rhetoric to do something it cannot. Trying to convince people you are empathetic by a political address is a little like trying to convince a dinner date you are attractive by sliding a particularly flattering photograph across the table. Did Mitt Romney really close the empathy gap with the American public, particularly with younger voters, by his touching revelation that "every day Dad gave Mom a rose, which he put on her bedside table"? Romney got more help on this point from his surrogates at the convention, above all his wife, than from his own efforts. His speech, though it was praised by many conservative commentators, could be seen as a missed opportunity.

The convention sought to convey an optimistic tone, which was meant to contrast with Obama's negative campaign. Of course some red meat was offered up, but it was lean by the standards of political conventions. Instead of leveling their own personal attacks, the convention focused largely on the possibilities of the next four years. The party continued to walk the tightrope between criticizing Obama the man, who remained well liked, and criticizing his policies. In his speech to the convention, Marco Rubio clarified, "Our problem with President Obama isn't that he's a bad person. . . . Our problem is he's a bad president."

In the days immediately after the convention, Romney had drawn even with Obama, though his "bounce" was relatively small by historical comparison. Now it was the Democrats' chance to respond. Going into their convention, many Democrats had grown uneasy about Obama's prospects. It appeared that the impact of the money they had spent had been erased, and some Democrats expressed fears that the president had too little cash on hand going into the fall. The attacks against Paul Ryan's plan for Medicare and Social Security, which the Obama campaign vowed to make a central focus of the campaign, had also failed to whip retirees into the hoped-for panic. While the timing of the Democratic convention gave the party a clear opportunity to stop Romney's perceived momentum, they had to make the most of it.

Yet it was unclear what new tactics were available to Obama. He did not have a strong record on the key issue of the campaign: the economy. Nor could he hope to run again as an outsider and an agent of change as he did in 2008. The only option was to stick with the strategy in place. Thus, the Democrats' convention was largely a continuation of the party's efforts throughout the summer. Romney, not Obama, seemed to be the focus as speaker after speaker made dire prophesies of what Romney's America would hold for the party's core constituencies. Romney was not only poised to wage war on women, but was also intent on assaulting minorities, teachers, the middle class, autoworkers, and grandma and grandpa.

Gender and class divisions received special attention. Lilly Ledbetter, the noted advocate of equal pay for equal work, and Sandra Fluke, the champion of the contraception mandate in Obamacare, both addressed the cheering audience. Twelve congresswomen also took the stage to warn of the Republican Party's war on women. Headline speakers Elizabeth Warren and Cory Booker, mayor of Newark, stressed the theme of class divisions, the widening gap between rich and poor, the shrinking middle class, and the unwillingness of "millionaires and billionaires" to pay their fair share of the nation's overwhelming financial burden. These speeches shed light on a major underpinning of the Obama campaign: that Obama was still just beginning and not responsible for many of the nation's woes. The problems facing the American economy, especially the problem of class difference, were not the result of any failure of Obama. These problems resulted from the old system, the system that Obama had been fighting to transform, and Mitt Romney would only take us back to those dark days. Democrats also pushed a new idiom in the lexicon of class warfare that joined together two sometimes antagonistic themes of the left: equality and nationalism. The slogan was "economic patriotism," which President Obama had been testing in campaign stops. Cory Booker asserted that after two expensive wars abroad and a debt crisis at home, "being asked to pay your fair share isn't class warfare, its patriotism."

Democrats realized, however, that their most dangerous opponent in November was not Romney or wealthy tax dodgers, but reality itself. It would not be enough to simply disqualify the Republican nominee; the Democrats also had to portray the last four years as promising success. Joe Biden pithily enumerated the two core elements of this effort when he reminded his audience that "Bin Laden is dead and GM is still alive." Getting Bin Laden was an unambiguous success of Obama's foreign policy, which shielded him from any serious foreign policy criticism. The survival of General Motors was proof that, even if Obama's economic policies had not yet created a broad-based recovery, Obama had provided relief where he could. He had defended the middle class. But to make the full argument that the past four years of slow economic growth were not a failure, but a step toward a real revival, Obama would have to turn to his great rival, Bill Clinton.

Not in modern times has there been a more intriguing pair of dueling partners than Clinton and Obama. During the 2008 primaries, when Hillary competed with Obama for the chance to be Bill's successor as Democratic president, the former president broke decorum several times, revealing his contempt for Obama. The Illinois senator returned the favor, indirectly demeaning Clinton's vaunted achievements. During Obama's first term, Clinton let it be known at several moments that he had not warmed very much to the new hero of the Democratic Party. Even in mid-2012, when the Obama campaign's attack on Romney's business record was reaching fever pitch, Clinton declared his judgment that the former Massachusetts governor had enjoyed a "sterling business career." And yet, when Obama was cornered, he often swallowed pride and turned to Clinton for an assist. This was true when Obama at a joint press conference in December 2010 ceded the floor to the former president, who carried on for the remainder as Obama slipped away. Now, again, Obama would enlist Clinton's help. Bill Clinton turned in the best performance of the Democratic convention—indeed, by common acknowledgement the best performance of either convention. Like Romney, whose wife's speech humanized him more than his own, Clinton's address was a stronger defense of Obama's first term than Obama could provide himself. Obama's speech was serviceable, but hardly memorable. Clinton, by contrast, stepped up to the plate and hit a home run. In making the case for Obama, Clinton argued that, though the economy was still in need of serious improvement, Obama's progress had to be judged in light of the conditions he faced as he took office. In a moment of feigned humility, which was simultaneously a reminder of his own success, Clinton noted "no president, not me, not any of my predecessors, no one could have fully repaired all the damage that he found in just four years."

The Republican bounce from its convention, if there was one, was immediately cancelled out by the Democratic convention, which received a larger bounce. Republicans were dismayed at the result and hoped that after the effects of Clinton's magic wore off, the "official" campaign could finally get under away. It was time, Republicans decided, to get back on message and return to the ground on which the campaign was supposed to be fought: Obama's economic failure. Events immediately foiled this hope.

## STAGE 3: BETWEEN THE CONVENTION AND THE DEBATES, SEPTEMBER 6–OCTOBER 2

Less than a week after the Democratic convention, riots broke out in Egypt—purportedly in reaction to a YouTube video, produced in California, that demeaned Mohammed. The American embassy in Cairo came under siege and was breached. Next door in Libya, on the night of September 11, the American consulate and the safe houses in Benghazi were attacked by a heavily armed group of assailants. Four were killed, including Ambassador Christopher Stevens, and ten more were injured. The day after the attack, President Obama held a Rose Garden press conference on the incident. What was most notable about the president's address is what he did not say. While condemning the incident as an "outrageous attack," he never clearly categorized it as a terrorist incident, portraying it instead as the fallout of a spontaneous riot spurred on by the inflammatory YouTube video. The next day, Secretary Hillary Clinton apologized to the Muslim world for the video, calling it "disgusting and reprehensible." And that weekend, U.S. ambassador to the United Nations, Susan Rice, made the rounds of the morning news shows repeating the claim that Benghazi had been about the video.

The night of the attack, Romney released a statement questioning the response of the American embassy in Cairo, which had blamed the video: "I think it's a terrible course for America to stand in apology for our values . . . the first response of the United States must be outrage at the breach of the sovereignty of our nation." The next day, as the Benghazi incident topped the news, Romney came under intense fire for intruding himself into a foreign-policy crisis at a sensitive moment and trying to exploit it for political gain. Romney was accused of breaking protocol and endangering national security. In the flood of news stories on September 12 and 13, coverage focused as much on Romney's comments; his putative and his alleged incompetence in foreign affairs, as on the riots in Egypt, the killings in Benghazi; and the accuracy of the administration's account of what had happened. A foreign-policy crisis was transformed into a domestic political story, all at the expense of Mitt Romney.

As time passed, however, details of the Benghazi attack sprinkled into the news cycle. The embassy's security cameras revealed that there had been no riot prior to the attack. Communiqués revealed that Ambassador Christopher Stevens pleaded for additional security. Within two weeks, the administration admitted that the original assessment, that the attack was a spontaneous response to a YouTube video, was incorrect. It had, in fact, been a terrorist act, carried out by an al-Qaeda affiliate. Though the president was never pressed on this issue by the mainstream media, and while an official investigation of what had happened and why was conveniently pushed off until after the election, one effect of these accounts was to dampen the Obama campaign's enthusiasm to speak as much about foreign affairs. Democrats continued to proclaim that they had saved GM, but they were more reluctant to boast that they had gotten bin Laden, for fear of bringing a slew of questions about terrorism and the Middle East to the forefront.[20]

Nevertheless, Benghazi's cost to Obama may still not have been as great as its cost to Romney. The event temporarily changed the focus of the campaign from the economy, which Romney would have preferred, to foreign policy. Even if Obama's strength on foreign policy was softening, Romney was not well positioned to capitalize on it. The events in Benghazi never achieved the status within the public's consciousness of a scandal or crisis for Obama. While Fox News pursued the story with great attentiveness (and forced some disclosures), no similar appetite was displayed in the rest of the mass media. Some Republicans pressed Romney to raise Benghazi as a major campaign issue, though such a step would have shifted attention away from the economy and turned the campaign into a debate on foreign policy.

Overall, the affair shows the difficulty that a partisan leader has, acting on his own, in lifting an event like this to the status of a general matter of inquiry. Any questions he raises can be dismissed as mere politics. Here one sees the remaining power of the mainstream media. Though its impartiality is doubted, the media, and the media alone, still tenuously holds the status of umpire, able to bring an issue into public focus and force discussion of it. Once the media has decided, so to speak, to take a play upstairs to the booth for review, a candidate can legitimately begin to raise questions, press for explanations, and offer criticisms. Absent this cover, an overtly political figure like a presidential candidate will struggle, and any expectations that Romney could turn Benghazi into the early October surprise were almost certain to be disappointed.

The real surprise arrived, nicely packaged, on September 17, when *Mother Jones* released a video of Romney speaking at a private dinner for donors four months earlier. The dinner had been held in Boca Raton, Florida, not exactly the Bronx, at the home of a private equity manager. The price of entry was evidently $50,000, putting the scene squarely in 1-percent land. In the video Romney stated, "There are 47 percent of the people who will vote for the president no matter what. All right, there are 47 percent who are with him, who are dependent upon government, who believe that they are victims." There was an uncanny resemblance between this statement and one that Barack Obama made four years earlier, at a private fund-raiser in San Francisco, when he referred to working-class voters in the Midwest: "They get bitter, they cling to guns or religion or antipathy to people who aren't like them or anti-immigrant sentiment. . . ." Both statements, delivered before a friendly audience (with the exception of the individuals who recorded and released the tapes), dripped of elitist disdain. Obama's comment very nearly cost him the nomination; Romney's may well have cost him the election.

The story of this video went viral. In the seventy-two hours following the leak of the Romney speech to donors, broadcast network morning and evening shows ran forty-two stories on the subject. The scientific study of gaffes, otherwise known as gaffeology, has shown that the most damaging of the breed are not the one-off remarks, however stupid, poorly timed, or insensitive, but those that have been "primed," that is, that reinforce and confirm an image or attitude that has already been brought to the public's attention. "All gaffes are not created equal," CNN's John Berman said on *Starting Point*. "The 47 percent, for his [Romney's] critics, speaks to what [voters] feel may be his inner beliefs, the character of Mitt Romney."[21] The Obama campaign had spent millions and millions of dollars trying to promote the picture of Romney the uncaring vulture capitalist who, if elected, would govern on behalf of the wealthy and the wealthy alone. This gaffe was priceless. The Obama campaign capitalized on its investment by an attack ad utilizing the clip that juxtaposed Romney's voice with a haunting score and images of a single mother, two woman factory workers, elderly VFW members in uniform, and a Latino for good measure.

The period between the conventions and the first debate had turned into a disaster for Romney. He had not really gained anything from the tragedy of Benghazi, and the 47 percent comment shifted the focus to exactly what the Obama campaign had wanted. Many in the media, conservatives as well as Democrats, were not shy to point out the dire straits of Romney's presidential bid. Peggy Noonan called the Romney campaign a "rolling calamity," while *Weekly Standard* editor William Kristol, no shrinking violet, publicly wondered if Romney should not step down and allow someone else to take over the lead bill on the Republican ticket. Polls showed the race to be slipping away, falling outside of the margin of error that provided small comfort to those in the embattled Romney's camp. Romney needed the first debate to be the start of a sea change, and they knew it.

## SECTION 4: THE DEBATES, OCTOBER 3–OCTOBER 22

Although there were a few ominous portents—Obama's uneven performances in the 2008 debates and reports that he was "bored" by his debate prep—no one could have predicted the unmitigated disaster that was to come. Much was made in the press of Obama's poor outing in the debate in Denver, and rightfully so. Obama seemed subdued, even sullen. His answers were rambling and tangential. His tone was professorial but, when challenged on details, he seemed to have a tenuous grasp on the facts. Liberal blogger Andrew Sullivan described the president's debate performance as "so execrable, so lazy, so feckless, and so vain it was almost a dare not to vote for him."[22]

As lackluster as Obama appeared, Sullivan's reaction was hyperbolic. Obama looked so outmatched in some measure because of his own uninspired performance, but also because his opponent turned in what was, arguably, the best debate performance in the era of television. Romney commanded the stage and the issues. He stayed on message, distilling and repeating the key elements of his economic agenda. Romney finally had success rebutting Obama's charges against him. He thwarted Obama's attempts to portray his tax plan as a gift for the rich at the expense of the middle class by explaining his pro-growth tax and regulatory policies in a way that wisely positioned the GOP as the party of small business and Main Street, and by attacking Obama on his fiscal profligacy, his "green energy" crony capitalism, and Obamacare. When Obama repeated for the *n*th time his central attack on Romney's tax policy, Romney responded with the best line of the night: "Look, I've got five boys. I'm used to people saying something that's not always true, but just keep on repeating it and ultimately hoping I'll believe it."

Conservatives were satisfied that Romney had finally articulated the essential difference between his vision and Obama's, fulfilling their plea to turn the election into a "choice." Yet the best thing about Romney's debate performance was that his positions did not sacrifice his appeal to moderates—in particular to the now iconic "independent women"—at the expense of the party's base. Just the contrary. One of Romney's most effective responses came on an issue where he was thought to be most vulnerable: Romneycare. When Obama claimed that Romney's bill and his own reform bill were essentially the same, Romney was quick to point out that while Romneycare may have been good state policy, it was not wise federal policy, a distinction he made throughout the primaries. But he then went on to point out that he had managed to get this bill, in a blue state, with support of an overwhelmingly Democratic legislature. In the midst of a divisive campaign, Romney here claimed the mantle of the postpartisan, one willing and able to reach across the aisle and work with the opposition. Some of Romney's most popular lines with independents, according to Frank Luntz's instant response panel of undecided voters, were those that emphasized his record of bipartisanship.

After the debate, the polls started moving in Romney's direction. Romney went from a consistent three- to four-point underdog, to leading every major national poll three days later. Concerned Democrats pinned their hopes on the next two debates.

There were a full thirteen days between the first and second debate of the 2012 race, which was the longest gap between the first two debates since 1988. Pundits, voters, and candidates had a long time to think about and discuss what had just happened. Obama's attempts to save face and recover ground during this period did little to help. Attack ads featuring Big Bird—a reminder of Romney's pledge to cut funding to PBS—were even too snarky for newscaster Jon Stewart, who claimed the most damning line in the ad was "I'm Barack Obama, and I approved this message." Then, at a Virginia campaign stop, Obama blamed his current difficulty in the campaign on his inability to recalibrate when Romney started "forgetting what his positions [were]," a condition he dubbed "Romnesia." Shifting the line of attack to Romney the flip-flopper from Romney the plutocrat, the Obama campaign began to look desperate. The Romney campaign pounced on the opportunity these weak attacks handed them: "They've been reduced to petty attacks and silly word games. Just watch it. The Obama campaign has become the incredible shrinking campaign."

The later debates were far more evenly matched, with a consensus that the president may have won on points. Still, they did not provide the Democratic ticket any clear victories, nor did they move the polls by much. One event between the first and second debates did help to stop the bleeding for President Obama: the jobs report on October 5. For the first time in forty-three months, the unemployment rate dropped below 8 percent. When Obama first took office in January 2009, unemployment was at 7.8 percent—the highest it had been in twenty-five years. At that time, while Obama's team was passing the 2009 stimulus package, his Council of Economic Advisers released a report explaining the administration's projections for the economy with and without the president's proposed stimulus legislation. Without the government spending, Obama's team argued, unemployment would reach as high as 9 percent in 2010. With Obama's legislation, however, the unemployment rate would stay below 8 percent and return back to 5 percent by the end of the president's first term. In reality, unemployment exceeded 8 percent the very month after the stimulus was passed, and it remained above there for the next three years and nine months.

In an interview on NBC's *Today Show* following the passage of the president's stimulus, Matt Lauer asked Obama how far the recession would have to deepen until he conceded that the government should change course from its stimulus approach to resolving the economic crisis. Obama responded, "If I don't have this done in three years, then there's going to be a one-term proposition." Three years after the passage of the stimulus legislation, in January 2012, the unemployment rate was still higher than he found it; this was a powerful talking point for Romney throughout the 2012 campaign. However, when the Department of Labor released the jobs report in October showing the unemployment rate back under 8 percent for the first time, Obama supporters could claim that the president was turning things around just in time. With the economy finally breaking through the 8 percent floor of unemployment, Obama took this victory into the next debates.

In the second presidential debate, with its town hall format, both candidates were fiercely argumentative, circling each other like boxers. Though Romney stood his ground, Obama benefitted from staying on subject and enumerating key points in a manner similar to Romney during the first debate. This time around, Obama was largely able to stave off Romney's attacks, with one notable assist from moderator Candy Crowley. When Romney asserted that Obama had evaded labeling the Benghazi attack an act of terror until two weeks after the event, Crowley interjected, "He did call it an act of terror," even though Obama had not directly made such an official proclamation. The Benghazi tragedy was reduced to a squabble over semantics. The debate on balance helped Obama. It showed that his first performance was an aberration, stanching Romney's momentum in the polls.

However, Obama was unable to fully capitalize on any of his "victories" in the later debates. Each bore with it problems and possibilities in near equal measure. In the vice presidential debate, for instance, Biden may have had the slight edge on content alone, but his demeanor during the debate was so odd that few scored it a decisive victory. (Indeed, most post-debate snap polls showed Ryan with a small advantage among viewers.[23]) While Biden stayed on the offensive and forced Ryan to equivocate on questions about his budget plan, and what, if anything, he would do differently regarding Syria or Iran, he seemed both flip and mean-spirited. The contrast of young, somber-faced Ryan with the older, riotously cackling Biden was bad optics for the Democratic ticket.

The final debate, which was meant to focus on foreign policy, fell somewhere between the first and second presidential debates. It was not the thunderous Romney victory the first debate was, nor was it the punching-match debate number two had become. Both candidates had their own points well rehearsed and were unsurprised by their opponent's retorts. Romney did not go on the offensive on issues like Benghazi or Iran, as many conservatives had hoped he would. It was a clear calculation that he would have been unable to pin down the president, who was surely ready for these moves. Instead, Romney was content to convey that he was knowledgeable enough regarding foreign affairs to plausibly serve as the commander-in-chief. This limited aim was appropriate given that the election would clearly turn on domestic policy, not foreign policy. Thus, while Romney did not bludgeon Obama with his failures, he did accomplish what he needed to while avoiding handing Obama an opportunity to achieve the full gravitas of the office.

The advantage Romney had won in the first debate was not repeated—it was unrepeatable. The later debates, it could be argued, had not stemmed the slow movement to Romney. In most snap polls, viewers said they thought Obama had "won" the last two debates; at the same time, most gave Romney the advantage on economic policy and previously undecided voters said they had edged closer to the challenger. Stung by criticism that his campaign had offered no agenda for a second term, Obama issued a hastily drawn document that was promptly panned by CNN reporter Jessica Tellin, who complained that "there's not anything significantly new in here."[24] At the same time, media questions about Benghazi began to bite, six weeks after the event. Above all was the issue of presidentialism. Obama's demeanor onstage and off only elevated his challenger. Following the model established after the first debate, Obama's campaign accused Romney of lying during the debates and disguising his true identity as a radical Tea Party–style conservative. In an interview with Douglas Brinkley for *Rolling Stone*, Obama said, "You know, kids have good instincts. They look at the other guy [a reference to Romney] and say, 'Well, that's a bullshitter, I can tell.'" The campaign's advertising drew scorn, as well, when actress Lena Dunham recorded an ad aimed at "first time" voters that likened voting to losing her virginity.

## STAGE FIVE: SANDY, OCTOBER 29–NOVEMBER 6

What neither the debates nor the rest of the campaign could do to make Barack Obama look presidential, Mother Nature would. The opportunity came in the form of Hurricane Sandy, which was a tragedy to many but a boon to President Obama. Sandy made landfall in the Northeast on October 29, destroying large swaths of the New Jersey shore, flooding portions of Connecticut and New York, and leaving many in the New York City area without power for over two weeks.[25] Staten Island was devastated. Many lives were lost, and billions of dollars in property were destroyed. For Governor Cuomo and Mayor Bloomberg, the storm was a sure sign of climate change, which was an indirect way of commending Barack Obama for his farsighted investments in wind and solar power.

The storm helped the president in three ways. First, it stopped the ordinary campaign in its tracks. Whatever movement or dynamic was at work inside the electorate ceased, as all attention turned to the natural disaster. The candidates had to essentially end regular campaigning. If one assumes—no one will ever know for sure—that there was either a glacial movement toward Romney, or that a final week of campaigning would have left the candidates where they were on October 28, then the election could have turned out differently.

Second, the sort of small-government arguments Romney had built his campaign on do not resonate nearly as well when you need government. When firefighters are saving city blocks, Coast Guard helicopters are pulling people from the roiling sea, and Republican governors are requesting FEMA aid, it is easy for Americans to see their taxpayer dollars at work. A natural disaster can aid "the party of government" over the "party of private action," providing that it handles the situation adequately.

Third, and more importantly, the storm gave Obama a chance to look presidential. Only the president can act, and the event placed him center stage on the airwaves, removing candidate Romney to the sidelines. Obama cut short a campaign visit to Florida and headed to Ground Zero of the storm in New Jersey, arriving on Halloween. Landing in Air Force One, with all its majesty, he was greeted by Governor Christie with an enthusiasm that went well beyond the requirements of a decent and modest reception. The mantle of bipartisanship, which for months the president had squandered, he now reclaimed. The press made much of the president's leadership in Sandy's aftermath, as network television and cable news were flooded with images of the president in motion. Christie's outsized praise for the president's actions was widely circulated and oft repeated, as were tales of Obama's skillful preparation and response to the hurricane. Seldom seen, at least until after the election, were scenes of the suffering thousands that might have been attributed to a slow delivery of federal relief efforts. The attention of the national media was, unsurprisingly, far kinder to President Obama than it had been to President Bush following Katrina, despite growing signs that the federal response was not much more effective. By the time President Obama left the epicenter of the disaster, he was a new man with a restored image.

Regular campaigning resumed the last weekend. Still, the spell had been broken nationwide, like the feeling in a stadium when a game is restarted following a rain delay. The lack of attention fell at the wrong moment for Mitt Romney. For the first time in his political campaign, Romney was connecting with his audience. In the final weekend, huge throngs clogged backroads in Virginia, Wisconsin, Pennsylvania, Colorado, and Ohio as people flocked to see the Republican nominee. His audiences were electrified; some Romney fans on Twitter even dubbed one such event "Mittstock." And, yet, the predominant story remained Sandy and Obama. By the time Romney had found his voice, the sound and fury of the hurricane drowned it out.

That said, it is difficult to gauge Sandy's effect with much accuracy. A Gallup poll of likely voters ending on eve of the storm gave Romney a substantial 51 to 46 percent lead; the same poll conducted immediately after the storm had Romney's lead fall to 49 to 48 percent. The October 26–28 Gallup measurement of presidential approval showed Obama at 48 percent approval, 48 percent disapproval; by the November 3–5 survey, his presidency was viewed favorably by a 52–44 percent margin. Though many things could have driven this shift—another jobs report, though mixed, contained enough good news to be helpful to the president—exit polls give another indication of the impact of Sandy on the electoral results. Forty one percent of voters reported that President Obama's handling of Hurricane Sandy was an "important" factor in their vote choice, with 15 percent of these saying it was "the most important" factor. It is likely that these are exaggerations, as people may recall more readily what is latest. However, there is yet another statistical anomaly that begs a consideration of Sandy's effect. Of those who made up their mind in the last three days, President Obama won by six points, fifty to forty-four. A debatable rule of thumb, shown to be wrong in this instance, holds that it is the challenger who typically wins among late deciders.[26]

## EXPLAINING THE RESULT

The narrative account of the 2012 campaign suggests that the election could have turned out differently than it did, even up to the final week. But all speculation about "could have beens" is just that: speculation. Turning to facts, what we do know is that Barack Obama was elected with some 3.5 million fewer votes than he received in 2008, but with a solid margin of 3.85 percent over his opponent Mitt Romney in the popular vote and a large victory in the Electoral College (332 to 206). What were some of the main reasons that account for Obama's victory?

## TURNOUT

One unexpected result of the 2012 election was the decline in voter turnout from 2008. The number of voters casting ballots *decreased* by over 2 million persons, despite an estimated increase of 8 million citizens in the voting-age population. Turnout among the voting age population fell over three points from 56.9 percent in 2008 to 53.6 percent in 2012.[27] This decline ended a trend in increasing voter turnout that began between 1996 and 2000.

Turnout has always been considered important in its own right, as a general measure of the health or well-being of democracy and an indicator of people's satisfaction with the current political class and the choice that is offered. The decline in 2012, despite the momentous choice at stake, suggests there were reservations among large parts of the public toward both candidates. For whatever reason, the campaign ended by pushing voters away in droves. Jay Cost offered a particularly gloomy assessment of what this means: "The United States of America in 2012 is a dyspeptic and disappointed nation, deeply frustrated and lacking confidence in either political coalition. As a consequence, we saw stark declines—in participation, in confidence, and in the vote."[28]

Yet the real importance of the turnout rate in 2012 has less to do with these general concerns than with the clues it provides about the outcome of the election. Investigating these clues supplies insights into some of the reasons why Barack Obama defeated Mitt Romney. One possible hypothesis is that the decline in turnout is explained in large part by less participation among minorities and young voters. The reasoning for this position would be as follows: Barack Obama generated an extraordinary amount of excitement and enthusiasm from these groups in 2008, resulting in a surge in turnout; in 2012, the process was reversed.

A nice hypothesis, only this is *not* what happened. According to exit polls, turnout among African Americans remained the same, while turnout among Hispanics and young voters actually went up from 2008. Each of these groups increased its turnout roughly in proportion with its increased share of the overall population.[29] In addition, these groups remained strongly for Obama in both elections: slightly more so in the case of Hispanics, near the same for African Americans, and dropping a bit for young voters.[30]

The fact that these strongly pro-Obama groups maintained their turnout rates, while other groups declined, was a critical factor in Obama's victory. Why they did so is another part of the story. Was it because they retained their enthusiasm relative to other groups, or for some other reason? Surveys before the election sought to measure the level of enthusiasm about the election among various groups, on the theory that it would serve as an indicator of the rate at which people would actually turn out to vote. Some of these surveys discovered that enthusiasm was low among Hispanics and especially among young voters, though not African Americans. Many concluded—in particular, many prominent Republican analysts—that turnout among pro-Obama groups would decline overall. They were wrong.

Here is where Obama's campaign organization proved to be so important. It targeted these groups for its turnout effort on the idea that it doesn't matter if a voter is enthusiastic or not, as long as he or she votes. Get people to the polls, and, enthusiastic or not, their votes all count the same. For example, although young voters were by far the least enthusiastic demographic group surveyed, they somehow increased their turnout by 6 percent, which showed that the enthusiasm indicator for voting was overcome in many of the Democratic voting blocs. By contrast, the higher enthusiasm found among Republican-leaning groups did not result in higher turnout rates. This pattern showed itself time and time again.[31] As GOP vice presidential candidate Paul Ryan commented after the election: "The surprise was some of the turnout, some of the turnout especially in urban areas, which gave President Obama the big margin to win this race."[32] Ryan was certainly not alone in misjudging the threshold level at which people would vote. The same reasoning, though not pushed to the same lengths, might help account for why the major polls systematically underestimated Obama's margin of victory.

It is a common error of political analysis to claim that the losing campaign is poorly run and the winning campaign does everything right. On the questions of campaign strategy in 2012, the judgment is still out as to which of the campaigns performed better. But when it comes to the quality of their "ground game" of getting out the vote, all admit—including those in the Romney campaign—that the Obama organization held a distinct advantage. The attention focused on building an effective machine began practically the day after the victory of 2008, when the highly touted Obama For America, which orchestrated Obama's fundraising and volunteer efforts in 2008, was rebranded as Organizing for America. It got immediately to work building professional systems of voter contact and turnout, especially in the battleground states. The Republican ground game for 2012 was playing catch-up all along, with some of its deficiencies dating back to management and financial problems at the Republican National Committee under the chairmanship of Michael Steele from 2008 to 2010. The Republican effort in 2012 may have been better than it was in 2008, but it was no match for the Obama organization. One telling example of the Republicans' lack of sound preparation was the failure of an expensive election-day software program that the Romney campaign developed to help monitor and get out the vote.

Named ORCA, after the whale, it was to be accessed by an app, which many in the field did not know how to operate; and at some point on Election Day, the whole system crashed, beaching ORCA and costing Romney many votes. The Obama campaign had Narwhal, a data platform that unified what it knew about voters, canvassers, event-goers, and phone-bankers.[33] It thus had a far greater ability to gather, analyze, and use information than the Romney campaign. The Obama campaign's technical superiority was especially helpful with those who cast their ballots by mail or at early voting centers. By "banking" millions of votes ahead of time, it insulated itself against any late-breaking adverse events or attack ads.

In part, this advantage reflected a cultural difference between the two camps. The Romney campaign focused on mass-market television advertising—rather like *Mad Men*, only without all the alcohol and sex. Recruiting from Silicon Valley instead of Madison Avenue, the Obama campaign focused on technology, analytics, and direct voter contact. But the Obama campaign's edge also had a more prosaic basis: it simply had much more time to prepare. In one form or another, it had been in operation for several years. Since the president had no opponent in the primaries, his campaign had the luxury of focusing on the general election even as Mitt Romney was still contending with the likes of Rick Perry and Herman Cain.

Since the decline in turnout in 2012 cannot be attributed to minority groups and the young, it took place among the rest of the electorate, which is to say nonminority citizens over the age of thirty. While the size of this category shrunk slightly as a proportion of the eligible electorate, the drop in turnout exceeded what the demographic shift alone would indicate. Nonminority voters as a whole (including young voters) decreased their share of the electorate from 74 percent in 2008 to 72 percent in 2012. Since nonminority voters in no sense constitute a group with any kind of identity or interest, it only makes sense to speak of some of the parts. Which groups from within this great mass of the electorate tended to go "missing" on Election Day?

Let us again consider some of the possible answers. One hypothesis is that the high levels of white evangelical support for Bush and McCain disappeared when the Republican Party nominated a moderate Mormon from Massachusetts, who had only recently aligned his political positions with social conservatives. This explanation does not seem to hold up: white evangelicals constituted 23 percent all voters in 2012, the same as in 2008. There is no evidence that disappointment in candidate Romney suppressed voter turnout among evangelicals. But a hoped-for surge in turnout, encouraged again by reported high levels of enthusiasm, did not occur either. As for the evangelicals who turned out, they supported Romney strongly, much more than they did John McCain in 2008 and on par with President Bush's evangelical vote share in 2004

Another hypothesis is that high levels of the white, working-class—including here many who had lost jobs or were underemployed—disappeared from the electorate in 2012. The argument here is that they exited from voting when the Republican Party nominated a wealthy businessman, who grew up as the son of a successful auto executive and governor of Michigan, and who the Obama campaign characterized as responsible for the loss of many jobs. Romney of course made a pitch to win over these voters, speaking continually throughout the campaign of the importance of creating new jobs and better jobs. But, the argument runs, his manner and his distance, added to some of his telling gaffes, made it difficult for him to "connect" with this stratum of voters. Voters who turned out for Bush and McCain did not turn out for Mitt Romney.

Although middle-class Americans making between $50,000 and $100,000 per year favored the Republican Party when they turned out to vote, many fewer actually did vote: 15 percent fewer in 2012. Part of this decline is probably due to the smaller relative size of this group as a portion of the total population, but a decline of this magnitude almost surely indicates a decline in turnout levels. In case after case, pro-Democratic demographic groups showed increases in turnout, while pro-Republican demographic groups, with the exception of Americans earning over $100,000 per year, registered decreases. The evidence is imperfect, and the measurements—exit polls—are less than precise. Still, what information exists lends a good deal of support to the interpretation that working-class white voters, a group that has been more favorable to Republicans in recent years, were, by comparison with previous Republican candidates, turned off by Romney and stayed home more often, especially in some of the Midwestern states. Turnout decreased by 5.4 percent in Michigan, by 2.2 percent in Ohio, and by 4.3 percent in Pennsylvania—the decreased turnout in each state was more severe than in the nation overall despite the fact that each was a swing state with greater mobilization efforts by the candidates. President Obama may not have won among white, working-class voters in these states, but many decided they would not vote for Romney either, and in so doing Obama was able to comfortably win these critical Midwestern swing states. Here, Obama's negative campaign may have worked particularly well. He did not have to persuade these voters in order to prevail; he only had to discourage them.

Mitt Romney by this account left a large number of possible votes on the table in 2012. There remains the great question of which party, if either of them, will be able to reactivate these voters in 2016. The most important lessons of the 2012 election may be discovered less in analyzing how those who did vote decided than in studying why some decided not to vote at all.

## VOTING BEHAVIOR AND THE OBAMA COALITION

Turning to an analysis of those who *did* vote, the exit-poll findings show that Obama's basic strategic objective for the campaign worked. The core of that strategy came into focus when Democrats realized that unfavorable economic conditions would not allow Obama to win the 2012 contest in a blaze of glory, improving on what he had accomplished in 2008. The plan was instead for an orderly retreat, holding on to all the key assets, and falling back to defensible positions. With a victory of 53 percent of the vote in 2008, Obama could give up a couple points and still comfortably win the election, which is exactly what he did.

A look at the breakdown of the various demographic groups shows that Obama's strategic retreat was generally followed across the board (see table 4.1). Obama lost vote share among almost every demographic group, dropping, for example, four points among men, one point among women, seven points among independents, three points among liberals, two points among African Americans, four points among whites, one point among high school graduates, three points among college graduates, three points among those with incomes between $50,000 and $100,000, five points among those with incomes over $100,000, four points among Catholics, nine points among Jews, and three points among Protestants. If the length of this list and the numbers make it appear that Obama must have lost more than two percent overall, the mirage is partly explained by the aforementioned growth in the relative size of some of the groups that gave him strong support.

There were a few exceptions to Obama's across-the-board retreat. Notable among the groups where Obama gained vote share were Hispanics (a net gain of 4 percent), Asian Americans (plus 9 percent), and those without a high school diploma (plus 3 percent). These cases shed light on two features of the 2012 election. One is the strong support of Democrats among minorities, larger even than in the past. Obama lost by twenty points among nonminority voters (who made up 72 percent of the vote), but he was able to overcome this deficit by piling up huge victory margins among minorities: he won by eighty-seven points among African Americans, forty-seven points among Asian Americans, and forty-four points among Hispanics. The other feature is the class appeal. Along with his gain of vote share among those without a high school diploma, Obama managed to hold constant his large share (60 percent) of voters whose income was under $50,000. The class divisions in voting behavior were accentuated in comparison to 2008, a consequence of the president's rhetorical appeals during the campaign and the status of the Republican candidate. In 2008, a less class-driven campaign allowed Obama to win voters making over $200,000 a year by six points. This advantage disappeared in 2012, but, fortunately for Obama, that group makes up only about 6 percent of voters. Much more important for Obama was

**Table 4.1. Demographic Groups' Vote Share, Electorate Share Changes (in percent)**

| *Demographic Group* | *Romney Vote Share* | *Obama Vote Share* | *Obama's Change from '08* | *Portion of Electorate 2012* | *Change Electorate* |
|---|---|---|---|---|---|
| Men | 52 | 45 | -4 | 47 | 0 |
| Women | 44 | 55 | -1 | 53 | 0 |
| Married Men | 60 | 38 | -8 | 29 | -4 |
| Married Women | 53 | 46 | -1 | 31 | -2 |
| Unmarried Men | 40 | 56 | -2 | 18 | 4 |
| Unmarried Women | 31 | 67 | -3 | 23 | 3 |
| Youth (18–29) | 37 | 60 | -6 | 19 | 1 |
| 30–44 Years Old | 45 | 52 | 0 | 27 | -2 |
| 45–64 Years Old | 51 | 47 | -3 | 38 | 1 |
| 65+ Years Old | 56 | 44 | -1 | 16 | 0 |
| Democrat | 7 | 92 | 3 | 38 | -1 |
| Independents, Other | 50 | 45 | -7 | 29 | 0 |
| Republican | 93 | 6 | -3 | 32 | 0 |
| Conservative | 82 | 17 | -3 | 35 | 1 |
| Moderate | 41 | 56 | -4 | 41 | -3 |
| Liberal | 11 | 86 | -3 | 25 | 3 |
| African Americans | 6 | 93 | -2 | 13 | 0 |
| Asian Americans | 26 | 73 | 9 | 3 | 1 |
| Hispanics | 27 | 71 | 4 | 10 | 1 |
| Non-Hispanic Whites | 59 | 39 | -4 | 72 | -2 |

| | | | | | |
|---|---|---|---|---|---|
| No High School Diploma | 35 | 64 | 1 | 3 | -1 |
| High School Graduate | 48 | 51 | -1 | 21 | 1 |
| Some College/ Assoc. Degree | 48 | 49 | -2 | 29 | -2 |
| College Graduate | 51 | 47 | -3 | 29 | 1 |
| Postgraduate Degree | 42 | 55 | -3 | 18 | 1 |
| Income < $50,000 | 38 | 60 | 0 | 41 | 3 |
| Income $50,000–$99,999 | 52 | 46 | -3 | 31 | -5 |
| Income > $100,000 | 54 | 44 | -5 | 28 | 2 |
| Catholic | 48 | 50 | -4 | 25 | -2 |
| Jewish | 30 | 69 | -9 | 2 | 0 |
| None | 26 | 70 | -5 | 12 | 0 |
| Protestant or Other Christian | 57 | 42 | -3 | 53 | -1 |
| Something Else | 23 | 74 | 1 | 7 | 1 |
| White Evangelical | 78 | 21 | -3 | 26 | 0 |

to keep voters making less than $50,000 because they made up 41 percent of the electorate in 2012.

There were exceptions on the other end as well, where Obama's retreat went well beyond the average range of 1 to 4 percent. Groups where Obama lost an inordinately large share of the vote from last time, and hence where Romney gained, included: Jews (minus nine points), young voters (minus six points), married men (minus eight points), and those earning incomes over $100,000 (minus five points). In the first two cases, Jews and young voters, these groups were strongly pro-Obama in 2008, and, even after the dropoff, remained strongly pro-Obama this time. Still, the signs of movement in 2012, in particular with many Jewish voters dissatisfied with aspects of Obama's Middle East policies, could portend a long-term change. For married men (and married voters overall), Republicans already had the advantage, and yet still gained by a considerable degree.

Finally, there was the movement among the different categories of partisans: Democrats, Republicans, and independents. Trying to measure partisanship in an exit poll is generally agreed to be one of the worst of times, since people tend more than usual to bring their partisanship in line with the vote they just cast. Still, the figures are instructive. They confirm, if any confirmation is needed, the intensifying polarization of American parties, as well, perhaps, as the polarizing effect of the figure of Barack Obama. Countering the general loss of vote share to the Republicans in 2012, Obama gained strength among Democrats. Republicans, who had four years to observe President Obama, voted for him by less than last time. More than nine of ten voters from each partisan group voted for its nominee, which is extremely high. Romney won the coveted vote of independents, improving substantially over McCain's showing in 2008. One of Romney's achievements as a candidate was to have kept social conservative voters while still increasing his support among independents.[34] Still, if the advantage of Democrats as reflected in this poll continues, Republicans will have to win independents by a larger margin in the future to capture the presidency.

## THE COALITIONS

More important for the future than changing margins in the demographic groups from 2008 to 2012 is the absolute level of support they gave to the Democratic and Republican candidates. Margins of victory can be reduced until kingdom come, but if a candidate still wins majorities in enough of them, as Obama did, he will win the election. It is important therefore to note a few elements of the coalitional support of each party and of where changes might take place.

The core of the winning Democratic coalition in 2012 comprised two overlapping groups: minority ethnic groups and lower-income voters. Minorities made up 28 percent of the electorate and Obama captured 76 percent of this vote (accounting for 21 percent of all voters). Voters with incomes less than $50,000 made up 41 percent of the electorate, and Obama won 60 percent of this group (25 percent of all voters). For large numbers of these voters, group and class appeals reinforced each other.

In addition to this base of support, Obama added certain key pieces from the rest of the population. These pieces in some cases relied on "cultural appeals" and other sets of interests. One notable group supporting Obama was unmarried women. While married women supported Romney by a margin of seven points, unmarried women supported Obama by thirty-six points, reinforcing the observation that there is not a "gender gap" so much as a "marriage gap." Younger voters continued to support Obama, in part because of his values appeals and hipper image. Religious "nones," those who are not affiliated with any organized religion, favored Obama by forty-four points. Finally, highly educated elites with postgraduate degrees favored Obama by thirteen points. Philosophical liberalism has a bastion in universities, particularly the universities that offer advanced degrees. As political scientists pointed out in the aftermath of the 2008 election, Obama seems to have brought together a "Great Society coalition" of racial minorities, the young, and the highly educated.[35]

Republican support is centered among the category of nonminority voters. Nonminorities made up 72 percent of the electorate and Romney captured 59 percent of this vote (42 percent of all voters). Within this category, white evangelicals made up a quarter of all voters in 2012, and Romney received 78 percent of their votes (18 percent of all voters). Catholics also made up a quarter of all voters in 2012, of which Romney won half, and a larger share if one removes the large portion of Catholics who are Hispanics, where Obama scored so well. As noted, Romney did slightly better than Obama among the relatively higher income voters ($100,000 and more). On some of the cultural issues, groups supporting the Republicans were a mirror image of those favoring Democrats. Republicans have majorities among the married, the more religious, and older voters.

There has been much talk, as there always is within the defeated party, about how Republicans might put together a winning presidential coalition in 2016. One obvious strategy would be to cut into some of the huge leads that Democrats have among minorities. Gains in just one more of the Democratic coalition's strongholds could swing the majority in a closely divided and polarized electorate. This thinking is sensible. Another strategy, not necessarily contradictory, is to increase voter share and turnout among groups already favorable. A surprising number of analysts seem to dismiss this possibility and despair of winning an election by any further appeals to the "white" group. According to a common formulation: "Trying to win a national election by gaining a larger share of a shrinking portion of the electorate is a losing proposition." This portion, which, to repeat, accounts for nearly three quarters of the electorate, is not fixed by any single interest. It is made up of different groups, and there are possibilities for gaining (or losing) significant shares among many of these groups, enough to change the national majority.

## THE REASONS FOR THE VOTE

Other than behavior of Mother Nature 2012, which, like most unmarried women, favored the Democrats, the exit polls provide some insight into *why* people voted as they did. The questions ask directly about issues and concerns that motivated individual voters and about the judgments they made on these issues.

On the top of the list of what people saw as the most important issue in their voting decision, 59 percent of voters listed the economy, dwarfing every other single issue (health care was second at 18 percent and the deficit was third at 15 percent). The salience of the economy fits with the obvious fact that this was a domestic-oriented election, in which foreign affairs and national security were of far less importance (only 5 percent listed foreign policy as their top issue). It can be called the first post-9/11 election. Perhaps 59 percent fell below what Republicans hoped, but the prominence given to the economy generally accords with the Republican model for the election, which was predicated on making it a referendum on the president's economic performance.

Why, then, didn't the Republicans win? Part of the answer is that while a focus on the economy helped Romney, it turned out to be much less of a boon than he expected. Among those who listed the economy as the nation's top issue, Romney bested Obama by four points—but only four points. Judgments of the economy and its prospects were not dismal. While less than a quarter of the population thought the economy was good—that was the bad news for Obama—the good news, or the good-enough news, was that 39 percent thought the economy was on the right track, while another 29 percent said the economy was staying about the same. Only 30 percent believed the economy was worsening. Even better news for Obama was the fact that 53 percent of voters still blamed Bush for the bad economy, while just 38 percent blamed the current occupant of 1600 Pennsylvania Avenue. For many voters, 2012 was an economic referendum—on the previous president. George W. Bush was the gift that kept on giving.

Enough Americans were willing to see Obama's experiment to its conclusion to allow him to hang on. Only four years earlier, the American economy fell into a deep crisis, nicely labeled for the Democrats' purposes as "the Great Recession." The crisis led many to conclude that the growth and apparent prosperity of the previous eight years had been illusory, built upon unregulated Wall Street profiteering and exotic financial products. Obama offered a change from those policies to another approach that, while vaguely specified, was at least different. Four years later, in the context of low growth and uncomfortably high unemployment, Obama was unable to claim that it is Morning in America. But he could attempt to sell the notion that it was 2:00 or 3:00 a.m.—and that with a little more time his policies might begin to produce tangible improvements. There were enough in the electorate who were satisfied by this logic. Thus, Romney's strategy was, at best, incomplete. To be successful, he needed to offer an alternative explanation for the 2008 financial crisis and make a case for why continuing economic troubles should be laid at Obama's feet. It was not enough to point at unemployment figures, which were themselves improving. This adaptation, however, would have forced him further onto the uncomfortable terrain of ideas.

An issue closely related to Obama's economic performance was the debt issue, which was the issue the Tea Party made prominent in 2010. But 2012 was not 2010. Romney got more than twice as many votes than Obama among the smaller group that considered the deficit the leading issue (66 percent to 32 percent). This might be grounds to question Romney's hybrid strategy, which, some have argued, hewed too closely to the referendum model and veered too far from the "big choice" between strictly limited government and a more interventionist state. The difference was of degree. But the reality of the day in 2012 was that the debt crisis had less salience than two years previously, and no leader may have been able to materially change that fact.

The economy was certainly the dominant factor in the 2012 election, but there were many other micro-issues that, combined, played an important role. Social issues like abortion and immigration certainly hurt Romney, as noted, with Hispanics and single women. Romney did not speak to these issues very much during the general election, but Democrats and the media did. Romney was continuously bludgeoned with the anti-immigration stands he took during the primaries in an effort to outflank Rick Perry, and while he deflected questions regarding abortion to the greatest extent possible, Democrats, with a little assistance from certain Republican senatorial candidates, were able to galvanize single women around the issue, though they may have been influenced just as much by considerations of economic security.

Spanning economic and social issues was the question of class division, which was the great new cultural question of 2012. While always a feature of mass politics to some degree, the Democrats' strong class appeal against the top 1 percent and Romney's own wealth made class issues even more salient in 2012. Portraying Romney as an out-of-touch plutocrat was a centerpiece of Obama's reelection strategy. After all, who could trust a corner office type to look out for the little guy? Exit polls suggest that Obama may have had some success; 53 percent of voters believed Romney's policies would "generally favor" the rich, while only 34 percent believed his policies would chiefly benefit the middle class. The Republican response was that by justly rewarding the rich, all would be rewarded. This was a more difficult argument. In the worst of lights for the Republicans, it looked like Obama had ceded 1 percent to the Republicans, while the Republicans had ceded 47 percent to the Democrats.

On foreign affairs, 57 percent of voters said that they would trust Obama to handle an international crisis. Romney fared just slightly worse at 50 percent. The significance of foreign affairs lies more in the realm of the *could have been* than the *was*. By "getting" Osama Bin Laden, Obama created a shield for himself. Recall that before the picture of Obama sitting with his close advisors watching a television monitor in the Situation Room, the defining image of the Obama Doctrine was of him bowing to Saudi King Abdullah at a G-20 meeting to London. Foreign policy and American exceptionalism offered some hope for Republicans. Three years and at least a dozen spikes of the football later, Obama had silenced much of the criticism that he was obsequious, even apologetic, when abroad. Even Benghazi was not enough to erase the memory of the greatest single victory in the war on terror. Americans were weary of these wars and of their expense, and though Obama was a war leader—he had introduced thousands of more troops in what he had once called the "good war" in Afghanistan—he never made much of an effort to mobilize public opinion on behalf of a war strategy. By the time of the election campaign, the president had managed to place himself on the anti-war side of the argument and dared the Republicans to go in the other direction. They would do so only gingerly.

Finally, in Americans' assessment of leadership qualities, Romney, as the challenger, surprisingly appeared more presidential than the president. Here, the quality of the competing campaigns in October undoubtedly played a part. Among voters who said that the top quality they looked for is "a strong leader," Romney beat Obama by twenty-three points; among those who listed "has a vision for the future," Romney won by nine points; and among those who listed "shares my values," Romney won by thirteen points. In the traditional leadership qualities, Romney was the preferred leader. But in a statistic that points to the success of the Obama campaign's portrayal of Romney, among those who listed their top quality as "cares about people like me" (21 percent of voters), Obama out-sympathized Romney by a remarkable sixty-three points. In a country facing economic hardship that was less and less interested in global military involvements, the pivotal subset of voters looking for a president who could "feel their pain" found their man in Barack Obama.

## NOTES

1. Both candidates were rated to have used a high percentage of negative ads, but Obama's percentage was considerably higher and in fact was the highest of all the candidates of the past three campaigns (2004, 2008, and 2012). See Donovan Slack, "RIP Positive Ads in 2012," *Politico*, Nov. 4, 2012, www.politico.com/news/stories/1112/83262.html.

2. Barack Obama, "Remarks by the President on the Economy in Osawatomie, Kansas," Office of the Press Secretary, Dec. 6, 2011, www.whitehouse.gov.

3. George Will, *ABC News Post-Debate Coverage*, ABC, Oct. 16, 2012.

4. In 2000 a number of the statistical models had Al Gore winning beyond the range of the campaign effect. His repeatedly poor or strange performances in the debates went as far as any modern campaign in stretching the campaign effect to its maximum. And of course he did win the popular vote.

5. Thirteen political science models can be seen in *PS* 45, no. 4 (Oct. 2012): 591–674. They are summarized in Larry J. Sabato, "Forecasting the Presidential Election: Other Crystal Balls," Sept. 13, 2012. Economist Ray Fair added his forecast in Marek Ramilo, "Fair Predicts Close Race," *Yale Daily News*, Sept. 25, 2012, accessed Jan. 3, 2013, http://yaledailynews.com.

6. Harry J. Enten, "Why the 2012 Election Is Set to Break All the Rules," *Guardian*, Apr. 18, 2012.

7. Neil Newhouse, *2012 Campaign Decision Makers Conference*, Harvard University Institute of Politics, Nov. 29, 2012.

8. Barack Obama, "Remarks by the President at a Skills for America's Future Manufacturing Event," Office of the Press Secretary, June 8, 2011.

9. Ken Walsh, "Romney Readies a Sprint to the Finish Line," *U.S. News and World Report*, www.usnews.com/news/blogs/Ken-Walshs-Washington.

10. So, while the Romney campaign was outspent nearly two to one throughout the summer, those close to him believed that Obama's early ad blitz would not have a lasting effect on independents. Source: Federal Elections Commission.

11. RealClearPolitics, accessed Jan. 6, 2013, www.realclearpolitics.com/epolls/2012.

12. "May 2012 Candidate Financial Summary," Federal Elections Commission, May 2012, www.fec.gov/finance/disclosure.

13. "August 2012 Candidate Financial Summary," Federal Elections Commission, May 2012, www.fec.gov/finance/disclosure.

14. CNN/ORC poll conducted on Aug. 7–8, 2012, released Aug. 9, 2012.

15. Obama balked before eventually proffering an exemption to the contraception requirement for religious employers. This proved unacceptable to the Catholic Health Administration, which claimed the exemption should be extended not only to religious employers, but also to Catholic hospitals, health care organizations, and other ministries of the church.

16. Beth Myers, *2012 Campaign Decision Makers Conference*, Harvard University Institute of Politics, Nov. 29, 2012.

17. Mitt Romney, "Campaign Speech in Boston Massachusetts," Aug. 16, 2012.

18. Rich Noyes, "Five Ways the Mainstream Media Tipped the Scales in Favor of Obama," Fox News online, Nov. 7, 2012, www.foxnews.com.

19. See Paul Bedard, "Record 19 Reporters, Media Execs Join Team Obama," *Washington Examiner*, Feb. 17, 2012, http://washingtonexaminer.com/record-19-reporters-media-execs-join-team-obama/article/1130971#.UPctqR1juSo and "Agribusiness: Long-Term Contribution Trends," Center for Responsive Politics, www.opensecrets.org/industries/totals.php?cycle=2012&ind=C1100.

20. For the survey data, see "On Eve of Foregin Debate, Growing Pessimism about Arab Spring Aftermath," Pew Research Center for the People & the Press, Oct. 18, 2012, www.people-press.org/2012/10/18/on-eve-of-foreign-debate-growing-pessimism-about-arab-spring-aftermath.

21. John Berman, *Starting Point*, CNN, Sept. 21, 2012.

22. Andrew Sullivan, "How Obama Gave the Campaign Back to Romney," *The Daily Beast*, http://andrewsullivan.thedailybeast.com.

23. "Snap Polls: Ryan 2, Biden 1," *Politico*, Oct. 11, 2012, accessed Jan. 17, 2013, www.politico.com/politico44/2012/10/snap-polls-ryan-biden-138249.html.

24. Noah Rothman, "CNN Reporter on Obama's Second Term Agenda: 'There Is Not Anything Significantly New in Here,'" Mediaite.com, accessed Jan. 17, 2013, www.mediaite.com/tv/cnn-reporter-on-obamas-second-term-agenda-there-is-not-anything-significantly-new-in-here/.

25. Christina Rexrode and Verena Dobnik, "Hurricane Sandy: New Jersey, New York Still Struggle with Power Outages," *Huffington Post*, Nov. 11, 2012, www.huffingtonpost.com.

26. The Election Day polls were based on questionnaires completed by voters as they left voting stations throughout the country on Tuesday, supplemented by telephone interviews with absentee and early voters. The polls were conducted by Edison Research of Somerville, NJ, for the National Election Pool, a consortium of ABC News, Associated Press, CBS News, CNN, Fox News, and NBC News. The national results are based on voters in 350 randomly chosen precincts across the United States, and include absentee voters and early voters interviewed by telephone.

27. There are a number of different ways of calculating turnout, with the major variable being what is used as the denominator. We use here the total voting-age population, while others sometimes use the total voting-eligible population, which subtracts those who are noncitizens, felons who can't vote, and the like. These differences are explained on the invaluable website of the United States Election Project at George Mason University, headed by Professor Michael McDonald (http://elections.gmu.edu/index.html).

28. Jay Cost, "After the Tumult and the Shouting," *The Weekly Standard* 18, no. 12 (Dec. 3, 2012).

29. About 0.3 million more African Americans cast votes in 2012 (making up 13 percent of the electorate in both 2008 and 2012), about 1.6 million more Hispanics cast votes in 2012 (increasing from 9 to 10 percent of the electorate), and young voters (aged eighteen to twenty-nine) similarly increased from 18 to 19 percent of the electorate.

30. According to exit polling, Obama's vote share among Hispanics increased from 67 percent in 2008 to 71 percent in 2012. Among blacks, Obama's unprecedented domination continued with only a very slight diminution; among this group his vote share moved from 96 percent in 2008 to 93 percent in 2012. Obama dropped 6 percent among young voters (between age eighteen and twenty-nine at the time of the election), falling from 66 percent in 2008 to 60 percent in 2012.

31. "Post Election Survey of Hispanic Voters," *Resurgent Republic*, Dec. 12, 2012. Incidentally, on the enthusiasm scores, African Americans, in contrast to young people and Hispanics, remained highly enthusiastic for Obama.

32. Michael D. Shear, "Ryan Surprised by Voters in 'Urban Areas,'" *The Caucus, the Politics and Government* (blog of the *New York Times*), Nov. 13, 2012, http://thecaucus.blogs.nytimes.com.

33. Alexis Madrigal, "When the Nerds Go Marching In," *The Atlantic*, Nov. 16, 2012, www.theatlantic.com/technology/archive/2012/11/when-the-nerds-go-marching-in/265325/.

34. It is true that the total number of voters did decrease in many evangelical-heavy states, but these states also tended to not be competitive: Alabama decreased by 1.21 percent, Arkansas by 1.58 percent, Georgia by 0.62 percent, Kansas by 6.14 percent, Kentucky by 1.61 percent, Mississippi by 0.33 percent, Missouri by 5.74 percent, Oklahoma by 8.74 percent, Tennessee by 5.43 percent, and West Virginia by 6.03 percent. States with heavy evangelical populations that were swing states tended to increase their number of votes: Colorado by 7 percent, Florida by 1 percent, Iowa by 2.93 percent, and North Carolina by 4.51 percent.

35. Phillip A. Klinkner and Thomas Schaller, "LBJ's Revenge: The 2008 Election and the Rise of the Great Society Coalition," *The Forum* 4, no. 6 (2008).

# FIVE

# Congressional and State Elections

While Barack Obama was holding onto the presidency, his party held onto the Senate with a surprising net pickup of two seats. Republicans, meanwhile, held onto their majority in the House. The state elections were something of a wash. Democrats made only modest inroads in the legislatures, and Republicans finished with one more governor than before. To understand these outcomes, we have to look beyond the 2012 presidential race and ponder the three preceding biennial elections.

In 2006, Republicans lost their majorities of both chambers of Congress. In the Senate, there had been a brief period of Democratic control in the early part of the decade. For Republicans in the House, the reversal followed a dozen straight years of dominance, so they felt it more sharply. Some reasons for the defeat were beyond their control, such as President Bush's unpopularity. But as they sifted through the political rubble, many of them concluded that they shared the blame. House Republican whip Kevin McCarthy (R-CA), who first won his seat that year, recalled that voters "were talking about the party's failures—our failures—from high profile ethical lapses to the inability to rein in spending or even slow the growth of government."[1] In various ways, Republicans were determined not to repeat those failures.

On the Senate side, the six-year term meant that the 2006 election would influence the lineup for 2012. Democrats beat GOP incumbents in Missouri, Montana, Ohio, Pennsylvania, Rhode Island, and Virginia. In the 2012 election, there were twenty-three Democratic seats (including those of nominal independents Joe Lieberman of Connecticut and Bernard Sanders of Vermont) and only ten Republican seats. With such lopsided exposure on the Democratic side, Republican prospects seemed robust at the start of the year.

But predicting gains or losses in the Senate can be tricky. When there are only thirty-three or so seats at stake, a handful of bad breaks or weak candidates can transform a party's fortunes. The GOP had an opportunity, but it would also need good luck.

Because the 2008 election brought Barack Obama to the White House, the 2012 congressional and state elections would take place during a presidential reelection contest. Such races tend not to yield big gains for the incumbent party; even the victory of a sitting president usually indicates a "status quo" election. In the last landslide reelection, that of Ronald Reagan in 1984, the Republicans gained a paltry fourteen seats in the House and suffered a slight net loss in the Senate. In 1996, Democrats hoped that Bill Clinton would sweep them back into a majority in the House. They fell short. As we argued in *Losing to Win*, some voters supported Republican congressional candidates to serve as a check on Clinton, who was a heavy favorite for reelection.[2] The 2012 presidential race was far from a landslide and the outcome was in doubt for much of the campaign, so neither the coattail effect nor the "check and balance" effect came into play. But Obama did leave a mark down the ballot. In places where his policies were unpopular, Republicans tried to tie Democratic candidates to him.

During the 2010 midterm, the GOP made historic gains in races for the US House and state legislatures. In the House, as in the Senate, these gains potentially exposed Republicans to losses in 2012; even under the best of circumstances, the prospects for large GOP gains were not high. Unlike their Senate co-partisans, however, House Republicans were now in a majority and thus were in a stronger position to raise money from individuals and groups that wanted access to power. The same was true in state capitals.

The 2010 midterm had an even more important impact on redistricting, thanks to state legislative pickups. Republicans unilaterally controlled redistricting for 210 House seats (in 18 states) and 2,498 state legislative seats (in 21 states). Democrats controlled the process for just 44 House seats (in 6 states) and 885 state legislative seats (in 8 states).[3]

One reason for the GOP's strong performance in the 2010 midterm was the growth in outside spending that stemmed from the *Citizens United* case, as well as other legal and regulatory decisions. Outside spending had existed before, but because of the arrival of super PACs and the easing of restrictions on 501(c)(4) groups, it was more than four times as great in 2010 as in the 2006 midterm. And whereas liberal groups had once done more outside spending than conservative ones, the financial advantage in 2010 was on the right.[4] As the 2012 campaign started, it was obvious that outside groups would spend even more. What was less clear was whether GOP groups would have the same edge that they had two years before.

In one way, the 2010 midterm created an opportunity for Democrats. Now that Republicans controlled the House and had more seats in the Senate, they shared responsibility for governing. In light of the enormity of the country's problems, "responsibility" potentially translated into "blame."

## OBAMA VERSUS "THE REPUBLICAN CONGRESS"

Newt Gingrich provided Democrats with a wonderful foil in the 1990s, combining real power with a habit of making outrageous statements. Democratic leaders could use him to stoke fear and anger, thus unifying their ranks and coaxing more money from their donors. During the first two years of the Obama administration, Democrats struggled to find an equally heinous villain. Republicans were in the minority in both chambers, and for a brief time, they did not even have the votes to sustain a filibuster in the Senate. Mindful of what happened to Gingrich, House Republican leader John Boehner (R-OH) and Senate Republican leader Mitch McConnell (R-KY) strove to avoid high-profile gaffes. Fortunately for their party, they were an undynamic duo. In the 2010 midterm campaign, Democrats tried and failed to rally voters against them. Tom Jensen of Public Policy Polling said that Boehner and McConnell "don't even have 50 percent name recognition nationwide. And for the most part, people who do know them are hard partisans whose voting preferences are pretty set in stone. This is the kind of thing where people who work in politics need to keep perspective about just how unfamiliar average people are with most of the movers and shakers in D.C."[5]

Things changed with the 2010 midterm, when Republicans won a majority in the House and gained several seats in the Senate. Republicans could not enact their own agenda, but they now had far more ability to block the president's program. Democrats could thus accuse them of obstructionism. Even before the election, Senate Republican leader Mitch McConnell supplied ammunition for this charge. In an interview with *National Journal*'s Major Garrett, he said: "The single most important thing we want to achieve is for President Obama to be a one-term president."[6] Over the next two years, many media stories repeated that line, usually omitting what McConnell said next: "If President Obama does a Clintonian backflip, if he's willing to meet us halfway on some of the biggest issues, it's not inappropriate for us to do business with him. . . . I don't want the president to fail; I want him to change. So, we'll see. The next move is going to be up to him."

In the lame-duck congressional session following the midterm, the president seemed to be taking a new approach when he agreed to a two-year extension of the Bush tax cuts. Hostilities resumed soon after the 112th Congress convened. On the Republican side, the Tea Party freshmen took a hard line on fiscal issues—deep spending cuts and no new taxes—which constrained Boehner in his budget talks with the administration. Some of the newcomers were nonchalant about the possibility of shutting down much of the federal government or defaulting on the national debt. Congress barely managed to avoid such outcomes. Because of the partisan stalemate, lawmakers also avoided a long-term solution to the deficit, instead providing for massive across-the-board cuts in 2013 if they did not reduce the budget shortfall.

In April of 2011, the House passed a fiscal plan by Budget Committee chair Paul Ryan (R-WI). Among other things, his budget resolution proposed to transform Medicare from a fee-for-service program into a subsidy for the purchase of private health insurance. No Democrats voted for it, and only four Republicans voted against it. The measure was largely symbolic, since it had no chance in the Democratic Senate (which would not end up passing any budget resolution at all). Its purpose was to set out the GOP position on economic issues, and Democrats happily reinforced that point. Just before the floor vote, President Obama attacked the plan during a speech at George Washington University, with Ryan sitting in the front row. Republicans did not believe the administration's subsequent claim that Ryan's invitation had been a staff mistake: they saw the move as a deliberate insult.[7]

Steve Israel (D-NY), chair of the Democratic Congressional Campaign Committee (DCCC), promised that Medicare would be the cornerstone of his party's efforts to regain a majority in the House. "We're going to hold every single Republican accountable for choosing to protect the special interests and turning their back on America's senior citizens by terminating their Medicare benefit," he said.[8] The next month, a Democrat won an upset victory in a special election for an upstate New York House seat that had belonged to a Republican. Israel said, "Today, the Republican plan to end Medicare cost Republicans $3.4 million and a seat in Congress. And this is only the first seat."[9]

News accounts of congressional stalemate seemed to give rise to a general sentiment of anti-incumbency, an ominous sign for the party with more incumbents. In December of 2011, about three-quarters of registered voters said that most members of Congress did not deserve reelection, the highest share that Gallup had measured in nineteen years of asking the question. Thirty-nine percent said the same of their own representative, just shy of the record 40 percent saying so before the tumultuous 2010 election.[10] And overall approval of Congress, which was not high to begin with, hit a record low of just 10 percent in February of 2012.[11] Obama tried to bundle this increasingly unpopular institution with the GOP. Notwithstanding Democratic control of the Senate, more than a dozen of his 2012 speeches included criticism of what he called "the Republican Congress."[12]

The president was setting himself up as the alternative to congressional Republicans, which was not quite the same thing as helping his own co-partisans. After the midterm, relations between the White House and Capitol Hill Democrats ranged between tepid and cool. In June of 2012, a top House Democratic aide said, "He's done nothing for us so we don't have to do anything for him."[13] Other presidents had faced similar complaints, but President Obama was averse to the chit-gathering that had helped his predecessors get their way. "I've been on Air Force One twice—with George W. Bush," a House Democrat told *Politico*.[14] At rallies, he rarely shared the stage with other candidates or urged supporters to work for them.[15]

In many places, the president's support might not have helped anyway. Nationwide, he actually had higher approval ratings than one might have predicted from the weak economy.[16] Those ratings, however, were lower in a number of states, including some holding key House and Senate contests.[17] The president's name and likeness were sure to be part of Republican attack ads in those races.

## HOUSE CONTESTS

The Democratic victory in the upstate New York special election caused anxious moments for congressional Republicans. They got some relief in September 2011, when they notched two special-election wins of their own. In Brooklyn, Bob Turner won the seat vacated by Anthony Weiner, who quit after a bizarre online sex scandal. More significant was a Nevada race in which GOP candidate Mark Amodei mounted a successful counterattack on the Medicare issue. Pete Sessions (R-TX), chair of the National Republican Congressional Committee (NRCC), advised Amodei to hit his opponent for backing the president's health care law.[18] The measure cut the future growth of Medicare spending by billions, thus providing an occasion to say that it raided Medicare to pay for Obamacare. (Democrats and media fact-checkers disputed this claim.) In one Amodei ad, the narrator asked, "Why is Democrat Kate Marshall lying about Mark Amodei's record on Medicare?" Then as the screen showed a photo of President Obama with his arm over Marshall's shoulder, the narrator answered, "Because Kate Marshall wants to cover up her support for a $500 billion Medicare cut."[19]

When Mitt Romney chose Paul Ryan as his running mate, NRCC produced an online slide presentation using the Nevada race as a case study of how to deal with the Ryan plan. "The media is eager to write stories that we are suddenly on defense and that choosing Ryan for VP will cost us votes with seniors," said NRCC political director Mike Shields in the presentation. "This is absurd since a. the Democrats were going to hit us on the Ryan plan anyway and b. we have proven you can successfully push back so long as you play offense."[20]

Meanwhile, redistricting was another source of Republican hope. The 2010 legislative gains seemed to put the GOP in its strongest redistricting position in decades, but Republicans had already learned not to overplay their advantage. During the previous decade, Texas, Florida, and Pennsylvania had GOP gerrymanders that eventually backfired. In drawing the maximum number of Republican districts, they spread their core voters too thinly and left their incumbents vulnerable to the kind of Democratic wave that struck in 2006.[21] This time, Republicans aimed to do things differently. "We don't need to overreach. We're trying to convince members to relay to their [state] legislators that, you know, this has got to be a 10-year map," said Lynn Westmoreland (R-GA), who headed redistricting oversight for the National Republican Congressional Committee.[22] In states such as Ohio, Pennsylvania, and North Carolina, Republicans drew maps that they hoped would lock in their previous gains for the next decade.

Some developments on the redistricting front worked against the GOP. In Texas, a Republican-drawn map fell to a legal challenge. In New York, the party hoped that its narrow control of the state senate would lead to a plan that would protect its House incumbents, but the senate could not reach an agreement with the state assembly. In both Texas and New York, federal courts drew the lines. In 2010, Florida voters approved a state constitutional amendment forbidding legislators from drawing congressional lines to favor a party or an incumbent. Noting that this measure would block a gerrymander by the GOP governor and legislature, DCCC chair Steve Israel said, "Our path to 25 seats flows straight through Florida."[23]

Illinois Democrats wrote a tough map that jeopardized several GOP seats, and Republicans fought back in court. Trial testimony confirmed that the Democratic Congressional Campaign Committee had helped draft the Illinois gerrymander, including emails explaining "how to destabilize Republican incumbents" and proclaiming that the plan "seemingly accomplished" its goal.[24] Although noting that the plan was a partisan power grab, the court ruled that it did not break federal law.

Two 2010 California ballot measures shaped elections for the largest House delegation. One took congressional redistricting out of the hands of the state legislature and assigned it to an independent commission. The commission was supposed to base its decisions on testimony from affected communities, not on the advice of political operatives. But Democrats quietly lined up local voters, unions, and community groups to testify for districts that served the party's interests.[25] Democrats might not have needed much help, however. By October of 2012, Democrats had a 44–29 percent voter registration edge over the Republicans, who were at their all-time low point.[26]

The other 2010 ballot measure established a "top two" primary system, in which all candidates for every office would run on the same primary ballot, with the top two vote-getters proceeding to the general election, regardless of party. (Presidential primaries were an exception, with each party having a separate contest.) The system resulted in ten contests pitting members of the same party against each other: eight with Democrats, two with Republicans. (One Democrat-on-Democrat battle drew national attention when YouTube showed Los Angeles–area lawmakers Howard Berman and Brad Sherman in a shoving match during a town-hall meeting.)

On the national level, another legacy of the 2010 election was the increased prominence of outside spending. In 2012, Republican groups such as the American Action Network and the Congressional Leadership Fund spent heavily on ads in House races. Learning from their midterm setback, Democratic outside groups also decided to ante up. In competitive House races, there was rough parity in spending between pro-Republican and pro-Democratic non-party groups.[27] The two sides spent their money differently, with Republican groups focusing on mass media and Democratic groups concentrating on voter contact. "There is a bias towards funding infrastructure as it relates to the elections," said Brad McKay, chair of the Democracy Alliance, a liberal donor group. "That means get-out-the-vote efforts" aiming at youth, Hispanics, African Americans, and single women.[28]

In an impressive performance for the minority party, the DCCC raised nearly as much money as the NRCC. The latter organization attempted something new in 2012. Early in the election cycle, Speaker Boehner told his political staff to launch a program through NRCC to help party organizations in the "orphan states," those that would not be in play in the presidential race. A political staffer explained to *The Hill* that "the whole orphan dilemma was that you've got, effectively, the majority hanging in the balance of states that are not going to get any attention from the presidential campaign. They are not going to get a single dollar . . . to do the voter identification, to do the turnout, to do those basic blocking and tackling."[29] The project set up thirty-eight local offices in key districts aimed at building a "ground game" to match what Democrats were already doing through unions and other outside groups.[30]

Candidate spending pointed to a problem for Democrats. In House races, the key test of competitiveness is not whether challengers can raise more than the incumbents, but whether they can raise enough to campaign effectively. In recent years, this threshold has been about $1 million. In 2010, fifty-eight GOP challengers had raised that much through the end of September while only fifteen Democratic challengers had done so. In 2012, when Democrats needed a net gain of twenty-five seats to regain a majority, just thirty-five Democratic challengers crossed the threshold, along with twenty Republicans.[31] In spite of the anti-incumbent sentiment that some polls had picked up in 2011, most incumbents remained front-runners in 2012—and that was good news for the GOP.

Some incumbents retired, resigned, or ran for another office. Even though Republicans held more seats, there were more voluntary Democratic farewells (twenty-three to the GOP's twenty), several of which were in districts ripe for a Republican takeover. The GOP advantage in retirements reflected the efforts of NRCC chair Sessions, who used the prospect of tough election battles to nudge some Democrats out of running while persuading veteran Republicans in swing districts to hang on for another term.[32]

## SENATE CONTESTS

Retirements loomed large in the other chamber as well. The thirty-three Senate seats up for election in 2012 not only were lopsidedly Democratic, but also produced a disproportionate number of Democratic departures. Seven Democrats (including Lieberman) called it quits, compared with only three Republicans. At first, these numbers made GOP gains seem almost inevitable.

One by one, however, several of the open seats slipped out of the party's grasp. In New Mexico, GOP nominee Heather Wilson had an excellent résumé (Rhodes Scholar, air force captain, former US House member) and took heart from the 2010 election of a Republican governor. In Hawaii, the Republican candidate was Linda Lingle, who in 2002 had become the state's first Republican governor in forty years and had won a second term in 2006. By fall, however, both were lagging in the polls. In Connecticut, which had elected a Republican governor in 2006, wrestling magnate Linda McMahon spent millions of her own money and did well in some early surveys, but also fell behind. These cases show that gubernatorial races are poor barometers for federal elections. Blue states may elect Republican governors from time to time, but are less likely to pick Republican senators.

In all three cases, moreover, the Democratic candidates had strong starts as incumbent House members from relatively small states. Mazie Hirono of Hawaii, Martin Heinrich of New Mexico, and Chris Murphy of Connecticut were already well known to large fractions of state voters and had campaign organizations in place. The Democratic Senatorial Campaign Committee officially or unofficially supported the trio in competitive party primaries.[33]

Virginia looked more promising for the GOP. After supporting Republicans in the previous ten presidential races, it had gone for Obama in 2008. A big GOP victory in the 2009 gubernatorial election suggested that 2008 might have been a one-off. Incumbent Democratic senator Jim Webb was stepping down after just one term, and the person he had defeated six years earlier thought that he could win his old seat back.

But George Allen's 2006 loss to Webb cast a shadow on his chances in 2012. Allen had created the most notorious moment of the 2006 Senate midterm election when he singled out the Democratic "tracker" videotaping a campaign appearance and sarcastically asked the audience to greet the young Indian American, whom he called "Macaca." Though no one in the audience probably knew it at the time, the word turned out to be an obscure ethnic slur. The tracker's video quickly appeared on YouTube. In the first major demonstration of the year-old site's potential power, the "Macaca Moment" exposed Allen to national criticism for racial insensitivity and probably was responsible for his narrow defeat. Six years later, Allen hoped that the 2006 incident had gone down the memory hole. His opponent was former governor Tim Kaine, who had served as President Obama's choice as chair of the Democratic National Committee.

In Wisconsin, Republican former governor and HHS secretary Tommy Thompson ran against Representative Tammy Baldwin to succeed retiring Democratic senator Herb Kohl. Though Obama had carried the state in 2008, Republicans were optimistic. Wisconsin had elected a Republican governor and US senator in 2010, and in June of 2012, the governor survived a fierce Democratic recall campaign. Thompson had won the governorship four times between 1986 and 1998, but now he was seventy years old and had not run for office in fourteen years. He scraped through a rough Republican primary, ending up with an anemic 34 percent of the vote.

Ads by Republican groups accused Baldwin of being an angry extremist. Democrats went after Thompson's time in George W. Bush's cabinet, where he helped win passage of the Medicare prescription drug bill. "Tommy Thompson was the 'point man' for a plan that prohibits negotiating lower drug prices," said one ad by the Democratic Senatorial Campaign Committee. "Thompson's plan gave billions in taxpayer handouts to the drug companies." The ad said that he had gone on to lobby for those same companies.[34] One topic was conspicuous by its absence from the campaign. Although Baldwin stood to be the first openly gay senator, Thompson did not make an issue of her sexual orientation, and gay-rights groups assumed a low profile in supporting her.[35]

In North Dakota, news of Democratic senator Kent Conrad's retirement led many in the Republican political community to regard his seat as an automatic pickup. President Obama was unpopular there and Republican candidate Rick Berg had strong name identification as the state's sole House member. But Democratic nominee Heidi Heitkamp was also a known quantity, since she had served two terms as the state's attorney general. She shrewdly positioned herself as a centrist, taking advantage of her tenure as a director of a synfuels plant to criticize the

Obama administration's energy policy. When surveys showed her pulling close to Berg, Republican groups ran television spots trying to portray her as an ally of the president. One Crossroads GPS ad said, "North Dakota Can't Afford an Obama Rubber Stamp," emphasizing her support for the Wall Street bailout.[36] The attack was odd, given that TARP was an initiative of President Bush.

Another likely GOP gain appeared when Nebraska's Ben Nelson announced that he would leave. Deb Fischer, a former state legislator, surprisingly won the GOP primary by depicting herself as champion of rural interests against two urban lawyers.[37] She also benefited from the endorsement of Sarah Palin, who still carried weight with many conservative primary voters. Despite Republican strength in Nebraska, Democrats thought they might have a winner in Bob Kerrey, who had served as both governor and senator. But like Tommy Thompson in Wisconsin, Kerrey was now a senior citizen who had not run for office in years. (His last election was 1994.) And he had lived in New York City for more than a decade, marrying a former *Saturday Night Live* writer. His wife did not help matters when she penned an article for *Vogue* that made fun of his state. Aside from one outlier survey in October, Fischer had a double-digit lead throughout the fall campaign.

Retirements caused some hardship for Republicans as well. Olympia Snowe, a moderate from Maine, would have probably won reelection. But when she said that she was stepping down, Republicans knew that they would probably lose a seat in a state that had not voted for a GOP presidential candidate since 1988. Running as an independent, former governor Angus King was a strong favorite, and would likely caucus with the Democrats if they kept their majority. In Arizona, highly regarded Senator Jon Kyl (who played workhorse to John McCain's showhorse) would also have won. When he decided not to run again, Representative Jeff Flake got the GOP nomination. Democrats thought that their candidate might be former representative Gabrielle Giffords, who had become a national heroine for her brave fight to recover from a gunshot wound. But she was not yet well enough to run. Instead Democrats nominated Richard Carmona, a former US surgeon general who hoped that the state's growing Hispanic population would carry him to the Senate. The race was competitive, and some surveys put Carmona ahead.

In Texas, Republican senator Kay Bailey Hutchison opted not to seek reelection after losing the 2010 gubernatorial primary to Rick Perry. There was little doubt that her successor would be a Republican, but which one? Ted Cruz defeated Lieutenant Governor David Dewhurst in the Republican primary runoff. Many stories depicted the race as a clash between the establishment that backed Dewhurst and the Tea Party outsiders who supported Cruz, but the picture was more complex. For one thing, Cruz had establishment roots: Princeton undergraduate degree,

Harvard law degree, clerkship with the chief justice of the United States, and stint as solicitor general of Texas. For another thing, much of the campaign money behind Cruz came from Washington-based conservative groups.[38] In short, Cruz was no peasant with a pitchfork, but a conservative in the familiar mold of former Texas senator Phil Gramm.

Early in the election cycle, Republicans thought that they might be able to oust Democratic incumbents in Michigan and Florida, but the GOP candidates failed to catch fire. Republican challengers did better in Pennsylvania and Ohio, but never led in any independent polls. All of these states had elected Republican governors in 2010, again illustrating the disconnect between federal and gubernatorial elections.

A few Republican incumbents were at more serious risk. In Nevada, Governor Brian Sandoval had appointed Dean Heller to replace the disgraced John Ensign, who had quit because of a scandal involving sex and hush money. Appointed senators have an uneven electoral record, and Democrats thought that they had a strong candidate in Shelley Berkley, who had represented much of the state in the House. But Heller had also served in the House, and Berkley had to deal with allegations that she had used her office to help her husband's medical practice. The race stayed close.

The most endangered Republican was Scott Brown of Massachusetts. Early in 2010, he had stunned Democrats by winning a special election for the seat that Edward Kennedy had held. He did have support from Tea Party activists in his campaign, but after he was in office for a while, a *National Journal* analysis of roll-call votes put him in the Senate's ideological center.[39] Despite his moderate positions and political skills, any Republican was bound to have a hard time, especially in a year when Barack Obama would carry the state by a thumping margin. His 2012 opponent was Elizabeth Warren, a Harvard Law School professor and former Obama administration official. Warren got some unfavorable publicity when news accounts revealed her dubious claim to Native American heritage. (Conservative *Boston Herald* columnist Howie Carr dubbed her "Fauxcahontas.") The issue faded, however, and as the election approached, Brown seemed likely to sink in a blue tide.

If Brown was a Republican fluke, Montana's Jon Tester seemed to be a Democratic fluke. In 2006, he had beaten Conrad Burns, an aging, gaffe-prone, scandal-tainted incumbent. Despite his problems, Burns came within 3,562 votes of holding on, and might well have won except for a Libertarian candidate who drew 10,377 votes. Six years later, two big challenges put Tester's reelection in doubt. First, he had a well-known opponent in Denny Rehberg, who had won six statewide elections as Montana's only US House member. Second, he was running a presidential election in which Mitt Romney was likely to carry the state by a large margin. Rehberg, however, had some liabilities, including a well-publicized drunken boating accident. And a Libertarian was again on the ballot, this time benefiting from an ad campaign. Montana Hunters and Anglers, consisting of a super PAC and a 501(c)(4) nonprofit, attacked Rehberg and asked voters to support the Libertarian as "the real conservative." The groups had ties to Democratic and liberal activists, and the ads were an obvious attempt to split the anti-Tester vote.[40]

It was not the first time in 2012 that Democrats ran ads to manipulate another party.

In Missouri, Democratic senator Claire McCaskill initially seemed likely to lose because of ethics problems and support for President Obama. Of the three Republicans who ran for the chance to oppose her, the weakest was Representative Todd Akin, a hardline conservative. Just before the primary, McCaskill aired a spot showing Akin in various settings as a narrator called him "Missouri's true conservative . . . a crusader against bigger government" with a "pro-family agenda." At the end, the narrator delivered the tag line that Akin was "too conservative." Nominally, it was an attack on Akin, but in effect it was a clever way of prodding social conservatives and Tea Party Republicans to vote *for* him. "That's music to their ears," said political scientist Ken Warren. "No one is 'too conservative' for a Tea Party Missourian."[41] Akin won the nomination, and McCaskill had the opponent she wanted.

When Akin led in post-primary polling, it seemed possible that McCaskill had outsmarted herself. But then, in a television interview, Akin blundered while trying to explain his opposition to abortion even in cases of rape. "It seems to be, first of all, from what I understand from doctors, it's really rare," he said. "If it's a legitimate rape, the female body has ways to try to shut the whole thing down."[42] The remark, which had no basis in science, drew fire from all sides. Akin was sure to cost the GOP a winnable seat, so calls for his withdrawal came from key Republicans, including Senate minority leader Mitch McConnell. The National Republican Senatorial Committee withdrew support from Akin, and American Crossroads stopped advertising in the race. Akin, however, refused to pull out, and polls showed him losing to McCaskill.

Only one Senate incumbent fell in a primary, with consequences for the general election.

In Indiana, Senator Richard Lugar lost the Republican nomination to state treasurer Richard Mourdock. During his thirty-six years in the Senate, Lugar had built a reputation as a bipartisan compromiser and expert in foreign policy—credentials that earned him respect in Washington and suspicion among GOP primary voters. Over time, he lost touch with his home state, and did not even own any property there. Mourdock beat Lugar by stressing his own Tea Party conservatism and ties to Indiana. Though Mourdock was not as strong a general-election candidate as Lugar, he seemed viable until he stumbled over the same issue as Akin. "I struggled with it myself a long time but I came to realize that life is a gift from God, that I think even when life begins in that horrible situation of rape that it is something that God intended to happen," he said during a debate with the Democratic candidate, Representative Joe Donnelly.[43] Though party leaders did not abandon him as they had with Akin, polls showed him losing ground.

By late October, practically no one expected Republicans to take control of the Senate. The only question seemed to be whether they could score any net gains at all.

## THE RESULTS

In spite of the public's earlier unhappiness with the institution, the 113th Congress would look much like the 112th. In the House, Democrats had a net pickup of eight seats, bringing their total to 201. Republicans stayed in the majority, with 234 seats. Senate Democrats gained bragging rights and confounded expectations by netting two seats. With the support of newly elected Angus King of Maine, they would have a 55–45 majority. The actual balance of power changed little, however. In the majoritarian House, a unified Republican party would always prevail. In the Senate, the GOP would have more than enough votes to sustain filibusters. The 2012 congressional elections ratified the status quo in another way, too. As usual, most incumbents who sought reelection were successful. Of the twenty-three senators who ran in 2012, the only losers were Lugar (R-IN) in his primary, and Scott Brown (R-MA) in the general election, for a reelection rate of 91 percent. Of 391 House members up for reelection, 13 lost primaries and 27 went down in the general election, for a reelection rate of 90 percent.[44] This rate had been higher in seven of the eight previous biennial elections for the House.[45] But the 2012 figure is artificially low because it includes thirteen races where redistricting pitted incumbents against each other in primaries or general elections. If we leave these races out of the calculation, the reelection rate goes up to *93 percent*.

Presidents with big popular-vote margins have sometimes shaken up the status quo by bringing many House members on their coattails. But 2012 was obviously not a coattail election like 1920, 1932, or 1964. President Obama's margin was modest, and in the net House gain for the winning presidential candidate's party, this election ranks seventeenth of thirty (see table 5.1). In this regard, 2012 was typical of presidential reelections, which usually bring smaller congressional party shifts than other presidential elections or midterms.

To the extent that House Democrats did make gains, they tended to come from big states with major redistricting changes:

- In California, they picked up a newly drawn open seat and defeated incumbent Republicans Dan Lungren, Brian Bilbray, and Mary Bono Mack. They expanded their edge from 34–19 to 38–15.

**Table 5.1. Gains or Losses in the House by the Party of the Winning Presidential Candidate, 1896–2012 (in Order of Seat Change)**

| | | | *Margin* | *Seat Change* |
|---|---|---|---|---|
| 1 | 1932 | Franklin D. Roosevelt | 17.76% | 93 |
| 2 | 1948 | Harry S. Truman | 4.48% | 75 |
| 3 | 1920 | Warren G. Harding | 26.17% | 63 |
| 4 | 1912 | Woodrow Wilson | 14.44% | 62 |
| 5 | 1904 | Theodore Roosevelt | 18.83% | 43 |
| 6 | 1964 | Lyndon B. Johnson | 22.58% | 37 |
| 7 | 1980 | Ronald Reagan | 9.74% | 34 |
| 8 | 1928 | Herbert Hoover | 17.41% | 30 |
| 9 | 1924 | Calvin Coolidge | 25.22% | 22 |
| 10 | 1952 | Dwight D. Eisenhower | 10.85% | 22 |
| 11 | 1944 | Franklin D. Roosevelt | 7.50% | 21 |
| 12 | 2008 | Barack Obama | 7.27% | 21 |
| 13 | 1984 | Ronald Reagan | 18.21% | 16 |
| 14 | 1900 | William McKinley | 6.12% | 13 |
| 15 | 1972 | Richard Nixon | 23.15% | 12 |
| 16 | 1936 | Franklin D. Roosevelt | 24.26% | 11 |
| 17 | 2012 | Barack Obama | 3.85% | 8 |
| 18 | 1940 | Franklin D. Roosevelt | 9.96% | 5 |
| 19 | 1968 | Richard Nixon | 0.70% | 5 |
| 20 | 1996 | Bill Clinton | 8.51% | 3 |
| 21 | 2004 | George W. Bush | 2.46% | 3 |
| 22 | 1976 | Jimmy Carter | 2.06% | 1 |
| 23 | 1956 | Dwight D. Eisenhower | 15.40% | -2 |
| 24 | 2000 | George W. Bush | -0.51% | -2 |
| 25 | 1908 | William H. Taft | 8.53% | -3 |
| 26 | 1988 | George H. W. Bush | 7.72% | -3 |
| 27 | 1992 | Bill Clinton | 5.56% | -9 |
| 28 | 1960 | John F. Kennedy | 0.17% | -20 |
| 29 | 1916 | Woodrow Wilson | 3.12% | -21 |
| 30 | 1896 | William McKinley | 4.31% | -40 |

- In Illinois, which lost a seat in reapportionment and where one Republican retired, four GOP incumbents went down: Joe Walsh, Judy Biggert, Bobby Schilling, and Robert Dold. As a result, the delegation went from eleven Republicans and eight Democrats to twelve Democrats and six Republicans.
- In Texas, where reapportionment added four seats and a federal court drew the lines, Republicans netted one seat and Democrats netted three.
- In Florida, which gained two seats, the Republican advantage dropped from 19–6 to 17–10. A couple of the Democratic pickups came from troubled GOP incumbents. David Rivera had multiple ethics issues. Allen West had become better known for over-the-top political attacks than for constituent service or competent campaign management. "Sometimes people don't want controversy," one Republican told *Politico*. "They just want a congressman."[46]
- In New York, which dropped two seats, two freshman Republicans lost. In the Syracuse area, the addition of Democratic territory helped former Representative Dan Maffei defeat Ann Marie Buerkle, who had beaten him two years earlier. Nan Hayworth lost her race in the northern suburbs of New York less because of redistricting than because of a poor campaign.

Republicans had a big redistricting conquest in North Carolina, where the House delegation flipped from a 7–6 Democratic edge to a 9–4 Republican advantage. As mentioned earlier, however, GOP redistricting success consisted mostly of holding seats in states such as Michigan, Ohio, and Pennsylvania. The Republicans' "orphan state" tactic may have helped keep some races tighter than they might have been, but still fell short in blue states. The GOP fared better in orphan red states, bolstering some shaky incumbents and grabbing Democratic seats in Arkansas, Indiana, and Kentucky.[47]

Overall, Democratic House candidates outpolled Republicans by more than a million votes, yet got only 46 percent of the seats. Some commentators blamed this unusual gap on GOP gerrymandering.[48] There were additional reasons for the seat-vote difference. Much of the Democratic vote was concentrated in urban areas, where landslide margins for Democratic House candidates resulted in many "wasted" votes.[49] GOP support was more efficiently distributed: fewer Republicans took over 80 percent of the vote, but more of them won. Political scientists Jowei Chen and Jonathan Rodden refer to such differentials as "unintentional gerrymandering."[50] In part because of incumbency advantages and the efforts of both parties to shore up their own seats in redistricting, only a minority of House elections were competitive. In about six races out of seven, the winner outpolled the loser by more than 10 percent.[51] Most of the losers failed to mount much of a campaign, writes Nathan Gonzales of the *Rothenberg Political Report*, "so victories in those districts didn't say much, if anything at all, about the public validating one party's ideas over the other."[52]

On the Senate side, the biggest upsets were Democratic victories in North Dakota and Montana. Heidi Heitkamp proved to be a gifted politician who foiled GOP efforts to tie her to President Obama. Jon Tester once again owed much to a spoiler. Libertarian Dan Cox pulled 31,287 votes while Denny Rehberg ran behind by 18,674. The ads by the Montana Hunters and Anglers Leadership Fund apparently succeeded in splitting Tester's opposition. Republicans took consolation from wins in Arizona, Nebraska, and Nevada. But Democrats ruined GOP hopes in Massachusetts, Virginia, and Wisconsin. And to no one's surprise, Republicans suffered throwaway losses in Indiana and Missouri. Absent devastating gaffes by GOP candidates in those two states, the party would have at least broken even. Add these two to the three seats that they arguably threw away in 2010, and Republicans could easily have started 2013 with a fifty/fifty tie in the Senate rather than a ten-seat deficit.

Could President Obama take credit for the Senate Democrats' good election night? To find out, we can look at the eleven Democratic victories in races that RealClearPolitics rated as "tossups" or "leans." Table 5.2 compares the percentage of the vote for the winning Senate candidate and President Obama. Only in Connecticut, Massachusetts, and Wisconsin did the president get a higher percentage of the vote than the winning Senate candidate, and only in Massachusetts was the difference more than 5 percent. Although the Obama campaign's turnout operation may have had the side effect of helping his party's Senate candidates, it would be hard to argue that Senate Democrats won on the president's coattails.

Democrats had good luck and smart candidates. The Massachusetts Senate race provides one example of how they outmaneuvered the Republicans. Scott Brown and Elizabeth Warren signed a "People's Pledge" to keep outside groups off the air. (Under the deal, each would have to make a charitable donation equal to half the cost of any TV or Internet ad by a supportive outside group.) The Brown campaign thought that the deal would put Warren at a disadvantage, but American Crossroads CEO Steven Law warned: "Because the agreement allows union phone banks, direct mail, and get-out-the-vote drives—all union core specialties—Warren's latest agreement has loopholes the Teamsters could drive a truck through, the longshoremen could steer a ship through, the machinists could fly a plane through and government unions could drive forklifts of paperwork through."[53] After the election, a report in the *Boston Globe* confirmed Law's prediction: "Over the course of the campaign, union members knocked on the doors of 327,936 union households, said Steven A. Tolman, president of the Massachusetts AFL-CIO. They made 242,000 phone calls to union households, distributed 250,000 leaflets to 175 work

**Table 5.2. Percentage of the Vote for Winning Democratic Senate Candidate and President Obama in Key States**

| | *Winner* | *Winner%* | *Obama%* |
|---|---|---|---|
| Connecticut | Murphy | 55.2% | 58.1% |
| Florida | Nelson | 55.2% | 50.0% |
| Indiana | Donnelly | 50.0% | 43.9% |
| Massachusetts | Warren | 53.3% | 60.7% |
| Missouri | McCaskill | 54.8% | 44.4% |
| Montana | Tester | 48.6% | 41.7% |
| North Dakota | Heitkamp | 50.5% | 38.7% |
| Ohio | Brown | 50.7% | 50.7% |
| Pennsylvania | Casey | 53.7% | 52.0% |
| Virginia | Kaine | 52.9% | 51.2% |
| Wisconsin | Baldwin | 51.5% | 52.8% |

*Source*: Ballotpedia, "United States Congressional Elections Results, 2012," http://ballotpedia.org/wiki/index.php/United_States_Congressional_elections_results,_2012; David Wasserman, "2012 National Popular Vote Tracker," https://docs.google.com/spreadsheet/lv?key=0AjYj9mXElO_QdHpla01oWE1jOFZRbnhJZkZpVFNKeVE&toomany=true#gid=19.

*Note*: In the Ohio race, rounding to two decimal places instead of one shows that Senator Sherrod Brown got a slightly greater share of the vote than President Obama: 50.70 percent to 50.67 percent.

sites, and worked 10,708 volunteer shifts, he said, often standing for hours outside Warren's events."[54]

After the election, American Crossroads and other outside GOP groups came under criticism for spending millions on behalf of losing candidates. The critics often left out a key piece of contextual information. These groups were not spending in a vacuum: Democratic Party organizations and outside groups reached a rough overall equivalence with the GOP counterparts. Table 5.3 shows independent expenditures by super PACs, other nonparty outside groups, and party organizations. The airwaves were boiling with ads on both sides. Perhaps the messages of Team Blue and Team Red ended up cancelling each other out, but if one side had pulled out, the other would have had air superiority.

It is harder for GOP party organizations and outside groups to dismiss the criticism that they should have spent less on broadcast advertising and more on field and get-out-the-vote operations. Even when they did engage in voter contact, they did not always do it well. In the Massachusetts race, for instance, Crossroads GPS sent out automated telephone messages against Warren, even though research has shown that such "robo-calls" have no effect.[55] Karl Rove later acknowledged, "Tactically, Republicans must rigorously re-examine their '72-hour' ground game

**Table 5.3. Senate Outside Money Totals, through October 23, 2012**

| | *Republican* | *Democratic* |
|---|---|---|
| Super PACs | 24.0 | 33.7 |
| Other Nonparty Groups | 56.2 | 24.6 |
| Party Organizations | 17.1 | 33.8 |
| Total | 97.3 | 92.1 |

*Source*: Lee Drutman, "Outside Money in the Senate: One Map, Four Graphs and Seven Takeaways," Sunlight Foundation, October 24, 2012, http://sunlightfoundation.com/blog/2012/10/24/outside-money-in-the-senate.
*Note*: Figures are in millions of dollars. Data for party organizations do not include direct contributions to candidates.

and reverse-engineer the Democratic get-out-the-vote effort in order to copy what works."[56] GOP consultant Patrick Ruffini warned against simply replicating the other side's last campaign: "Just as venture capitalists would reject pitches from companies aiming to become the next Facebook or Google, as their business models seem fairly secure, Republican donors should apply a similar framework to evaluating technology projects. Is the project trying to solve a problem which has already been solved, or whose relevance is on the decline? If so, they shouldn't invest."[57]

## STATE ELECTIONS

The most important state-level contest took place months before the general election. In 2011, newly inaugurated Republican governor Scott Walker asked the legislature to curb collective bargaining rights for most public employees. Thousands of union members and their supporters staged protests at the state capitol. Lawmakers who backed the measure received death threats. After the bill passed, *Time* described this scene: "Gone were the throngs of protesters who had occupied its marble floors like it were a summer campground. The midnight honking of cars circling the white building had ceased. The chalk outlines around fake dead bodies etched with Wisconsin Governor Scott Walker's name remained in dismembered parts, not yet completely washed away by hoses."[58]

Wisconsin allows for the recall of elected officials after they have served at least a year. In November, the unions started a recall drive and by early 2012, they had 931,000 signatures, far more than they needed to force a vote. On both sides, the race drew money and attention from all over the country. One figure was absent: President Obama. He did not go to Wisconsin to stump for Democratic candidate Tom Barrett, though he did tweet a message of support just before the election. Walker defeated Barrett, who had run against him in 2010. Compared with the earlier race,

Walker won the recall by a bigger margin and with more votes. He even carried 38 percent of union households—a slight improvement from his 2010 showing.[59]

The eleven regular gubernatorial elections gave the Republicans a net gain of one, bringing their total to thirty governorships. The pickup came in North Carolina, where former Charlotte mayor Pat McCrory defeated Lieutenant Governor Walter Dalton to succeed Bev Perdue, an unpopular incumbent who did not seek reelection. The GOP had a couple of disappointments. In Washington State, Democratic former House member Jay Inslee narrowly defeated Rob McKenna, the state's Republican attorney general. In Montana, it was the sitting attorney general who beat a former House member, as Democrat Steve Bullock won a close race over Republican Rick Hill.

Montana Democrats had a special reason to gloat. A conservative outside-spending group had challenged Montana's law banning independent political spending by corporations. As attorney general, Bullock defended the law all the way to the US Supreme Court, losing in a *per curiam* decision that effectively applied *Citizens United* to state elections. Republicans criticized Bullock and defended outside spending. As we have seen, however, a sneaky tactic by an outside group thwarted the GOP's effort to defeat Senator Jon Tester.

Shortly after the election, the Democratic Legislative Campaign Committee issued a release saying that the party had gained a total of 170 seats in legislative elections across the country.[60] But 119 of those seats were in the 400-member New Hampshire House, where the average constituency size is about 3,300. All 119 seats together have fewer people than one state assembly district in California.

What matters is control of state legislative chambers, and here the news was only mildly encouraging for the Democrats. A total of eighty-six of the ninety-nine chambers held elections in November 2012. Twelve changed party hands, with four switching to the GOP, eight to the Democrats. After the election, however, Republicans in the New York and Washington senates built cross-party coalitions with insurgent Democrats, thereby reducing the Democrats' net gain of legislative chambers from four to two. Both before and after the election, Republicans controlled both houses in twenty-six states—or twenty-seven, if one counts Virginia, where a Republican lieutenant governor could break ties in an evenly divided state senate. Republican state legislators thus kept most of their midterm gains and remained at an historic high point. Before the 2010 election, Republicans had not run that many legislatures since the 1920s.[61]

Party polarization was evident, with a number of states becoming more strongly Republican or Democratic. As a result of the election, one party would hold the governorship and both legislative chambers in thirty-six states, the largest number in decades.[62] Republicans would hold twenty-four states (again, including Virginia), and Democrats would have a dozen. After the election, half of the state legislatures had two-thirds supermajorities in both chambers, up from thirteen four years earlier.[63] Some of these changes were unprecedented in recent times. In Tennessee, for instance, Republicans would have supermajorities for the first time since Reconstruction.

The Tennessee result was part of a larger trend. By picking up both chambers in Arkansas, Republicans now had control of the legislatures of all eleven states of the Old Confederacy (including Virginia). And with McCrory's election in North Carolina, Republicans would also have every governorship in the region as well, with the single exception of Arkansas.

As Republicans were surging in much of the South, they faced the danger of a death spiral in California. After the 2010 election, they no longer held any statewide offices, but GOP legislators still had some leverage because the state constitution required a two-thirds vote to approve tax increases. With the election of Democratic supermajorities in 2012, they were now irrelevant. Fundraising from special interests would be tougher, because access to GOP lawmakers had become essentially worthless. The state's powerful pro-Democratic labor unions were riding high. They mobilized supporters to beat an initiative that would have curbed their ability to collect political money. They also helped Governor Brown pass a ballot measure to raise sales taxes and the top marginal income tax rate.

Voters in Maryland, Washington, and Maine approved same-sex marriage, marking the first time that ballot measures had extended marriage rights to same-sex couples. (In other states, the decision had come from courts or legislatures.) Minnesota voters defeated a constitutional amendment defining marriage as a union between one man and one woman. These results reflected a dramatic shift in public opinion. According to Gallup, support for same-sex marriage nearly doubled between 1996 and 2012, going from 27 percent to 50 percent.[64]

Colorado and Washington voters approved measures to legalize the recreational use of marijuana, making them the first states to do so. Oregonians turned down a similar measure. Massachusetts voters approved medical marijuana but the Arkansans voted no. The practical effect of the successful measures was questionable, since possession remained illegal under federal law.

## CONSEQUENCES OF THE VOTE

Despite the ebb and flow of power in individual capitals, Republicans still maintained power in more states than not. They could use that power to alter election law (e.g., on voter identification and allocation of electors), develop talent, stake out alternative policy agendas, and resist Obama administration policies. Within a few weeks after Election Day 2012, a significant number of states with Republican governors had announced that they would not participate in the statewide health exchanges called for in the Affordable Care Act.

The election changed some things in Washington. With President Obama in the White House for another four years and with an enlarged Democratic majority in the Senate, congressional Republicans knew that they could not repeal the key legislative accomplishment of the president's first term: the health care law. Although they had held the House, they were disappointed. Wishful thinking and bad polling had created unrealistic expectations about the presidential and Senate races.

But for the 113th Congress, however, the fundamental story was one of continuity. Things did not change, and trends continued in the same direction as before. The parties were already polarized and would likely become even more so in the next couple of years. In the Senate, the departures of Republicans Scott Brown and Olympia Snowe, along with Democrats Joseph Lieberman and Ben Nelson, meant that the center would be an even lonelier place.[65] In the House, similarly, there would continue to be an ideological divide between liberal Democrats and conservative Republicans.[66] Consider what happened to two groups of moderates in the House. The Republican Main Street Partnership is a caucus of pragmatic members who place more emphasis on economics than social issues, even though most of them have fairly conservative voting records.[67] Of its fifty-three House members in the 112th Congress, fifteen either retired or lost reelection bids, and it seemed unlikely that an equal number of freshmen would sign up. The shrinkage of the Democratic Blue Dog Coalition was even more remarkable.[68] In the 111th Congress it had fifty-two members. At the start of the 112th Congress, there were twenty-seven. After the 2012 election, only fourteen came back.

Lawmakers sometimes spoke about seeking "common ground," but they had less and less in common. Women and minorities now made up most of the House Democratic Caucus while white males were an even larger majority of the House Republican Conference than before.[69] The defeat of Florida's Allen West and the Senate appointment of South Carolina's Tim Scott left the House GOP without a single African American. In a geographical sense, the parties literally came from different places. Democrats accounted for 88 percent of House members and 93 percent of senators from New York and New England. In the eleven states of the Confederacy, 71 percent of House members and 73 percent of senators were Republicans. Among Democratic House members from the South, most were African American or Hispanic.

The two sides interpreted the 2012 election in different ways. Democrats saw a national vote in favor of their party. Republicans, especially in the House, looked at individual constituencies. "Pretty much everyone in our conference is returning with a bigger margin of victory than the president of the United States," Tim Huelskamp (R-KS) told *National Journal*.[70] In the 113th Congress, only fifteen of them would come from districts that Obama won in 2012. Of the fourteen Republican senators whose seats would be up for election in 2014 (including appointed Senator Tim Scott), only Susan Collins of Maine represented a state that Obama carried in 2012.[71] Compromise would be difficult. Even if the president wanted to cut deals with Republicans, he might have a hard time getting Democratic lawmakers to go along. He did not make a priority of winning the House, and most Democratic senators in tough races actually ran ahead of him.

Inevitably, lawmakers would soon look ahead to the 2014 midterm. Thanks to defensive redistricting and the tendency of midterms to go against the president's party, House Republicans could be reasonably confident that they would keep the majority. By holding onto most of their midterm gains in the state legislatures, Republicans also ensured themselves a good "farm club" of challengers and open-seat candidates.

In the Senate, the peculiar six-year cycle would leave its mark once again. Because of their party's success in 2008, Democrats held twenty of the thirty-four seats that would be up in 2014. The GOP would have another shot at a majority, provided that it could somehow avoid a repeat of the Akin and Mourdock fiascoes. Senate politics in the 113th Congress would surely revolve around the fight for control.

Republican outside groups such as American Crossroads and the Koch-financed Americans for Prosperity (AFP) might be reviewing their strategy and tactics, but they would continue to spend big money. So would their Democratic counterparts. "To the extent that Crossroads isn't going anywhere, AFP isn't going anywhere, and they will have programs in the midterm elections, then I don't think we can cede that ground even for a second," said Rodell Mollineau, president of American Bridge 21st Century, a liberal super PAC. "You have to fight with all the tools you have."[72]

To those who saw partisan conflict as a sign of democratic health, these developments were positive. To those who lamented polarization and attack politics, there was little hope for change. By mid-2011, both parties had essentially given up on governing, leaving it to American voters to break the deadlock in 2012. Instead of breaking the deadlock, Americans voted to reinstate it for at least another two years.

## NOTES

1. Paul Ryan, Eric Cantor, and Kevin McCarthy, *Young Guns: A New Generation of Conservative Leaders* (New York: Simon and Schuster, Threshold Editions, 2010), 148.
2. James W. Ceaser and Andrew E. Busch, *Losing to Win: The 1996 Elections and American Politics* (Lanham, MD: Rowman and Littlefield, 1997), 141–42.

3. Morgan Cullen and Michelle Davis, "5 Trends Shaping Redistricting," *State Legislatures*, Oct./Nov. 2012, www.ncsl.org/legislatures-elections/redist/5-trends-shaping-redistricting.aspx.
4. "Total Outside Spending by Election Cycle, Excluding Party Committees," Center for Responsive Politics, www.opensecrets.org/outsidespending/cycle_tots.php.
5. Matt Negrin, "White House Searches for a Villain," *Politico*, Aug. 17, 2010, www.politico.com/news/stories/0810/41180.html.
6. Major Garrett, "Top GOP Priority: Make Obama a One-Term President," *National Journal*, October 23, 2010.
7. Bob Woodward, *The Price of Politics* (New York: Simon and Schuster, 2012), 106–7.
8. Z. Byron Wolf, "DCCC Chair Steve Israel Says Ryan Budget, Medicare Will Cost Republicans the House," ABC News, Apr. 15, 2011, http://abcnews.go.com/blogs/politics/2011/04/dccc-chair-steve-israel-previews-democrats-2012-campaign-strategy-on-abcs-top-line/.
9. Siobhan Hughes and Neftali Bendavid, "Democrat Captures House Seat," *Wall Street Journal*, May 25, 2011, http://online.wsj.com/article/SB10001424052702304520804576344103139763790.html.
10. Frank Newport, "Record High Anti-Incumbent Sentiment toward Congress," Gallup Poll, Dec. 9, 2011, www.gallup.com/poll/151433/Record-High-Anti-Incumbent-Sentiment-Toward-Congress.aspx.
11. Frank Newport, "Congress' Job Approval at New Low of 10%," Gallup Poll, Feb. 8, 2012, www.gallup.com/poll/152528/Congress-Job-Approval-New-Low.aspx.
12. John J. Pitney Jr., "Obama and the Republican Congress," *Bessette-Pitney Text*, Oct. 17, 2012, www.bessettepitney.net/2012/10/obama-and-republican-congress.html.
13. John Bresnahan and Manu Raju, "Some Dems Keep President Obama Far, Far Away," *Politico*, June 27, 2012, www.politico.com/news/stories/0612/77920.html. Read more: www.politico.com/news/stories/0612/77920.html#ixzz2BgdwKnEq.
14. Glenn Thrush and Jonathan Allen, "Obama: Party of One," *Politico*, Sept. 2, 2012, www.politico.com/news/stories/0912/80555.html.
15. Laura Meckler, "Obama Hits Hustings on His Own," *Wall Street Journal*, Aug. 31, 2012, http://online.wsj.com/article/SB10000872396390444772804577623452628195804.html.
16. John Sides, "Is Obama More Popular Than He Should Be?," *New York Times*, May 2, 2012, http://fivethirtyeight.blogs.nytimes.com/2012/05/02/is-obama-more-popular-than-he-should-be/.
17. Jeffrey M. Jones, "Thirteen States and D.C. Give Obama Majority Approval," Gallup Poll, Aug. 1, 2012, www.gallup.com/poll/156389/thirteen-states-give-obama-majority-approval.aspx.
18. Alex Isenstadt, "How Pete Sessions Helped Keep a GOP House," *Politico*, Nov. 8, 2012, www.politico.com/news/stories/1112/83612.html.
19. Mark Amodei for Nevada, "Mom," Aug. 8, 2011, http://youtu.be/TnSEiDOFfrE.
20. Charles Mahtesian, "Inside the Ryan Budget Pushback," *Politico*, Aug. 13, 2012, www.politico.com/blogs/charlie-mahtesian/2012/08/inside-the-ryan-budget-pushback-131951.html.
21. Jeanne Cummings, "Redistricting: Home to Roost," *Wall Street Journal*, Nov. 10, 2006, http://online.wsj.com/article/SB116312053645719332.html.
22. Reid Wilson, "Curbing Their Enthusiasm," *National Journal*, March 31, 2011, www.nationaljournal.com/member/magazine/hispanic-gains-dim-gop-redistricting-hopes-20110331.
23. Joshua Miller, "Democrats Betting Big on Florida Redistricting," *Roll Call*, Nov. 8, 2011, www.rollcall.com/issues/57_55/Democrats-Betting-Big-on-Florida-Redistricting-210095-1.html.
24. James Warren, "Democratic Dreams of Big Wins in Illinois Fading," *The Daily Beast*, Oct. 13, 2012, www.thedailybeast.com/articles/2012/10/13/democratic-dreams-of-big-wins-in-illinois-fading.html.

25. Olga Pierce and Jeff Larson, "How Democrats Fooled California's Redistricting Commission," ProPublica, Dec. 21, 2011, www.propublica.org/article/how-democrats-fooled-californias-redistricting-commission.

26. California Secretary of State, "Historical Voter Registration and Participation in Statewide General Elections 1910–2010," www.sos.ca.gov/elections/sov/2010-general/04-historical-voter-reg-participation.pdf; "15-Day Report of Registration," Oct. 22, 2012, www.sos.ca.gov/elections/ror/ror-pages/15day-general-12/hist-reg-stats1.pdf.

27. Campaign Finance Institute, "Independent Spending Roughly Equaled the Candidates' in Close House and Senate Races; Winning Candidates Raised More Than Any Previous Election," Nov. 9, 2012, www.cfinst.org/Press/PReleases/12-11-09/Early_Post-Election_Look_at_Money_in_the_House_and_Senate_Elections_of_2012.aspx.

28. Nicholas Confessore, "Liberals Steer Outside Money to Grass-Roots Organizing," *New York Times*, May 7, 2012, www.nytimes.com/2012/05/08/us/politics/liberals-putting-super-pac-money-into-grass-roots.html.

29. Molly K. Hooper, "Speaker Boehner Uses Karl Rove-Like Strategy to Hold House GOP Majority," *The Hill*, Oct. 2, 2012, http://thehill.com/homenews/campaign/259625-boehner-uses-rove-like-strategy-to-hold-majority.

30. Reid Wilson, "Chasing Nancy," *National Journal*, November 15, 2012, www.nationaljournal.com/member/magazine/boehner-is-emulating-pelosi-in-one-thing-fundraising-20121115.

31. Bob Biersack, "House Races Less Financially Competitive Than in 2010," *Open Secrets Blog*, Oct. 21, 2012, www.opensecrets.org/news/2012/10/2012-house-race-summary-through-sep.html.

32. Isenstadt, "How Pete Sessions Helped Keep a GOP House."

33. David Catanese, "Translating Patty Murray's Briefing," *Politico*, Dec. 6, 2011, www.politico.com/blogs/davidcatanese/1211/Translating_Patty_Murrays_briefing_.html.

34. "Cameron Joseph, DSCC Accuses Tommy Thompson of Cronyism in New Ad," *The Hill*, Oct. 16, 2012, http://thehill.com/video/campaign/262351-dscc-accuses-thompson-of-cronyism-in-new-ad.

35. Jesse McKinley, "A Gay Voice, on the Edge of History," *New York Times*, Nov. 2, 2012, www.nytimes.com/2012/11/04/fashion/tammy-baldwin-on-the-edge-of-making-history.html.

36. Crossroads GPS, "Rubber Stamp Bailout ND," Oct. 16, 2012, http://youtu.be/C8kO8Wk8uuE.

37. Rachel Weiner, "How Deb Fischer Pulled an Upset in Nebraska," *Washington Post*, May 16, 2012, www.washingtonpost.com/blogs/the-fix/post/how-deb-fischer-pulled-an-upset-in-nebraska/2012/05/16/gIQAtDQwTU_blog.html.

38. Zachary Courser, "Tea Party Surge in Texas or the Usual Conservative Suspects?," *Detailing Democracy*, Aug. 1, 2012, http://detailing-democracy.blogspot.com/2012/08/tea-party-surge-in-texas-or-usual.html.

39. "Centrist Senators: The Most Moderate Members," *National Journal*, March 2, 2012, www.nationaljournal.com/pictures-video/centrist-senators-the-most-moderate-members-pictures-20120302.

40. Mike Dennison, "Group Sympathetic to Tester Drops $500K on TV Ad—for Libertarian," *Billings Gazette*, Oct. 26, 2012, http://billingsgazette.com/news/state-and-regional/montana/group-sympathetic-to-tester-drops-k-on-tv-ad-for/article_4419 7da9-b6d2-5e8a-ae05-7442aef0a45d.html; Kim Barker, "In Montana, Dark Money Helped Democrats Hold a Key Senate Seat," ProPublica, Dec. 27, 2012, www.propublica.org/article/in-montana-dark-money-helped-democrats-hold-a-key-senate-seat.

41. Kevin McDermott, "Is Claire McCaskill Helping Todd Akin in the GOP Primary?," *St. Louis Post-Dispatch*, Aug. 1, 2012, www.stltoday.com/news/local/govt-and-politics/is-claire-mccaskill-helping-todd-akin-in-the-gop-primary/article_5b4c 2bcc-85d0-5893-820e-ebad045fe159.html.

42. Charles Jaco, "The Jaco Report: Full Interview with Todd Akin," KTVI-TV, Aug. 19, 2012, http://fox2now.com/2012/08/19/the-jaco-report-august-19-2012.

43. Cameron Joseph, "Mourdock: Pregnancy from Rape Can Be 'Something God Intended to Happen,'" *The Hill*, Oct. 23, 2012, http://thehill.com/blogs/ballot-box/senate-races/263727-mourdock-says-pregnancy-from-rape-can-be-something-god--intended-to-happen.

44. Of 435 members, 14 sought other office, 25 retired, and 5 died or resigned without replacement before the election. The figure for general-election losers includes a runoff in Louisiana. "Casualty List: 112th Congress (2011–2012)," *Roll Call*, Nov. 21, 2012, www.rollcall.com/politics/casualtylist.html.

45. "Reelection Rates over the Years," Center for Responsive Politics, www.opensecrets.org/bigpicture/reelect.php.

46. Alex Isenstadt, "How Allen West Blew It," *Politico*, Nov. 20, 2012, www.politico.com/news/stories/1112/84108.html.

47. Wilson, "Chasing Nancy."

48. Harold Meyerson, "GOP's Gerrymandered Advantages," *Washington Post*, Nov. 13, 2012, www.washingtonpost.com/opinions/harold-meyerson-gops-gerrymandered-advantages/2012/11/13/4785e4d6-2d2f-11e2-a99d-5c4203af7b7a_story.html.

49. Rob Richie, "Clashing Mandates and the Role of Voting Structures," Center for Voting and Democracy, Nov. 20, 2012, www.fairvote.org/clashing-mandates-and-the-role-of-voting-structures.

50. Jowei Chen and Jonathan Rodden, "Unintentional Gerrymandering: Political Geography and Electoral Bias in Legislatures," www.personal.umich.edu/~jowei/florida.pdf.

51. Mike Maciag, "Analysis: Redistricting Mostly Protected Incumbents in 2012 Congressional Races," *Governing*, Nov. 16, 2012, www.governing.com/blogs/by-the-numbers/redistricting-gerrymandering-effect-2012-congressional-elections.html.

52. Nathan L. Gonzales, "Why the National House Vote Is Completely Irrelevant," *The Rothenberg Political Report*, Nov. 21, 2012, http://rothenbergpoliticalreport.com/news/article/why-the-national-house-vote-is-completely-irrelevant.

53. Dave Wedge, "Karl Rove-Allied Group Rips Scott Brown-Elizabeth Warren Pact," *Boston Herald*, Jan. 24, 2012, http://bostonherald.com/news/regional/view/20220124rove-allied_group_rips_brown-warren_pact.

54. Stephanie Ebbert, "Better Organized Mass. Democrats Roll Over Rivals," *Boston Globe*, Nov. 8, 2012, http://bostonglobe.com/metro/2012/11/08/mass-democratic-machine-wins-big-takes-seats/AXzrsQkr5m6wJshAIHeQgO/story.html.

55. Institute for Social and Policy Studies, "Lessons from Recent GOTV Experiments," Yale University, http://gotv.research.yale.edu/?q=node/10.

56. Karl Rove, "The Lessons of Defeat for the GOP," *Wall Street Journal*, Nov. 15, 2012, http://rove.com/articles/435.

57. Patrick Ruffini, "The GOP Talent Gap," *The Atlantic*, Nov. 16, 2012, www.theatlantic.com/politics/archive/2012/11/the-gop-talent-gap/265333/.

58. Dawn Reiss, "Wisconsin's Governor Wins, but Is He Now Dead Man Walker?," *Time*, March 12, 2011, www.time.com/time/nation/article/0,8599,2058601,00.html.

59. Josh Kraushaar, "Red Flags All Over for Obama in Wisconsin," *National Journal*, June 6, 2012, http://decoded.nationaljournal.com/2012/06/red-flags-all-over-for-obama-i.php.

60. Democratic Legislative Campaign Committee, "Democrats Gain 170 Seats in Legislative Elections," Nov. 8, 2012, http://dlcc.org/node/11082012/democrats_gain_170_seats.

61. Tim Storey, "2011 Legislative Elections," Council of State Governments, http://knowledgecenter.csg.org/drupal/system/files/tim_storey_2012_0.pdf.

62. Monica Davey, "One-Party Control Opens States to Partisan Rush," *New York Times*, Nov. 22, 2012, www.nytimes.com/2012/11/23/us/politics/one-party-control-opens-states-to-partisan-rush.html.

63. David A. Lieb, "Powerful Supermajorities Elected to Statehouses," Associated Press, Nov. 19, 2012, http://bigstory.ap.org/article/powerful-supermajorities-elected-statehouses.

64. Frank Newport, "Half of Americans Support Legal Gay Marriage," Gallup Poll, May 8, 2012, www.gallup.com/poll/154529/Half-Americans-Support-Legal-Gay-Marriage.aspx.

65. "The 113th Senate," *Voteview* blog, Nov. 8, 2012, http://voteview.com/blog/?p=602.

66. "The 113th House," *Voteview* blog, Nov. 13, 2012, http://voteview.com/blog/?p=609.

67. Republican Main Street Partnership, www.republicanmainstreet.org.

68. Blue Dog Coalition, http://mikeross.house.gov/bluedog; Ron Thompson, "Blue Dogs on Last Legs?," *Daily Kos*, Nov. 17, 2012, www.dailykos.com/story/2012/11/17/1162725/-Blue-Dogs-On-Last-Legs.

69. Halimah Abdullah, "New U.S. House: Women and Minorities to the Left; White Men to the Right," CNN, Nov. 14, 2012, www.cnn.com/2012/11/14/politics/house-diversity/index.html.

70. Ben Terris, "A Presidential Mandate? How about 435 Congressional Ones?" *National Journal*, Nov. 15, 2012, http://mobile.nationaljournal.com/magazine/a-presidential-mandate-how-about-435-congressional-ones--20121115.

71. Chris Cillizza, "As 'Fiscal Cliff' Looms, Republicans Have No Political Incentive to Make Deal with Obama," *Washington Post*, Dec. 30, 2012, www.washingtonpost.com/politics/as-fiscal-cliff-looms-republicans-have-no-political-incentive-to-make-deal-with-obama/2012/12/30/6e260104-52a3-11e2-8b9e-dd8773594efc_story.html.

72. Matea Gold, "Outside Groups Changing the Political Game for Good," *Los Angeles Times*, Oct. 21, 2012, www.latimes.com/news/nationworld/nation/la-na-outside-influence-20121021,0,3068748.story.

# SIX

# The Future of American Politics and Institutions

In 2008, Barack Obama won election to the presidency promising "Hope and Change" to a country tired of partisan disputes and mired in a financial crisis. By 2012, the crisis had passed, but so had the Hope and Change. The economy had stabilized and improved, but recovery remained slow and long-term unemployment was a serious problem. Moreover, the promise of a "postpartisan" politics, never very realistic, was long gone. Pursuing a less-noticed 2008 promise to "transform" America, Obama had proven himself the most polarizing president of modern times. From November 2009 to November 2012, his approval ratings were only rarely above 50 percent, and Americans believed the country was on the wrong track. In the midterm elections of 2010, Democrats lost sixty-three seats (and the majority) in the House and six seats in the Senate, serving as a rebuke to the president and a check on further policy departures. Obama's reelection campaign, unable to rely on an unambiguously successful term in office or popular programmatic achievements, was characterized by a relentless (and successful) assault on his opponent's character. On Election Day, it was an open question whether he would win; ten days before Election Day, before a hopeful jobs report and a hurricane that burnished his image, he may well have been losing.

When the votes were counted, Obama won by a popular vote margin comparable to George W. Bush's in 2004. It was a comfortable win, made more comfortable in the Electoral College by Obama's winning streak in the swing states, but it was also one of the smallest margins and lowest vote percentages for a reelected president in US history, and was the only time a president had won reelection with fewer votes than in his initial election. Democrats gained a modest eight seats in the House, as Republicans held onto the vast majority of the seats taken two years before, and two seats in the Senate, a gain traceable to the self-destruction of Republican candidates in Indiana and Missouri.

Despite the relatively close outcome and the unattractive means of obtaining it, Obama's win was important, for two reasons. Although further big policy moves to the left had been foreclosed since 2010 and would remain so in the aftermath of 2012, the election meant that the health care law and the large increase in federal spending since 2008 would probably be locked into place. Even if Obama accomplishes nothing more for the remainder of his presidency, these policies put on automatic pilot will represent a significant shift toward a more centralized and redistributionist state. Not only did Obama's victory secure his own policy achievements, but it also meant that Republicans would be blocked from advancing their own agenda. Thus, little would be done to address the growth of the entitlement state for at least another four years. Beyond his influence on the legislative process, Obama will also continue to possess significant levers of regulatory power and will continue to make judicial appointments. Second, the election indicated, at a minimum, that 2008 was not merely a fluke. An Obama coalition was able to win under much less propitious circumstances than before. What these facts portend for American politics remains open to debate, but no one could argue that they were unimportant.

## THE FUTURE OF AMERICAN ELECTORAL INSTITUTIONS

At the same time, nearly every presidential election opens or reopens institutional questions having to do with the constitutional provisions, federal and state laws, and party rules that govern presidential nominations and elections. The 2012 election was no exception, and produced a number of institutional issues with which the nation will grapple for at least the next four years.

### *Electoral College*

In the aftermath of the 2000 election controversy, the Electoral College was a major topic of political discussion. The 2000 presidential election was only the second in US history in which it could unambiguously be said that the winner of the electoral vote was not the winner of a plurality of the nationally aggregated popular votes; the other case had been in 1888. (Three other cases, 1824, 1876, and 1960, are sometimes considered to be in this category as well, but their claims are shakier.[1]) After the Bush-Gore dispute was settled, opponents of the Electoral College amplified their arguments, contending that the election proved the institution's unsuitability (e.g., George C. Edwards III and Neal R. Peirce in *Why the Electoral College Is Bad for America*[2]). Defenders of the Electoral College responded with a number of books, such as Gary Gregg's *Securing Democracy: Why We Have an Electoral College* and Tara Ross's *Enlightened Democracy: The Case for the Electoral College.*[3] The arguments were familiar: opponents argued that the Electoral College was archaic and undemocratic, supporters that it undergirded federalism, forced candidates to try to build broad coalitions, and typically reinforced the popular verdict rather than reversed it.

Opponents quickly accepted that a constitutional abolition of the Electoral College is extremely difficult and unlikely. They would have to get either two-thirds of both houses of Congress to propose an amendment or two-thirds of state legislatures to call for a convention to propose an amendment. Then, three-fourths of states—currently, a total of thirty-eight—would have to ratify the amendment, despite the fact that many more than thirteen (the minimum needed to block an amendment) benefit from the system. There is a reason that over seven hundred amendments to the Electoral College have been proposed since 1788, and only two have been adopted.[4]

As a result of the challenges associated with passing a constitutional amendment, opponents of the Electoral College began promoting an alternative means of making the nationally aggregated popular vote decisive, but without altering the language of the Constitution. They hoped to take advantage of the flexibility within the Constitution for states to determine how to elect and allocate their electors. The idea was to create a "compact" among states that would bind those states that agree to cast their electoral votes for the winner of the national popular vote. The National Popular Vote Interstate Compact would only start operating once enough states were participating to command the 270 electoral votes required to win the presidency. Seen by supporters as a constitutionally permissible means of indirectly making the nationally aggregated popular vote decisive, the compact is seen by some detractors as "utter madness" in which "states would be committing themselves in the Electoral College to preferring votes elsewhere to those cast by their own citizens."[5] The first state, Maryland, signed on in 2007. By 2012, eight states and the District of Columbia, with a total of 132 electoral votes, had joined the compact. Two additional legislatures had passed the measure but had seen it vetoed by the governor, and in another ten states one house of the legislature had passed it.[6] To succeed it needs 138 more electoral votes, which in theory could be gotten with only eight more states: New York, Florida, Pennsylvania, Ohio, North Carolina, Virginia, Indiana, and Minnesota. Six of the eight voted for Barack Obama in both elections, though most currently have a Republican legislature and/or governor. Then the Constitution would be effectively amended with the support of only sixteen states (and DC) instead of the constitutionally required thirty-eight.

The compact is still a possibility, but has lost momentum, for a number of reasons. With no repetition of a plurality loser in the last three elections, the sense of urgency of the reformers has lessened. Moreover, the plan has taken on a decidedly partisan cast. Although a number of Republicans have endorsed the plan, including former Tennessee senator and presidential aspirant Fred Thompson, former American Legislative Exchange Council chair Ray Haynes, and a significant number of state legislators, the states that had signed on by 2012 lean heavily Democratic—California, Illinois, New Jersey, Washington, Massachusetts, Hawaii, Vermont, and the District of Columbia. For the most part, Republican legislatures were already philosophically suspicious of the reform, and now ask why they should join what seems to be a partisan venture. Other Democratic states have been reluctant to join, perhaps because they do not want to facilitate a mechanism that would only operate with a practical effect if a Democrat were to lose the popular vote but be on the verge of winning the Electoral College. (Given the cast of states that have already endorsed the compact, it would have been ironic indeed if its first operation would have been to have given the popular vote winner Romney the presidency against electoral vote winner Obama, an outcome that seemed plausible in late October.) Casting a long shadow over the proposed reform, the Constitution also forbids compacts among states unless those compacts are approved by Congress—approval that has not yet occurred and seems unlikely to occur anytime in the near future. Some Supreme Court decisions indicate that congressional approval may only be required if the compact infringes on federal powers, and scholars are divided on whether the NPVIC would qualify, but the question will continue to hang over the project.[7]

Just as formal abolition of the Electoral College by constitutional means or informal evisceration by nonconstitutional means seemed to be fading from view, a new challenge has arisen to the institution. As usual, it has arisen as a partisan contrivance to solve someone's short-term problem, though it will undoubtedly be colored in terms of some important principle of democracy. This time, it is Republicans who feel aggrieved and seek redress by altering the current operation of the Electoral College.

The problem, as they see it, is that a number of large and medium states, operating under the at-large plurality system (or, as it is often called, the "winner take all" system), regularly give great prizes of electoral votes to Democratic presidential candidates despite the existence of substantial pockets of GOP strength within those states. (Of course, there are also pockets of Democratic strength in most Republican-leaning states.) The opportunity for Republicans is that the GOP made major gains in state government in many of these states in the 2010 elections, giving them the power to change state law regarding the allocation of electors. Consequently, after the 2012 elections, reports surfaced that Republican governors and legislatures in states such as Pennsylvania, Michigan, and Wisconsin intended to move their states to a congressional district system of electors, as is used in Maine and Nebraska. In such a system, the presidential candidate who wins each congressional district is given one electoral vote, and whoever wins the state as a whole gains the other two "at large" electors. If the three had used such a system in 2012, Mitt Romney would have won twenty-six electoral votes among them to only nineteen for Barack Obama. Other states such as Florida, Ohio, and Virginia might not be far behind.

The system is a way to allow expression of local differences, and its proponents claim it could boost voter participation as well. Moreover, it has a long history, as many states used such a method rather than winner-take-all prior to the 1840s. Nevertheless, the current drive for districted allocation of electors has a clearly partisan motivation. As one Republican strategist noted, "If you did the calculation, you'd see a massive shift of electoral votes in states that are blue and fully [in] red control. There's no kind of autopsy and outreach that can grab us those electoral votes that quickly."[8]

Such a system could cause congressional redistricting to begin turning on presidential election considerations and would also make it at least somewhat more likely that the leader of the nationally aggregated popular vote would lose in the Electoral College. Going back to 1968, a districted system would have made every election except 2000 and 2004 closer. Gerald Ford would have come tantalizingly close to winning in 1976 (with 268 electoral votes) and George W. Bush would have beaten Al Gore in 2000 by an even larger margin in the Electoral College, despite both Ford and Bush trailing in the popular vote.[9] By the estimate of David Wasserman, had the entire country used a districted system in 2012, Romney would have defeated Obama 278–262 in the Electoral College, for the same reason that Republicans easily held onto control of the House of Representatives—because their votes are much more efficiently spread around the country.[10] States such as California, New York, and Illinois, under Democratic control, will not be entertaining such a proposal, nor will Republican-leaning states with Republican state governments; West Virginia is the only state voting Republican at the presidential level that is under the unified control of a Democratic state government.

As an antidote to short-term thinking, recall that after Republicans won the 1988 presidential election—their fifth win in six tries—Democrats, in a situation analogous to the one that confronts Republicans now, seriously considered pushing for a districted plan in states such as Florida that at that point were reliably Republican at the presidential level but had Democratic legislative majorities. Under attack as opportunists, they backed off in the end, and in the very next election won without the reform. Republicans, if they succeed in enacting the reform in a number of states, may win short-term gains from it. But they run the risk of appearing as opportunists who would rather win by changing the rules than by making a better argument or running a better campaign with a better candidate. They will have chosen trying to squeeze every last electoral vote out of their current support rather than trying to expand their level of support. And if they do win this way, while again losing the nationwide popular vote, they may find the victory not worth the price that they will pay for it. Indeed, the negative consequences might go beyond an anti-Republican backlash that could ruin the presidency of the winner and damage the party's reputation; to the extent that plurality-loser elections undermine the legitimacy of the Electoral College and feed calls for its abolition, a move toward a districted system could end up badly damaging the Electoral College itself over time.

*Campaign Finance*

After the January 2010 *Citizens United v. Federal Election Commission* case, outraged liberals and campaign finance reform advocates predicted a surge of outside spending by corporations that would tilt the playing field toward Republicans and enhance the power of corporations in Washington. Democratic Senator Charles Schumer of New York, for one, called *Citizens United* "the worst [Supreme Court] decision since *Plessy v. Ferguson*," the 1896 decision that upheld racial segregation.[11] Aside from the partisan implications asserted by some, the issue revolves around deeper issues of political philosophy: Are individuals organized into corporations and labor unions "persons" under the Constitution? Is more money in politics a corrupting influence to be avoided, an expression of free speech to be encouraged, or morally neutral? In a country in which the federal government spends $3.5 trillion a year, extracts $2.5 trillion in taxes, and issues tens of thousands of pages of new regulations a year, is it realistic (or even just) to expect those with something at stake to refrain from attempting to influence the political process? Or are campaign finance restrictions attempts to stop water from flowing downhill?

There have now been two elections since *Citizens United*, and some conclusions can be reached. First, there has indeed been an influx of outside spending by groups such as Americans for Prosperity and American Crossroads on the right and Priorities USA and Majority PAC on the left. According to the Center for Responsive Politics, outside spending went from about $250 million in 2008 to about $1 billion in 2012.[12]

Second, spending has not tilted the playing field. In 2010, pro-Republican groups outspent pro-Democratic groups, but most of the time the money simply added resources to already-well-funded races on both sides. In other cases, the effect was to give some Republican challengers an even shot when they would otherwise have been underfunded. Rarely did outside money allow a Republican congressional candidate to simply overwhelm a Democratic opponent.[13] By 2012, Democratic groups caught up, and there was no obvious partisan impact of outside spending. In congressional races, the parties benefitted roughly equally. Moreover, in close Senate races between incumbents and challengers, unsuccessful challengers had more outside spending help than the successful incumbents who defeated them. In the presidential race, Romney received more help from outside spending than Obama did, but this aid merely closed the gap between the two campaigns, as the Obama campaign outspent Romney by about $250 million.[14] In the end, Obama narrowly won reelection, and Democrats retained control of the US Senate.

Third, outside spending has consisted of a combination of corporate spending (though most corporations have remained very cautious about expending their treasuries on political causes), spending by organized labor, which was also freed from controls under *Citizens United*, and wealthy individuals, who have been free to finance independent expenditures since *Buckley v. Valeo* in 1976. Most surprising to observers has been the prominence of wealthy individuals, who played a major role in outside spending in both the Republican nomination race and the general election.

Finally, studies have shown that television advertisements by outside groups are more often negative than ads by the candidate's campaign.[15] Consequently, although outside spending has not produced the partisan tilt or corporate influence that critics feared, it has contributed to a more negative tenor to campaigns. This point should not be exaggerated, at least in respect to the presidential race, where both candidates emphasized negative messages in their own advertising as well. Nevertheless, at the very least, outside groups can blur accountability in unfortunate ways; the notorious "Mitt-Romney-killed-a-steelworker's-wife" ad was run by an outside group, Priorities USA, allowing Obama to disclaim any responsibility.

Calls for reforms in response to the *Citizens United* decision came as soon as it was announced. Although some proposed a constitutional amendment to reverse the decision, this was always a long shot. The more likely of the proposed reforms, at least for a time, was offered by Senator Chuck Schumer, whose "DISCLOSE" bill ("Democracy Is Strengthened by Casting Light on Spending in Elections") would have required outside groups to disclose their top five donors, forced corporate CEOs to appear in ads funded by a corporate treasury, and prohibited ads by companies benefitting from TARP, with government contracts, or that are more than 20 percent foreign owned. The Republican takeover of the House that November ended any serious possibility of enactment.

A reasonable alternative approach might be to substantially increase the individual contribution limit, so that some of the money now flowing to outside groups might flow instead to the campaigns themselves. Whatever its logic, such an approach will be strongly resisted by those who see money in politics as inherently corrupting.

Given the impasse, the most plausible route for a substantial change in the campaign-finance regime will come through the Supreme Court. *Citizens United* was decided by a 5–4 margin. If any member of the majority leaves the court and is replaced by an Obama appointee, *Citizens United*—and possibly other cases treating campaign spending as a free-speech matter—will be vulnerable to reversal. In order to fully undo the campaign spending system in place in 2012, however, the court would have to reverse decisions going back to 1976.

### *Voter ID*

Throughout American history, there have been conflicts between the competing claims of voter access and ballot security. Measures that make it easier to vote sometimes make it easier to commit fraud; measures that aim to reduce the potential for fraud can also have the effect of creating barriers to use of the franchise. This tension came into relief during the 2012 campaign, and will continue to spawn debate.

Recent years have seen increased concerns about voter fraud. Numerous instances of fraud were apparent in 2000, including illegal voting by several thousand felons in Florida.[16] In 2008, the left-wing group ACORN was found to have engaged in massive and systematic voter registration fraud, leading to the collapse of the organization. During the midst of the 2012 campaign, an Arkansas state representative and three others plead guilty to voter fraud perpetrated to help the representative's father.[17] Journalist John Fund and others have documented the growth of the phenomenon, though some analysts have called the threat exaggerated.[18]

The 2002 Helping Americans Vote Act (HAVA) required that voters show identification when voting for the first time after registering by mail. In 2006, Indiana became the first state to require a government-issued photo ID as a condition of voting at the polling place. Partially in response to the ACORN scandal, numerous additional states adopted similar laws after 2008. In 2011, legislators in thirty-four states sought to impose or toughen a voter ID requirement. About half a dozen now have the strictest version, like Indiana's requiring photo ID. Other states allow alternative means of identification, and most allow voters without valid identification to cast provisional ballots and produce ID later. Supporters of the measures—mostly Republicans—argued that the laws were an important means to prevent voter fraud and posed a minimal risk of disenfranchising genuinely eligible voters. Opponents of the laws—almost entirely Democrats—contended that the photo ID requirement would exclude from the electorate large numbers of poor people, mostly racial minorities, and should therefore be seen as attempted "voter suppression." Indeed, some analysts argued that the high level of African American turnout in Ohio, Virginia, and elsewhere was owed in part to a reaction against the perception that Republicans were engaged in voter suppression. There are wildly varying estimates of how many Americans would be unable to vote if every state adopted strict photo ID rules. The Brennan Center estimated that 21 million otherwise eligible citizens would be unable to vote, but a Reuters/IPSOS survey found that only 2 percent of those who planned to vote either lacked proper identification or were not sure if they had it.[19]

In several states, the dispute ended up in court, with somewhat mixed verdicts. Indiana's law was upheld; Pennsylvania's law was suspended for the 2012 election, on the grounds that it placed too high a burden on voters with little notice. The court upheld the law going forward, however, as long as the state offered low-cost opportunities for all eligible voters to obtain an ID. Liberals tended to emphasize the first half of the Pennsylvania decision, and indeed it was the first half that had an immediate impact on the election. Conservatives noted that courts continued to uphold the general principle of voter ID, and that the laws would be in force by 2014. As more states impose strict photo ID requirements, it will be possible to see whether the impact on turnout will actually be large or small. Of course, if turnout goes down, it will take additional research to ascertain whether the decline represented legitimate voters turned away unfairly or fraudulent voters prevented from voting.

Although these laws will undoubtedly drive down voter fraud, supporters should not expect too much. First, voter ID laws can only be applied to voting at the polling place. They cannot affect absentee or other mail-ballot voting, since that voting takes place from home without the supervision of election officials. And it is clear that much of the voter fraud of recent years has taken place in mail voting. "Absentee vote brokers" have emerged, paying people for absentee ballots and then casting all for the candidate who hired them.[20] In Oregon in 2000, mysterious men collected mail ballots in downtown Portland, then disappeared—along with the ballots.[21] Second, voter ID laws can only prevent fraud if polling-place officials enforce those laws. It is possible—indeed, it seems more likely than not—that those officials in some locales will choose not to enforce the ID mandate, out of either sympathy for the voter or some less noble impulse. On Election Day in Philadelphia in 2012, Democratic election officials threw out 75 Republican observers until being forced by court order to readmit them several hours later.[22] One can only speculate how carefully voter identification would have been scrutinized during those hours had Pennsylvania's voter ID law been in operation. Altogether, as election law expert Rick Hasen notes, "When you do see election fraud, it invariably involves election officials taking steps to change election results or it involves absentee ballots which voter ID laws can't prevent."[23]

*Primary Schedule and National Convention*

Finally, there is reason to imagine that the nominating system, particularly as it relates to the schedule of primaries and caucuses, might undergo yet another change in 2016. The nominating system is wholly extra-constitutional, except to the extent that basic voting qualifications are the same as for the general election. Otherwise, the nominating system is formed by a patchwork of federal campaign finance law, national party rules, state law, and state party rules.

As outlined in chapter 3, after the 2008 election Republicans concluded that it had been disadvantageous for their nominating contest to wrap up so quickly. Barack Obama, they reasoned, had been aided by remaining in the public spotlight during his ongoing struggle with Hilary Clinton long after John McCain had become the de facto GOP nominee and dropped from sight. Concerns about this picture arose in the context of broader concerns about presidential primary front-loading that had developed over the previous twenty years. As a result, Republicans adopted rules that they hoped would partially reverse front-loading and prolong their nominating process.

After a long and bruising 2012 primary contest, a number of key Republicans contemplated returning to a more front-loaded schedule. In their judgment, the length of Mitt Romney's primary campaign hurt rather than helped him. And, looking ahead to prospects for an extended nomination challenge as an incumbent president, Mitt Romney did not like what he saw. Consequently, Republicans quietly revisited the post-2008 rules at their 2012 convention. They gave the winning primary or caucus candidate more control over delegate selection in that state and, more importantly, repealed the rule requiring early voting states to use some form of proportional representation.[24] The elongated calendar provided some benefits to Romney as well as imposing some costs, but in defeat, Republicans were even more determined to move away from the 2012 system. (Had Romney won, there might have been a chorus of Republican voices praising the new calendar for having toughened him and allowing Republican voters more opportunity to reach a high comfort level with the putative nominee.)

Republicans were, of course, in danger of refighting the last war, just as many think they did after 2008. As many Republican critics of the 2012 rules have pointed out, the party's rules reflected a reaction against the scenario in 2008, when there was no incumbent opponent. In 2012, Republicans did face a well-financed incumbent opponent who had his nomination wrapped up the moment voting started in Iowa. But in 2016, Republicans will once again be in or near the situation they faced in 2008. What this conundrum might illustrate better than anything is the folly of making quadrennial adjustments to the nominating rules in response to short-term factors. This, too, Democrats did in their season of loss from 1968 to 1992, with disappointing results.

Both parties are likely to take a second look at the timing and length of the nominating conventions. For decades, Republicans and Democrats held four-day conventions, with nominations taking place on the penultimate night and acceptance speeches on the final night. From the 1950s until the early 2000s, the parties also adhered to a norm in which the challenging party held its convention in July and the incumbent party held its convention in August. Then, about a decade ago, the parties began holding their conventions later and closer together, in late August or early September.

Both of these "convention conventions" are now in doubt. Convention viewership is down, as the networks have scaled back coverage, and both the parties have experimented with three-day conventions either deliberately or as an emergency measure. Republicans cut their national conventions to three days from a planned four days in 2008 and again in 2012, in both cases dropping the planned first day due to a hurricane. Democrats actually planned for a three-day convention in 2012. Both are now questioning whether they might make the change permanent. Some observers, looking farther ahead, ask whether the national convention will survive at all, though it is difficult to imagine either party surrendering the free publicity altogether.

There is also building support for moving the conventions back to mid-summer. The move to the end of summer came about when the major party nominees were still receiving public funding for the general election but had gone toward completely private financing of their nomination campaigns; holding the convention later allowed them to continue raising and spending private money for an extra month or two and kept them from running out of the limited amount of public funding after the conventions. In 2012, neither candidate accepted public funds for the general election, and Romney found himself having "maxed out" his top donors long before the convention. In his situation, an earlier convention would have been better. From now on, serious candidates are likely to decline public funds. Those facing expensive nomination contests—most nonincumbents—will benefit from an earlier rather than later convention. Look for both parties to make their calculations and seriously consider repositioning their national conventions in 2016.

## THE FUTURE OF AMERICAN POLITICS

The 2012 election results provoked a flood of commentary on the future of American politics. That commentary was divided between predictions of apocalypse for Republicans and suggestions that mere gloom was appropriate. There are, indeed, many reasons for Republicans to worry about their electoral future, and perhaps more reasons for conservatives to fear the policy consequences of 2012. Nevertheless, it also bears remembering that nearly every election is followed by overheated estimates of perpetual victory for the winners and imminent doom for the losers. A short eight years before, panicked liberals (and some triumphalist conservatives) met George W. Bush's reelection—by a nearly identical popular vote margin to Obama's in 2012—as the sign of permanent Republican ascendancy. While 2012's election signals important shifts, we have not arrived at the end of history quite yet.

First, this election demonstrates that the Democrats' presidential coalition is durable. In 2012, it weathered significant hardships such as a slow economy, unpopular legislative initiatives, and a disastrous midterm election. President Obama's strategists fastened on to Harry S. Truman's 1948 strategy and made it work. Truman gambled that the New Deal Democratic coalition was sufficient to carry him to victory if it was adequately mobilized. Among the public at large, Truman's antipathy to the Taft-Hartley labor act, support for desegregation of the military, and full backing of farm subsidies were not popular. But those policies, in combination with a hard-hitting, arguably demagogic, negative campaign, helped mobilize the coalition, and it was strong enough to win. The true test of a coalition is if it can hold together in a 2012 as well as a 2008. Obama's coalition passed the test. And some of the portions of the electorate most heavily disposed toward Democrats—Hispanics, unmarried women, the highly secular—are growing.

Another advantage for Democrats lies in their superior ground game. Their party has proven better able to identify and mobilize their voters through a more effective use of modern information technology. This advantage was pressed again in 2012, and probably contributed significantly to Obama's (narrow) winning margin.

Some analysts held that the Democratic coalition would remain powerful, perhaps dominant, due to the increasing dependence of Americans on the largesse of the federal government. In this view, America may have reached a tipping point in which the "takers"—recipients of government programs—outweigh the "makers"—the producers of economic wealth—and will continue to use their electoral power to support the party of big government. It was this concern that animated Mitt Romney's "47 percent" comment, and that characterized some post-election commentary (including Romney's).

There was a strong basis of plausibility in the observation. Under Obama, the number of Food Stamp recipients had doubled, federally guaranteed student loans became available only through direct lending from the federal government, and the percentage of income tax paid by the bottom 60 percent of taxpayers had fallen to 14 percent in 2012.[25] According to some estimates, over half of Americans had received a payment of some sort from the federal government's primary entitlement programs, and that was before millions more were going to become dependent on Washington for health care.[26] There could be little question that Democratic policymakers had for decades expected that an expanded welfare state would yield an expanded Democratic vote share. Though perhaps apocryphal, Harry Hopkins' motto of "Tax and tax, spend and spend, elect and elect" certainly captured the essence of FDR's political strategy.[27]

However, things are never so simple. One political problem with entitlement programs is that, by their very nature, they induce their recipients to see them as entitlements rather than gifts. It is difficult to obtain long-lasting gratitude for providing something that has been sold as an essential "right." To put it another way, even if dependency on government can be analogized to addiction, addicts never have better than a love-hate relationship with their suppliers. As a result, the partisan impact of reliance on government programs is ambiguous. One study showed that 59 percent of Obama's voters had received money from a federal entitlement program—but so had 53 percent of Romney's voters.[28] If there was a straight line between increased dependency and voting for Democrats, Republicans would not have won five of six presidential elections following the enactment of the Great Society.

Other pieces of the structural environment may actually provide a bigger long-term payoff to Democrats. Above all, the left has something nearly approaching a stranglehold on higher education, popular culture, and mass media.[29] Conservative hopes that the "new media" would provide a counterweight have not yet been fulfilled; "new media" have probably helped establish a higher floor for the Republican vote, can debunk egregious tales such as the 2004 CBS forgeries, and can launch guerrilla forays such as Andrew Breitbart's takedown of ACORN, but it cannot go toe to toe with the major networks for control of the news agenda. The highest-rated Fox News program still gets fewer viewers than the lowest-rated broadcast network evening news program.[30] Education and popular culture have also combined to shift social values to the degree that many conservatives now see themselves as the new counterculture, and question whether even the most competent campaigns can succeed in that environment. At the least, this advantage for Democrats means that to succeed Republicans must nominate candidates who can serve as articulate educators—a quality that is in surprisingly short supply among politicians.

Nevertheless, Obama's coalition, consisting of 51.06 percent of the vote in 2012, leaves Democrats little margin for error. Moreover, how much of Obama's coalition is a Democratic coalition, transferable to other Democrats, and how much owes to his personal appeal cannot be known until 2016 or even 2020, when he is no longer in the White House. The winning coalition of 2008 and 2012 bears a striking resemblance to that outlined in 2002 by John Judis and Ruy Teixiera in *The Emerging Demo-*

*cratic Majority*, before anyone had ever heard of Barack Obama.[31] The coalition has brought victory at the presidential level and in the Senate, where in 2012 most Democratic winners ran ahead of Obama's vote in their states. But it has not worked in the House or the statehouses taken as a collective whole. If it is a party (and not just personal) coalition, it is one that is highly dependent on large numbers of favorable voters concentrated in a few pockets around the country. And it broke down in 2010 with catastrophic results for the party. As political scientist John Sides notes, "Realignments don't take midterm elections off."[32]

A practical limitation that may be faced by Democrats in the future, and that will have more impact the more Obama himself was central to the 2008 and 2012 wins, is that their pool of potential presidential candidates in the near future does not seem particularly deep. In athletic terms, Democrats have a "weak bench." Looking to 2016, one could easily imagine as aspirants Hillary Clinton, who will have been in the public eye for twenty-four years and may be damaged by both health difficulties and her association with the Benghazi fiasco, as well as New York governor Andrew Cuomo and perhaps a handful of other governors. One might also imagine Joe Biden, who will be seventy-three and would have to overcome a reputation for gaffes. Of course, the party only needs to find one good candidate at a time; it is generally forgotten that Bill Clinton was often dismissed as merely the strongest candidate in the field of second-tier hopefuls that remained in 1992 after first-tier names such as Mario Cuomo, Bill Bradley, Richard Gephardt, and Al Gore took themselves out of the running.

In the short run, Democrats will be vulnerable in the 2014 Senate elections. The president's party typically faces rough sledding in Senate elections in a president's second midterm. The so-called six-year itch wreaked havoc in 1938, 1958, 1974, and 1986, as relatively weak incumbents in tough territory, brought to power by the president's coattails in his initial election, were swept out. In 2014, there will be twenty Democratic seats up for election and only thirteen Republican seats. Although they dodged a bullet in 2012, Democrats will have to fight hard to hold control of the Senate with two years remaining in Obama's term.[33] (On the other hand, if Republicans do not make significant gains in 2014, Democrats running against the large GOP class of 2010 could find themselves within reach of a filibuster-proof majority in 2016.[34])

In addition, even in the best case, there will be complications and difficulties associated with Obamacare as it is implemented. As Brookings Institution health care analyst Henry J. Aaron argued, "The 2012 election settled the immediate fate of the Affordable Care Act (ACA). The candidate who swore to repeal it lost." However, "Like those in the eye of a hurricane, a deceptive and short-lived calm is upon us." Implementation will be complex, difficult, and probably controversial, even if the disaster predicted by ACA opponents does not materialize.[35] Like the

Great Society and the War on Poverty, it is possible that the health care law will be a major legislative victory that nevertheless turns into (or in this case, remains) a political liability. Democrats not only will be responsible for the extension of health insurance coverage to those who were previously uninsured, but will also be held to account for whatever happens, good or bad, to the health care of the 85 percent who were already covered.

In the longer run, Democrats will have to face the difficulties posed by the intellectual exhaustion illustrated by Obama's presidential campaigns.[36] In 2008, that vacuum was covered by a financial crisis, a gauzy campaign of "Hope and Change," and a cult of personality; in 2012, it was covered by a negative campaign of personal attack. That the two campaigns represented two opposing approaches aesthetically does not change the fact that both were contrived as answers to the same strategic problem. Indeed, exit polls made it clear that Obama won reelection in spite of the intellectual underpinnings of his presidency, not because of them. By a 49 to 45 percent margin, even a pro-Obama electorate continued to say that it wanted to repeal all or part of Obamacare; by a 51 to 43 percent margin, voters said that government was doing too many things better left to individuals or businesses.[37] The president won because a quarter of the people who agreed with that view voted for him anyway. When Obama achieved the chief point on his 2012 policy agenda by persuading the lame duck Congress to accept a 3.6 percent increase on the tax rates of those making $400,000 a year or more, one could be forgiven in wondering if there was any point remaining in his taking the oath of office for a second term.

That Democrats lack a clear path to undisputed political dominance does not mean that Republicans are fated to make a big comeback soon. Their situation is largely, though not wholly, a mirror image of that facing Democrats. As many analysts noted after Election Day, the Republican presidential coalition gives the GOP a smaller base at the outset. The party also faces a real risk of additional decline, as key elements of its coalition are likely to continue shrinking as a share of the electorate. Republicans are also behind in the technology wars. Thus, taken together, there are fewer Republicans and GOP organizations are less proficient at mobilizing them. Until these deficiencies are corrected, or at least mitigated, Republicans can look forward to more election nights like November 6, 2012.

Fortunately for them, these weaknesses are not an immutable part of the political landscape, nor are Republicans beginning from a historically weak position. As recently as 2004, analysts were pointing to the long-term advantages accruing to Republicans from their strength in the country's fastest-growing counties and among religious groups with higher-than-average birth rates; George W. Bush had just captured around 40 percent of the Hispanic vote; and it was the Republican get-out-the-vote drive, featuring an early form of micro-targeting and personalized application of technology, that was drawing attention from envious Democrats. As election analyst Sean Trende argues, even in the 2012 vote, "Just looking at the numbers the Republican Party, overall, is actually in pretty good shape. Of course, that doesn't mean it isn't set for a major decline; this could be a high point. But it does mean the Party would be starting its decline from a pretty high peak." Along with losing the presidential race by a margin that was not only narrow but also well within the range forecast by econometric models, Republicans were near their post–World War II peak of House seats and governorships, within their normal range of Senate seats, and only slightly below their (2010) postwar peak in state legislatures.[38]

Few features of political life are more subject to swift reversal than technological advantage, and one can expect that Republicans will work hard to close the gap. Coalitions, though not as easily shifted, are not immutable, either. Indeed, as Sean Trende has shown, political parties in America are adaptive and capable of forging new, countervailing coalitions that balance their opponents' gains.[39] Another way of looking at the big advantage held by Democrats among young and minority voters is that Republicans only need to make modest inroads among those groups to change outcomes; Democrats must sustain unnaturally large margins to keep winning—and they have to pursue this racially polarizing strategy without driving up the GOP share (and turnout) of the white vote, only a little of which is also needed to put Republicans over the top.

Of course, Republicans will also have to try to increase their percentages among these groups without losing votes elsewhere. Immigration poses a large test for Republicans here, but is not the only barrier to GOP strength among Hispanics, whom surveys show to be much more favorable toward paternalistic government than other Americans.[40] Appealing to socially liberal younger voters without alienating their socially conservative base is another challenge. But the social liberalism of the young is not as uniform as some analysts think: while they strongly favor same-sex marriage, they are ambivalent about abortion.[41] Success on this ground does not seem any more impossible than finding common ground between environmentalists and organized labor or between aggressive secularists and evangelical African Americans, which the Democratic Party manages to accomplish on a regular basis. It takes the right circumstances and creative leadership, which one can never rule out in either party.

Indeed, in comparison with Democrats, Republicans would seem to have the stronger "bench" going forward. The 2009–2010 elections put forward a bevy of potential future leaders including New Jersey governor Chris Christie, Virginia governor Bob McDonnell, Senator Marco Rubio from Florida, New Mexico governor Susana Martinez, South Carolina governor Nikki Haley, and Senator Tim Scott of South Carolina, a Tea

Party favorite and the first African American Republican senator since Edward Brooke left office thirty-four years before.[42] Other strong figures include 2012 VP candidate Paul Ryan, Indiana governor and former House member Mike Pence, Louisiana governor Bobby Jindal, and Ted Cruz, who was elected to the US Senate from Texas in 2012. If, as seems probable, party strength in the modern era is substantially dependent on the image put forward by the party's most visible leaders, Republicans have reason for some optimism.

Although the two parties pose mirror images in certain ways, Republicans share something with Democrats as well. Like Democrats, Republicans are suffering from a certain degree of intellectual exhaustion. Some key GOP positions have turned from conviction into dogma and, as Republican figures including Mitch Daniels and Jeb Bush have acknowledged, reliance on the memory of Ronald Reagan threatens to become reflexive and irrelevant to younger voters rather than illuminating or inspiring.[43] The 2012 election demonstrated the degree to which the Republican establishment and its stable of candidates and consultants are very nearly allergic to ideas, a shortcoming that brought and will continue to bring a high price. Among other things, Mitt Romney's refusal to engage Obama in a serious contest of ideas about the causes and nature of the 2008 financial crisis conceded to the president the one argument that could exonerate him from the economic torpor of his presidency: it was the fault of George Bush, Wall Street robber barons, and unfettered capitalism. Now cemented into the public mind, this explanation of events will be very hard to undo, and will doubtless continue posing a headwind for Republican presidential candidates in the future.

Thus, both parties will have to work to chart a philosophical course going forward. The centrist Clintonian wing of the Democratic Party no longer exists or has gone into hiding. Even the Clintons themselves, who are never in hiding, have clothed themselves in the fashion of their party's current leadership. They have retained their sharp partisan edge, which remains in keeping with the spirit of Obama's presidency, but are no longer concerned with things like balanced budgets, welfare reform, or presenting a more moderate image on cultural issues, all of which the president himself has rejected. What remained of the elected base of Clintonism was very nearly annihilated in the 2010 midterms, and made no comeback in 2012. As the losing party, Republicans are under more immediate pressure, and the late 2012 "fiscal cliff" debate put them at each other's throats. After having lost with a moderate who reconfigured himself as a conservative, Republicans will now get down to the task of sorting out whether Romney lost because he was a moderate, because he ran too conservative a campaign, because he ran too nonideological a campaign, or because he was simply too reconfigured. At the end of the day, one can expect that Democrats will remain left of center and Republicans right of center, but that general characterization leaves considerable room for variation on each side.

Republicans and Democrats also continue to coexist in a general political environment characterized by severe political polarization. Both sides are increasingly cocooned and increasingly unable to trust the other; survey data on media usage, for example, shows large gaps along party and ideological lines in terms both of the sources on which people rely and their view of the trustworthiness of varying sources.[44] Indeed, they seem to inhabit different political worlds, and see the same events in totally different ways. After George W. Bush's reelection in 2004, a number of liberal commentators, including Bob Beckel, Lawrence O'Donnell, and Michelle Goldberg, discussed with some earnestness the option of "blue state secession." After Barack Obama's reelection in 2012, one poll showed that 25 percent of registered Republicans wanted their state to secede, and secession petitions in states such as Texas and Louisiana secured tens of thousands of supporters.[45] While few think secession is a serious possibility, these petitions are a troubling sign of the deep fault line dividing red America from blue. It means that a nontrivial contingent on each side believes the other is aiming to impose a vision of society that is so radically different from their own that they find it deeply disturbing to contemplate having to live under it. This is a polarization that has gone beyond policy and small politics into the realm of culture and great politics.

For progressives, what is at stake is a vision of a society in which justice is defined by egalitarianism, personal "autonomy" in moral matters, and the values of the (French) enlightenment above all else. To this view, the American Founding, with its emphasis on natural rights and limited government, is an anachronism and an obstacle. The great danger is concentration of wealth, which active government must combat and control. The European social democracies, featuring high taxes on wealth and income, a large public sector, omnipresent guidance from administrative experts, and high levels of secularization, are a model to be emulated. Hence Barack Obama's pledge to transform America and his dogged insistence on government-controlled health care. Hence as well the deep hostility of progressives to the Tea Party, to Paul Ryan's rhetorical reassertion of natural rights, and to any sign of traditional religious or cultural views in the public sphere. Michelle Obama was far from the only progressive who was really proud of America for the first time when Barack was elected. In this view, Obama has put the United States on a long-overdue course to join the social democratic and secular trajectory of a suitably modern democracy.

For conservatives, what is at stake is a vision of a society in which justice is defined, or at any rate secured, by liberty and by many of the things that progressives disdain: decentralized and limited government aiming for the preservation of natural rights (including property rights) under a fixed constitution, a political economy in which effort and enterprise regularly lead to unequal wealth, and a social order undergirded by enduring morals derived from the Judeo-Christian tradition. To this view, concentrated government power itself is the greatest danger—the problem, not the solution.

These two views are so different that victory by the adherents of one can lead to despair, sometimes apocalyptic in character, by the adherents of the other. Where liberal *Washington Post* columnist E. J. Dionne saw in Obama's reelection the potential to end the decline of America,[46] conservative commentator Mark Steyn saw one more sign of the end of America as a free society and a serious global power.[47] The alienation felt by some conservatives in November 2012 was palpable. Some felt they no longer knew their fellow Americans, or declared a Michelle Obama moment in reverse: Barack's reelection was the first time they had ever really been ashamed of their country.[48]

Conservatives had real reason to be concerned, even if not all of them embraced despair. As a party, Republicans may well bounce back, adjusting their tactics and taking advantage of a backlash against Obamacare or other liberal policies, but conservatives feared that those policies were now locked into place and would represent yet another irreversible giant step toward centralization and loss of self-government. The problem, as they see it, is a domestic version of the old Soviet Brezhnev Doctrine: when conservatives lose, the left's vision advances; when they win, the best they can do is hold the line. And even winning is no guarantee of holding the line. Conservatives must be asking themselves what the point is of holding the presidency in order to control judicial appointments if, at the end of the day, Reagan appointee Kennedy is the swing vote to uphold *Roe v. Wade* and Bush appointee Roberts is the swing vote to uphold Obamacare. For social conservatives, the first-ever statewide ballot victories by proponents of same-sex marriage also meant that the last line of defense against the social experimentation of the elites—the residual traditionalist sense of the people themselves—had been breached, with no easy repair in sight. And signposts from the HHS contraception mandate to the war against Chick-fil-A waged by big-city mayors and gay-rights activists appeared to many as ominous warnings of what might lie in store for the rights of those who were unwilling to conform themselves to the new moral order imposed by the victorious progressives.

From this point of view, the end result of this process, which was strengthened and accelerated by Obama's reelection, will not be progress. It will be nothing less than the ultimate decline of the American Republic into economic stagnation and national insolvency (presaged by the fate of European social democracies like Spain and Greece and American blue states such as California and Illinois), second-rate status abroad, social decay, and a kind of soft totalitarianism in which progressive lawmakers and bureaucrats in Washington will claim the right to decide everything about everything in a version of Alexis de Tocqueville's "democratic despotism." In *Democracy in America,* Tocqueville issued a warning about a government that, in the pursuit of equality, "takes upon itself alone to secure [the people's] gratifications and to watch over their fate," seeking "to keep them in perpetual childhood. . . . Such a power does not destroy, but it prevents existence; it does not tyrannize, but it compresses, enervates, extinguishes, and stupefies a people, till each nation is reduced to nothing better than a flock of timid and industrious animals, of which the government is the shepherd."[49]

It is no wonder conservatives saw the election as the most important in a generation, and felt the loss so deeply.

Progressives were glad that Obama had won, but the exhilaration of 2008 was long gone. They realized that Republican control of the House would thwart their ambitions to extend their early policy victories. And if conservatives worried that Obama had grand ambitions to move the country to the left, some on the left worried that Obama lacked those very ambitions. Instead of establishing the single-payer system that they wanted (and that Obama himself once endorsed), the Affordable Care Act left the private health insurance industry intact for now. The "fiscal cliff" legislation raised taxes on wealthy individuals, but at White House insistence, it also contained billions in corporate tax breaks. And as for national security policy, one liberal writer lamented: "Guantanamo remains open, warrantless wiretapping continues, and drone strikes have accelerated, leading to the deaths of innocent civilians and a burst in support for anti-American forces in Yemen, Pakistan and Somalia. Instead of breaking with the Bush era, Obama has codified and permanently institutionalized the 'war on terror' framework that has characterized American foreign policy since the September 11, 2001 attacks."[50]

The question going forward, of course, is just what the future holds under Obama and beyond, now that Obama is mostly reduced to protecting policies that have been put on autopilot, and whether the end result will be the happy land of the progressive vision, the dystopian decline that has gripped the conservative imagination, or something in between. It is also unclear what conservatives will do to reanimate their own alternative vision. Conservatives have yet to discover a way to reverse the policy results of progressive victories. Although they have made significant intermittent gains for the last century, progressives have had to rely for major advances on unusual circumstances (such as depression, presidential assassination, and financial crisis) and the unusually large legislative majorities that have followed. Consequently, stalemate, though perhaps one tilting toward one side or the other, is a more likely outcome than some sort of final victory by either, at least for a time.

In theory, one possible way to relieve the nation's political polarization is to reinvigorate federalism. As law professor Glenn Harlan Reynolds argues, "Let the central government do the things that only central governments can do—national defense, regulation of trade to keep the provinces from engaging in economic warfare with one another, protection of basic civil rights—and then let the provinces go their own way in most other issues."[51] The national stakes would be lowered, and no one would fear that a single way of life would be imposed on all Americans. If Texans want a low-tax, low-regulation state with more opportunity and less economic security, they could have it; if Californians prefer a high-tax, high-regulation environment with a sturdier welfare state but less opportunity and dynamism, they could have it. No one would try to turn the entire country into Texas or California. Such a solution has advocates across the political spectrum.[52] However, many on the progressive half of the political equation see federalism not as the solution but as a problem to be overcome on the road to a centralized future, and even most conservatives embrace federalism as only a secondary value, subordinate to other aims. Ultimately, both sides would have to foreswear using the power of national majorities, when they have them, to impose a vision on contrary local majorities.

Shortly after Lyndon Johnson's 1964 landslide—a reelection victory much broader and more impressive than Obama's—commentators laid out a scenario in which Democrats would win every presidential election through at least 1988. As it turned out, they lost every election in that period save one. Shortly after George H. W. Bush's 1988 win, major newsmagazines asked if the Democratic Party was beyond hope. Republicans have won the popular vote in one presidential election since then. It could well be that demographics and internal shortcomings will doom them to the minority for years to come, as a raft of pundits proclaimed after the 2012 election. Or it could be that we will see another unexpected turn of the wheel. No one in 1964 (except perhaps Barry Goldwater) predicted the catastrophe of Vietnam, the rise of crime and the counterculture, or the failures of the War on Poverty; few in 1988 predicted the imminent fall of the Berlin Wall and collapse of the Soviet Union. By definition, one cannot say in the wake of the 2012 election exactly what contingencies, if any, will surprise us next and have the potential to disrupt coalitions and the current trajectory of politics and policy. A new recession, the rise of inflation, or a foreign-policy crisis are all real possibilities.

Just as we cannot see the future, it is far too early to know how we will ultimately come to view the election of 2012. In 1992, Bill Clinton's election with 43 percent of the vote appeared flukish, a deviation from the norm established from 1968 to 1988. Clinton's relatively moderate presidency reinforced the impression of a Democratic president adapting to the requirements of a Republican era. Twenty years later, 1992 looks more like the beginning of a new electoral era that produced a winning demographic and geographic coalition for Democrats. If that is the case, though, 2012 may prove to be closer to the end than to the beginning of a period of Democratic advantage at the presidential level. Only time will tell.

What is clear is that Hope and Change is over. In 2008, Barack Obama embarked on an epic journey, complete with fanfare and visions of glory. In 2012, the journey continued through storm and wave, and the captain was given command for another four years, but the glory was gone and he barely put down mutiny by the passengers through the political equivalent of keelhauling the leader of the mutineers. He doubtless hopes that the hard part is past, but the history of presidential second terms is not reassuring. There is no guarantee that the sailing will get any smoother, or the passengers any happier.

## NOTES

1. In 1824, Andrew Jackson had more popular votes but lost the presidency in the House of Representatives, but popular vote was not used to select electors in six of the twenty-four states; in 1876, Samuel Tilden lost the election despite winning the official popular vote tally, but claims of fraud put twenty-one electoral votes in the hands of an extra-constitutional commission, which awarded all twenty-one disputed votes to Rutherford B. Hayes; in 1960, John F. Kennedy won the electoral vote and apparently won the popular vote tally, but that tally was complicated by the fact that Alabama elected each of its electors individually, and Kennedy's electors won only five of the eleven available spots.

2. George C. Edwards III and Neal R. Peirce, *Why the Electoral College Is Bad for America* (New Haven: Yale University Press, 2004).

3. Gary L. Gregg II, ed., *Securing Democracy: Why We Have an Electoral College* (Wilmington, DE: ISI, 2001); Tara Ross, *Enlightened Democracy: The Case for the Electoral College* (Dallas: Colonial Press, 2004).

4. These two were the Twelfth Amendment, separating the presidential and vice presidential votes, and the Twenty-Third Amendment, allotting three electoral votes to the District of Columbia.

5. Matthew Schmitz, "The Utter Madness of the National Popular Vote Interstate Compact," *First Things*, Nov. 6, 2012, www.firstthings.com/blogs/firstthoughts/2012/11/06/the-utter-madness-of-the-national-popular-vote-interstate-compact/; Brandon Watson, "Traditional EC vs. NPV," Oct. 12, 2012, accessed Dec. 29, 2012, http://branemrys.blogspot.com/2012/10/traditional-ec-vs-npv.html.

6. See www.nationalpopularvote.com.

7. For an opposing view, see Derek T. Muller, "The Compact Clause and the National Popular Vote Interstate Compact," *Election Law Journal* 6, no. 4 (2007): 372–93. For a view supporting the notion that no congressional approval is needed, see "Background on Interstate Compacts," www.every-vote-equal.com/pdf/EVE-CH-5.pdf.

8. Reid Wilson, "The GOP's Electoral College Scheme," *National Journal*, Dec. 17, 2012, accessed Dec. 29, 2012, www.nationaljournal.com/columns/on-the-trail/the-gops-electoral-college-scheme-20121217.

9. For 1968–2000, see http://sagarin.com/sports/electoral.htm. For 2000–2008, see http://law.marquette.edu/facultyblog/2010/02/28/a-different-way-to-run-the-electoral-college/; http://frontloading.blogspot.com/2009/03/2008-electoral-college-by-congressional.html.

10. https://twitter.com/Redistrict/status/279038728972947456.

11. Matt Cover, "Schumer: Citizens United Worse Than Racial Segregation Case *Plessy v. Ferguson*," CNS News, Apr. 20, 2012, accessed Dec. 28, 2012, http://cnsnews.

com/news/article/schumer-citizens-united-worse-racial-segregation-case-plessy-v-ferguson.

12. "Outside Spending," www.opensecrets.org/outsidespending/index.php.

13. See "Non-party Spending Doubled in 2010 but Did Not Dictate the Results," Campaign Finance Institute, Nov. 5, 2010, accessed Dec. 30, 2012, www.cfinst.org/Press/PReleases/10-11-05/Non-Party_Spending_Doubled_But_Did_Not_Dictate_Results.aspx.

14. See "Independent Spending Roughly Equaled the Candidates' in Close House and Senate Races; Winning Candidates Raised More Than Any Previous Election," Campaign Finance Institute, Nov. 9, 2012, www.cfinst.org/Press/PReleases/12-11-09/Early_Post-Election_Look_at_Money_in_the_House_and_Senate_Elections_of_2012.aspx; "Independent Spending Wars Fought to a Standstill in 2012," Campaign Finance Institute, Nov. 7, 2012, accessed Dec. 28, 2012, www.cfinst.org/Press/PReleases/12-11-07/Independent_Spending_Wars_Fought_to_a_Standstill_-_House_and_Senate_2012.aspx. "2012 Presidential Race," Center for Responsive Politics, accessed Dec. 30, 2012, www.opensecrets.org/pres12/index.php#out.

15. Paul S. Herrnson, "A New Era of Interest Group Participation in Federal Elections," in *Interest Groups Unleashed,* ed. Paul S. Herrnson, Christopher J. Deering, and Clyde Wilcox (Washington, DC: CQ Press, 2013), 25–26.

16. "Hundreds of Felons Cast Illegal Votes in Florida," *Los Angeles Times,* Dec. 2, 2000, accessed Dec. 30, 2012, http://articles.latimes.com/2000/dec/02/news/mn-60123.

17. Gavin Lesnick, "State Representative Pleads Guilty to Election Fraud," *Arkansas Online,* Sept. 5, 2012, accessed Dec. 30, 2012, www.arkansasonline.com/news/2012/sep/05/state-representative-pleads-guilty-election-fraud/.

18. John Fund, *Stealing Elections: How Voter Fraud Threatens Our Democracy* (New York: Encounter, 2008); John Fund and Hans von Spakovsky, *Who's Counting? How Fraudsters and Bureaucrats Put Your Vote at Risk* (New York: Encounter, 2012). An opposing view is offered by Lorraine Carol Minnite, *The Myth of Voter Fraud* (Ithaca, NY: Cornell University Press, 2010).

19. "Everything You've Ever Wanted to Know About Voter ID Laws," ProPublica, Nov. 5, 2012, accessed Nov. 28, 2012, www.propublica.org/article/everything-youve-ever-wanted-to-know-about-voter-id-laws.

20. Glenn R. Simpson and Evan Perez, "As Absentee Voters Increase in Number, Fears of Fraud Grow," *Wall Street Journal,* Dec. 19, 2000, A1.

21. Bryan Gruley and Chip Cummings, "Election Day Became a Nightmare, as Usual, for Bernalillo County," *Wall Street Journal,* Dec. 15, 2000, A1.

22. Dave Boyer and Jim McElhatton, "Problems, Panthers Surface at Pa. Polls," *Washington Times,* Nov. 6, 2012, accessed Dec. 30, 2012, www.washingtontimes.com/news/2012/nov/6/problems-black-panthers-surface-pa-polling-places/?page=all.

23. "Everything You've Ever Wanted to Know About Voter ID Laws."

24. See Doug Mataconis, "GOP to Change Rules for 2016 Primaries and Beyond," *Outside the Beltway,* Aug. 25, 2012, accessed Dec. 30, 2012, www.outsidethebeltway.com/gop-to-change-rules-for-2016-primaries-and-beyond/.

25. "Current Law Distribution of Taxes," Tax Policy Institute, accessed Jan. 5, 2013, www.taxpolicycenter.org/taxtopics/currentdistribution.cfm.

26. Rich Morin, Paul Taylor, and Eileen Patten, "A Bipartisan Nation of Beneficiaries," Pew Research Center, Dec. 18, 2012, accessed Jan. 5, 2013, www.pewsocialtrends.org/2012/12/18/a-bipartisan-nation-of-beneficiaries/.

27. See www.bartleby.com/73/1793.html, accessed Jan. 9, 2013.

28. Morin, Taylor, and Patten, "A Bipartisan Nation of Beneficiaries."

29. As one indication, according to the Center for Responsive Politics, 76 percent of 2012 election cycle contributions from individuals or organizations in education went to Democrats, as did 72 percent of contributions from the TV/movies/music industry and 71 percent from the books/magazines/newspapers industry. See www.opensecrets.org/industries/totals.php?cycle=2012&ind=W04; www.opensecrets.org/industries/totals.php?cycle=2012&ind=B02; www.opensecrets.org/industries/totals.

php?cycle=2012&ind=C1100, accessed Jan. 9, 2013. See also Thomas Edsall, "Journalism Should Own Its Liberalism," *Columbia Journalism Review*, Oct. 8, 2009, accessed Jan. 9, 2013, www.cjr.org/campaign_desk/journalism_should_own_its_libe.php. John Tierney, "The Left-Leaning Tower," *New York Times*, July 22, 2011, accessed Jan. 9, 2013, www.nytimes.com/2011/07/24/education/edl-24notebook-t.html?_r=0.

30. See "The State of the News Media 2012, Network: By the Numbers," Pew Research Center, http://stateofthemedia.org/2012/network-news-the-pace-of-change-accelerates/network-by-the-numbers/; "The State of the News Media 2012, Cable: By the Numbers," Pew Research Center, accessed Jan. 9, 2013, http://stateofthemedia.org/2012/cable-cnn-ends-its-ratings-slide-fox-falls-again/cable-by-the-numbers/.

31. John B. Judis and Ruy Teixeira, *The Emerging Democratic Majority* (New York: Scribner, 2002).

32. John Sides, "The Perils of Democrats' Euphoria, Or Why the 2012 Election Is Not a Realignment," *The Monkey Cage*, Nov. 12, 2012, accessed Jan. 7, 2013, http://themonkeycage.org/blog/2012/11/12/the-perils-of-democrats-euphoria-or-why-the-2012-election-is-not-a-realignment/.

33. Charlie Cook, "History Favors a 2014 Republican Comeback," *National Journal*, Dec. 6, 2012, accessed Jan. 7, 2013, www.nationaljournal.com/columns/cook-report/history-favors-a-2014-gop-comeback-20121206.

34. Stuart Rothenberg, "Supermajority within Reach for Senate Democrats," *Roll Call*, Nov. 28, 2012, accessed Jan. 7, 2013, www.rollcall.com/news/supermajority_within_reach_for_senate_democrats-219472-1.html.

35. Henry J. Aaron, "Health Reform: The Political Storms Are Far from Over," Brookings Institution, Dec. 27, 2012, accessed Jan. 4, 2013, www.brookings.edu/blogs/up-front/posts/2012/12/27-health-reform-aaron.

36. See Charles Kesler, *I Am the Change: Barack Obama and the Crisis of Liberalism* (New York: Broadside/HarperCollins, 2012).

37. National Exit Poll, accessed Dec. 5, 2012, www.foxnews.com/politics/elections/2012-exit-poll.

38. Sean Trende, "The Political Landscape After 2012," RealClearPolitics, Nov. 16, 2012, accessed Jan. 7, 2013, www.realclearpolitics.com/articles/2012/11/16/the_political_landscape_after_2012.html.

39. Sean Trende, *The Lost Majority: Why the Future of Government Is Up for Grabs—and Who Will Take It* (New York: Palgrave MacMillan, 2012).

40. Stephen Dinan, "Data Show Hispanics More Likely to Relate to Democrats," *Washington Times*, Nov. 26, 2012, accessed Jan. 7, 2013, www.washingtontimes.com/news/2012/nov/26/data-show-hispanics-more-likely-to-relate-to-democ/?page=all.

41. See David Karol, "The Myth of the 'Social Issues': The Politics of Abortion and the Politics of Gay Rights Are Different," *The Monkey Cage*, Aug. 9, 2012, accessed Jan. 9, 2013, http://themonkeycage.org/blog/2012/08/09/the-myth-of-the-social-issues-the-politics-of-abortion-and-the-politics-of-gay-rights-are-different/.

42. Scott was elected to the House of Representatives in 2010, then appointed to fill a Senate vacancy when Senator Jim DeMint resigned his seat at the end of 2012.

43. "Jeb Bush, GOP: Time to Leave Reagan Behind," *Washington Times*, May 3, 2009, www.washingtontimes.com/news/2009/may/03/gop-listens-in-drive-to-thrive/; Alan Greenblatt, "Mitch Daniels: Let Go of the Gipper," *Governing*, Apr. 25, 2008, accessed Jan. 9, 2013, www.governing.com/blogs/politics/Mitch-Daniels-Let-Go.html.

44. For media segmentation by ideology and party, see "In Changing Media Landscape, Even Television Is Vulnerable," Pew Research Center, Sept. 27, 2012, www.people-press.org/2012/09/27/section-4-demographics-and-political-views-of-news-audiences/; "Further Decline in Credibility Ratings for Most News Organizations," Pew Research Center, Aug. 16, 2012, accessed Jan. 9, 2013, www.people-press.org/2012/08/16/further-decline-in-credibility-ratings-for-most-news-organizations/.

45. See Charles C. W. Cooke, "Threats of Secession: A Bipartisan Game," *National Review*, Dec. 4, 2012, accessed Dec. 4, 2012, www.nationalreview.com/blogs/print/334768.

46. E. J. Dionne, "Obama and the End of Decline," RealClearPolitics, Nov. 19, 2012, accessed Jan. 7, 2013, www.realclearpolitics.com/articles/2012/11/19/obama_and_the_end_of_decline_116195.html.

47. Mark Steyn, "The Edge of the Abyss," *National Review* online, Nov. 9, 2012, accessed Jan. 7, 2013, www.nationalreview.com/articles/333116/edge-abyss-mark-steyn.

48. See Jay Nordlinger, "From Us, the Bitterati," *National Review* online, Nov. 8, 2012, accessed Jan. 5, 2012, www.nationalreview.com/corner/332994/us-bitterati-jay-nordlinger.

49. Tocqueville suggests that "for their happiness such a government willingly labors, but it chooses to be the sole agent and the only arbiter of that happiness; it provides for their security, foresees and supplies their necessities, facilitates their pleasures, manages their principal concerns, directs their industry, regulates the descent of property, and subdivides their inheritances: what remains, but to spare them all the care of thinking and all the trouble of living?" Alexis de Tocqueville, *Democracy in America*, vol. 2, sec. 4, chap. 6, accessed Jan. 4, 2013, http://xroads.virginia.edu/~Hyper/DETOC/ch4_06.htm.

50. Alex Kane, "5 Ways President Obama Has Doubled Down on Bush's Most Tragic Mistakes," AlterNet, Jan. 8, 2013, accessed Jan. 9, 2013, www.alternet.org/civil-liberties/5-ways-president-obama-has-doubled-down-bushs-most-tragic-mistakes.

51. Glenn Harlan Reynolds, "A Solution to Secession Fever: Federalism," *USA Today*, Nov. 19, 2012, accessed Jan. 9, 2013, www.usatoday.com/story/opinion/2012/11/18/texas-secession-obama-canada/1712241/.

52. For a progressive perspective, see Heather K. Gerken, "A New Progressive Federalism," *Democracy*, Spring 2012, www.democracyjournal.org/24/a-new-progressive-federalism.php; "Liberal Federalism," Nov. 13, 2010, accessed Jan. 10, 2013, www.bessettepitney.net/2010/11/liberal-federalism.html. For a conservative perspective, see Reynolds, "A Solution to Secession Fever: Federalism."

# Index

# About the Authors

**James W. Ceaser** is Harry F. Byrd Professor of Politics at the University of Virginia and a senior fellow at the Hoover Institution, Stanford University. He is the author of several books on American politics and American political thought, including *Reconstructing America* (1997), *Nature and History in American Political Development* (2006), and *Designing a Polity* (2010).

**Andrew E. Busch** is Crown Professor of Government and George R. Roberts Fellow at Claremont McKenna College, where he teaches courses on American government and politics and serves as director of the Rose Institute of State and Local Government. Busch has authored or coauthored a dozen books on American politics, including most recently *Truman's Triumphs: The 1948 Election and the Making of Postwar America* (2012) and *Epic Journey: The 2008 Elections and American Politics* (revised 2011), along with more than thirty articles and chapters in edited volumes.

**John J. Pitney Jr.** is professor of government at Claremont McKenna College. He is the author of *The Art of Political Warfare* (2001) and coauthor of *Congress' Permanent Minority? Republicans in the U.S. House* (1994) and *Epic Journey: The 2008 Elections and American Politics* (revised 2011). Professor Pitney is a frequent contributor to the popular press and hosts the widely read blog *Epic Journey*.